MEDIEVAL DREAM-POETRY

MEDIEVAL
DREAM-POETRY

A. C. SPEARING

FELLOW OF QUEENS' COLLEGE, CAMBRIDGE
AND UNIVERSITY LECTURER IN ENGLISH

CAMBRIDGE UNIVERSITY PRESS
CAMBRIDGE
LONDON · NEW YORK · MELBOURNE

Published by the Syndics of the Cambridge University Press
The Pitt Building, Trumpington Street, Cambridge CB2 1RP
Bentley House, 200 Euston Road, London NW1 2DB
32 East 57th Street, New York, NY10022, USA
296 Beaconsfield Parade, Middle Park, Melbourne 3206, Australia

First published 1976

Printed in Great Britain
at the
University Printing House, Cambridge
(Euan Phillips, University Printer)

Library of Congress Cataloguing in Publication Data
Spearing, A. C.
Medieval dream-poetry.

Bibliography: p.
Includes index.
1. English poetry – Middle English, 1100–1500 –
History and criticism. 2. Dreams in literature.
I. Title.
PR317.D786   821'.1'09353   75-46114
ISBN 0 521 21194 8 hard covers
ISBN 0 521 29069 4 paperback

CONTENTS

CONTENTS

PREFACE

Though I have been working towards this book, through an unfinished dissertation and several courses of lectures, for many years, it remains no more than an essay, outlining an approach to a large and complex subject which has never been treated in full. I am indebted to many friends, colleagues and students for various suggestions of which I have made use, and not least to my children for telling me about their dreams.

In quoting from medieval texts, I have removed ʒ and þ, regularized the use of i/j and u/v, and occasionally altered editorial punctuation, without comment. In quoting from translations, I have sometimes made changes where this seemed desirable, again without comment. Unattributed translations are my own.

Queens' College
Cambridge

A. C. SPEARING

I

DREAMS AND VISIONS

The nature of dream-poetry

The chief subject of this book is the dream-poem in English (including the 'Inglis' of Scotland) from the fourteenth to the sixteenth century. Many medieval poems include, as incidents in the stories they tell, dreams dreamt either by the narrator of the poem (as in Dante's *Divine Comedy* or Froissart's *Espinette Amoureuse*) or by one of his characters (as in Layamon's *Brut* or Chaucer's *Troilus and Criseyde*). But by dream-poems I mean not works of this kind, but poems whose main substance is a dream or vision, dreamt invariably by the 'I' of the poem. In order to approach the English dream-poems, it will be necessary to survey earlier works of a similar type in Latin and French, so as to define the traditions within which the English poets were working; but this is a subordinate purpose, and I do not discuss English poems, such as Chaucer's *Romaunt of the Rose* or Lydgate's *Reason and Sensuality*, which are mere translations. Two facts led me to my subject: the astonishing popularity of the dream-poem among medieval English poets, and the fact that so many of these poems are major works of literature. It would be generally agreed, I think, that the greatest period of medieval English literature is the later fourteenth century, and that its three greatest poets are Chaucer, Langland, and the author of *Sir Gawain and the Green Knight.* Dream-poems form an important part of the work of all three of these writers. Langland's only known poem, probably his life's work, is *Piers Plowman*; the *Gawain*-poet in all probability wrote *Pearl*; and from Chaucer we have four dream-poems – *The Book of the Duchess, The House of Fame, The Parliament of Fowls,* and the *Prologue* to *The Legend of Good Women* – together with a partial translation of the *Roman de la Rose.* From Chaucer's lifetime down to the work of Skelton in the early sixteenth century there exist many dream-poems written in a tradition which may broadly be called 'Chaucerian'. From the same period come a number of alliterative dream-poems, all anonymous. And Scotland in the fifteenth and sixteenth centuries also produced many dream-poems, some major and some minor, by King James I, Henryson,

Dunbar, Douglas and Lindsay. If we look back as far as the seminal thirteenth-century French work, the *Roman de la Rose*, we see that the dream-poem had as long a run as a major literary form as has been granted to the novel so far. Nor is the end of the Middle Ages a period of decline; I hope it will emerge from this book that the dream-poems of Skelton and Douglas vigorously put the old tradition to new uses.

My plan is not to attempt a comprehensive survey of all medieval dream-poems, or even of all those in English. Nor do I intend, on the other hand, to construct a generalized account of the dream-form, in which specific poems would function merely as examples or illustrations. There is some doubt whether the dream-poem can properly be considered an independent literary genre. One recent scholar has argued that it can: 'The special characteristics of the dream-vision poem establish it as a distinct literary kind, which had acquired, by the fourteenth century, a set of clearly discernible conventions.'[1] Against this, another has asserted that, 'Despite the common assumption of critics, dream poems did not constitute a separate category of love narratives.' Among the French love-poets who influenced Chaucer many of the conventional characteristics associated with poetic dreams are also found in poems about love which did not adopt the dream-form. 'Thus,' this scholar concludes, 'Chaucer was free to put his story in a dream or not, and to select conventional details as suited his artistic purpose. The conventions provided important tools, but they did not control'.[2] For this second view there is much to be said. Among English poems, the fifteenth-century *The Flower and the Leaf* might be mentioned as one example which includes many of the features associated with courtly dream-poetry – an ideal springtime landscape, a courtly company performing actions with an allegorical significance, an authoritative guide who explains this significance to the narrator – and yet it is not set in a dream. Dante's *Divine Comedy* is widely referred to as a dream-poem, even though the narrator does not represent himself as falling asleep and experiencing his story in a dream. And it is possible to read even Gower's *Confessio Amantis*, and to be so absorbed in its courtly treatment of love and its mythological fiction as to mistake that too for a dream-poem.[3] Many of the themes, genres and conventions of medieval literature – romance narrative, allegory, debate among symbolically embodied principles, religious revelation, and so on – are non-realistic. They belong to the world of the mind, could not be part of anyone's objective experience, and might therefore appropriately be framed in dreams. In dreams we undergo experiences in which we are freed from the constraints of everyday possibility, and which we feel to have some hidden significance;

and much of the content of medieval literature is of that kind too. It is unlikely, then, to be possible to establish the dream-poem as a *completely* 'distinct literary kind'; but this is not to say that the dream-framework was merely a gratuitous or optional component of a wide range of kinds of medieval literature.

For one thing, the authors of medieval dream-poems themselves seem to have been conscious of writing within a distinct literary tradition of dreams and visions. Guillaume de Lorris begins the most influential of all medieval dream-poems, the *Roman de la Rose*, by referring to

> An authour that hight Macrobes,
> That halt nat dremes false ne lees,
> But undoth us the avysioun
> That whilom mette kyng Cipioun. (7–10)[4]
>
> *authour...hight* authority named; *halt* held; *lees* lying; *undoth us* discloses to us; *whilom mette* once dreamed

'Macrobes' is Macrobius, the widely-read commentator on Cicero's *Somnium Scipionis*; and Chaucer in turn begins *The Parliament of Fowls* by describing at some length this vision of Scipio as it is recorded in a book entitled

> 'Tullyus of the Drem of Scipioun' –
> Chapitres sevene it hadde, of hevene and helle
> And erthe, and soules that therinne dwelle. (31–3)
>
> *Tullyus* Cicero

And later in the *Parliament*, when he comes to the appearance in his dream of the 'noble goddesse Nature' (303), Chaucer does not describe what she looked like, but simply refers us to an earlier literary vision in which she was described in great detail, the *De Planctu Naturae* of Alanus de Insulis:

> And right as Aleyn, in 'The Pleynt of Kynde,'
> Devyseth Nature of aray and face,
> In swich aray men myghte hire there fynde. (316–18)
>
> *Pleynt* lament; *Kynde* Nature; *deviseth* describes; *aray* dress

In *The House of Fame*, the first part of the dream is a description of the story of the *Aeneid*, as the dreamer saw it pictorially represented in a temple; and he passes quickly over the part of the story in which Aeneas had the visionary experience of visiting the underworld, telling us simply that if we want to know about that we must read

> On Virgile or on Claudian,
> Or Daunte, that hit telle kan (449–50)

– Virgil, or Claudius Claudianus (in the *De Raptu Proserpinae*), or Dante

3

(in the *Divine Comedy*). These are not dream-poems in the strict sense; but shortly afterwards he compares his own dreams with the visions seen by Isaiah, by Scipio (again), by Nebuchadnezzar, by Pharaoh, and by the more obscure 'Turnus' and 'Elcanor'. In *The Book of the Duchess* too, Chaucer compares his dream with 'th'avysyoun' of 'kyng Scipioun' (285–6) and with the dreams of Pharaoh and Joseph, and when the dream itself begins the room in which he finds himself has its walls decorated with pictures of the *Roman de la Rose*. Nor is it only Chaucer, that notorious name-dropper, who gives references of this kind to earlier dreams. In *Pearl* there is an allusion to the *Roman de la Rose*, and many references to the vision of the other world seen by St John in the Apocalypse. And in *Piers Plowman* there is a discussion of the dreams of Nebuchadnezzar and Joseph. It appears, then, that medieval writers of dream-poems were conscious of writing in an ancient tradition, going back to Scriptural and Classical sources, to which they felt a need to establish the relationship of their own poetic visions.

I do not wish to argue that this is a fully homogeneous tradition. The dream-framework may be used for a number of different purposes, and in some cases, no doubt, it is no more than a literary convention, taken over through sheer inertia on the poet's part. The modern editor of the fifteenth-century *Assembly of Ladies* writes in his introduction, 'The dream-framework...needs no explanation: the device was universal'.[5] In this book, except for purposes of contrast, I shall be mainly concerned with poems in which the dream-framework deserves some further comment than this, because it has a distinct and interesting function. This function will by no means always be the same; but from the fourteenth century onwards there is a growing tendency for major poets to use the dream-poem for one general purpose, though in a variety of different ways. I shall attempt a preliminary indication of this purpose now, because in my view it is the core of the subject 'dream-poetry'. It may well be that the dream-poem does not constitute a 'distinct literary kind', though it does tend towards a certain complex of subject-matter: an ideal and often symbolic landscape, in which the dreamer encounters an authoritative figure, from whom he learns some religious or secular doctrine, and so on. But essentially a dream-poem, from the fourteenth century on, is a poem which has more fully realized its own existence as a poem. Compared with other poems, it makes us more conscious that it has a beginning and an end (marked by the falling asleep and awakening of the narrator); that it has a narrator, whose experience constitutes the subject-matter of the poem; that its status is that of an imaginative fiction (whether this is conceived as a matter of inspiration, or of mere fantasy, or somewhere between the two); in short that it is not a work of nature but a work of art. It is a poem which does not take for granted its own existence, but is continuously aware of its own existence and of the need, therefore, to justify that existence (since it is not part of the self-justifying world of natural objects). Roland Barthes has written that 'around 1850, Literature begins to face a problem of self-justification',[6] but he seems to be wide of the mark by some five centuries. In England, a new consciousness of and interest in the nature and status of literature begins to develop in the fourteenth century. Earlier, vernacular poets had been no more than minstrels and story-tellers, entertainers who were of no special interest or dignity in themselves and whose mode of existence was justified simply by the satisfaction they gave to their audiences. In the fourteenth century, poets become more self-aware, more conscious of the peculiar status of works of literature, and of the need to define, or pretend to define, that status for their audiences. This new self-consciousness emerges partly under the impact of ideas filtering in from Italy of 'a new importance and seriousness in vernacular poetry',[7] and this is probably part of the explanation for its presence in Chaucer. It cannot be the whole explanation, however, for a similar self-consciousness is recurrently expressed by Langland, and even the author of *Winner and Waster*, writing in the 1350s, embarks on a brief discussion of the difference between mere entertainers and genuinely creative writers. There is no reason to suppose that either of these alliterative poets had come into contact with the work of Dante, Petrarch or Boccaccio; but it is no accident that they are both writers of dream-poems.

The dream-framework, in the first place, explains the mere fact of the existence of a poem; it exists as an account of the narrator's dream. As we shall see later, however, this explanation is potentially highly ambiguous, since a dream may be considered as the product of divine inspiration or as the expression of a merely human mood or fantasy. Secondly, the dream-framework inevitably brings the poet into his poem, not merely as the reteller of a story which has its origin elsewhere, but as the person who experiences the whole substance of the poem. As Susanne Langer has put it, 'The most noteworthy formal characteristic of dream is that the dreamer is always at the center of it'.[8] But this leads to further ambiguity, because though the poet can in this way discuss the problems of his art (often under the guise of considering the status and validity of dreams), and even advertise himself, calling attention to his other productions and his reputation, he also, by appearing in his dream, disappears, since he becomes part of his own fiction.

The double appearing and disappearing act of the dream-poet is performed to perfection by Chaucer, who is unmistakably present in his own dream-poems, and is even named (as in *The House of Fame*) and has works attributed to him (as in the *Prologue* to the *Legend*), but is present *as someone else* – someone excessively humble, timid, clumsy, uncomprehending. Chaucer comes more and more to use the dream-poem as a means of meditating on his own situation as a courtly poet of love; and similarly Langland uses the dream-poem to explore his vocation as a religious poet and the difficulties he had in writing the kind of poem he felt called on to write. In late dream-poems such as Skelton's *Garland of Laurel* and Douglas's *Palice of Honour* the focus comes to be explicitly on the role and worth of the poet himself. (I do not mean to imply that every detail in such poems is literally autobiographical. We are frequently intended to guess at an autobiography from a dream-poem, but we can rarely be sure how far it is ideal and how far literal.) In many different ways, then, the dream-poem becomes a device for expressing the poet's consciousness of himself as poet and for making his work reflexive. I shall return to these topics on later pages.

Spiritual adventure

Meanwhile I wish to look more closely at the tradition of visions which, as medieval poets were aware, lay behind their dream-poems. The tradition in question is one not specifically of dream but of spiritual adventure. The medieval dream-poem may seem something of an oddity, if we think of the main tradition of Western literature as being one of action in the outer, physical world. In our own time perhaps this is ceasing to be so. There has been a greatly increased interest in recent years in the expansion and exploration of consciousness itself, by drugs and other means, and, as a symptom in the field of literature, one might consider how science fiction, which used to consist largely of physical adventure, has turned from outer to inner space, in the work of William Burroughs, J. G. Ballard, and others. But, from the time of the Homeric poems down to the modern novel, it is surely true that the scene of the great bulk of Western literature has not been the internal world of the mind, in which dreams transact themselves, but the outer, public world of objective reality. This is not to suggest a predominance of mere brainless adventure. Mind and spirit have been active, of course, but they have usually derived their activity from interaction with the physical world. The underlying assumption of the main tradition of Western literature has perhaps been one which Aristotle states in his *Poetics*, and states briskly, as if he expected no argument: 'Our end is a certain kind of doing'.[9] In this context, the importance of the dream-poem as a kind of literature in the Middle Ages may seem strange. But if we then look further afield, to the context of world literature as a whole, the perspective changes. We learn from anthropologists that in primitive societies everywhere poets are the same as seers or prophets. Their compositions come to them in a state of trance or ecstasy, in which they are oblivious to the outer world, and their role in society is to see what cannot be seen by ordinary men. The main theme of the original literary traditions of Asia, Polynesia and Africa – which are, of course, oral, not written – is not physical but spiritual adventure: the journeys of the soul into the past, the distant or hidden present, and the future.

The forms which these spiritual adventures take are many and various; but they tend to follow traditional lines. The principal themes are the journeys of mortals to the bright Heavens above, the abode of the gods; to the Underworld with its mysterious darkness, the abode of the dead; to remote and inaccessible spheres of the Universe.[10]

Here, in this ancient literature of spiritual adventure, we find something much closer to the dream-poetry of the Middle Ages.

There is no need, however, to envisage any direct influence from ancient oral literature on the written literature of the Middle Ages. Medieval literature is highly bookish: we have already noted how frequently old books are mentioned in some medieval dream-poems, and we shall see later what an important part books and reading play in the economy of the dream-poem from Chaucer onwards. The fact is that there has existed in the West, too, a written literature of spiritual adventure alongside and even within the more prominent tradition of physical adventure. On the face of it, perhaps the last place we should expect to find this is in the classical epic poems, for epic is supremely the form of physical adventure. Yet in the figure of Homer, the blind bard who cannot see the outer world and who can yet be inspired by the Muse to re-create the heroic past to the eyes of the mind, there are still vestiges of the poet as prophet or seer. This makes it less surprising, perhaps, that in the *Odyssey* one part of Odysseus's wanderings should take him out of the 'real' world of the Mediterranean, into the 'other' world, the underworld, Tartarus. He goes there, in book x, so as to gain hidden knowledge from the soul of Teiresias, the blind prophet – a kind of double of Homer himself, in whom we recognize again the connection, as in dreams, between the closed outward eyes and the clear inward sight. He performs a ritual which calls up various ghosts, and, after he has spoken with some of the dead, including his own mother, Anticleia, he sees the torments being undergone by the souls of the impious: Tityus being eaten alive by vultures, Sisyphus forever pushing his stone up the hill, and so on. This episode in the *Odyssey*, with its vision of what so many people through the ages have longed to know – the fate of men after their deaths – was to be a major influence on medieval dream-poems. But it was an indirect influence. Homer's work itself was hardly known in the Middle Ages, and this underworld episode conveyed its influence through the scene written in imitation of it by Virgil in the *Aeneid*. In book VI, Aeneas receives instruction from the Cumaean Sybil on how to visit his dead father, Anchises, in the underworld. She goes down with him, and there he sees the damned undergoing the same torments as in Homer; but now the vision of judgment is made more comprehensive, for he also sees the homes of the blessed, where 'an ampler air clothes the plains with brilliant light, and always they see a sun and stars which are theirs alone'.[11] Finally, he is allowed to see the souls of people unborn: that is to say, he sees the future, and Anchises is able to inform him about his own destiny and about the future of Rome, the city he has not yet founded. Like much else in Virgil, this vision of the other world as a hell for the damned and a heaven for the blessed was readily susceptible of Christian interpretation in the Middle Ages. That is why it is Virgil who in the *Divine Comedy* accompanies Dante to hell and purgatory (though not to paradise, from which he is excluded through not having been a Christian), and why Chaucer refers to Virgil as well as Dante as an authority on the other world.

Macrobius on Scipio's dream

We can find episodes of spiritual adventure, then, in the very strong-holds of the Western literature of physical adventure; but in the *Odyssey* and the *Aeneid* these episodes are smuggled in, disguised as physical exploits. The journey to the underworld is presented as a physical journey, one ordeal among others that the epic hero must undergo before he reaches his home or founds a new city for his people. But there are other places in classical literature where spiritual adventure is presented as such, in the form of dream-experience. One such place is the *Somnium Scipionis*, which, as we have already seen, is referred to in the *Roman de la Rose* and in three of Chaucer's dream-poems. The *Somnium Scipionis* is the closing portion of a longer work, the *De Re Publica*, written by Cicero as a Latin equivalent to Plato's *Republic*. Just as Plato closed his work with a vision, the vision of judgment seen by Er when he was apparently on the point of death, so Cicero concluded

8

his work with the dream of Scipio. This conclusion was the only part of the *De Re Publica* known in the Middle Ages. In it Scipio the younger, after long conversation with King Masinissa about his late grandfather, Scipio Africanus the elder, falls asleep and has a dream, set in the heavens, in which his grandfather appears to him. Africanus foretells his grandson's future, and speaks to him of the nature of the heavens (including the nine spheres of Ptolemaic cosmology, and the harmony they make in their motion), the smallness of the earth, the vanity of earthly fame, and the immortality of the soul. Like the journeys to the underworld in Homer and Virgil, this vision includes information about the fate of human souls after death. Those who acted well, and especially those who served their countries, go to heaven, while those who have given themselves up to sensual pleasures, and have broken the laws of gods and men, are whirled round the earth and tormented for many ages before they can be saved. Once again, then, we have a pagan vision which could easily be understood or reinterpreted in Christian terms; and the *Somnium Scipionis* was made all the more attractive to medieval writers of dream-poems by the fact that it was known in the Middle Ages as incorporated in a commentary by Macrobius, dating from about 400, which included an elaborate classification of different kinds of dream.

Macrobius felt obliged to begin his commentary by justifying Cicero for his use of so 'fabulous' or fictitious a device as a dream to convey weighty subject-matter, and it is in order to do this that he attempts to classify the different kinds of dream. He distinguishes five types altogether: two insignificant and three significant. The two insignificant types are the nightmare (*insomnium*) and the apparition (*visum* or *phantasma*), and Macrobius says that these are not worth interpreting because they have no prophetic significance. The nightmare, he writes, 'may be caused by mental or physical distress, or anxiety about the future: the patient experiences in dreams vexations similar to those that disturb him during the day' (p. 88).[12] Macrobius's brief dismissal of this type of dream may seem strange nowadays, but a lack of interest in possible links between the dream and the psychology of the individual dreamer is normal in medieval dream-literature until the fourteenth century. The assumption that the outward form of a significant dream may be influenced by the dreamer's waking preoccupations is indeed found in the *Somnium Scipionis* itself, though not in Macrobius's commentary, for Cicero makes Scipio suggest that he dreamed of his grandfather because he and Masinissa had been talking of him the night before (p. 70). Of the other meaningless type of dream, the *visum*, Macrobius writes that it 'comes upon one in the moment between wakefulness and slumber,

9

in the so-called "first cloud of sleep". In this drowsy condition a person thinks he is still awake, and imagines he sees spectres rushing at him or wandering vaguely about, differing from natural creatures in size and shape, and hosts of diverse things, either delightful or disturbing' (p. 89). Such dream-experiences, naturally enough, seem to have been of no more interest to medieval poets than they were to Macrobius.[13]

The *insomnium* and the *visum*, then, can be fully explained in naturalistic terms, either psychologically or physiologically, and are of no prophetic value. The three types of dream which are of prophetic value are as follows. The *somnium*, or enigmatic dream, 'conceals with strange shapes and veils with ambiguity the true meaning of the information being offered, and requires an interpretation for its understanding'; the *visio*, or prophetic vision, shows something which 'actually comes true'; and the *oraculum*, or oracular dream, is one in which 'a parent, or a pious or revered man, or a priest, or even a god' appears and gives information or advice (p. 90). These three types of prophetic dream are not mutually exclusive, and indeed Macrobius explains that Scipio's vision belonged to all three. Probably most people have seen nearly all dreams as belonging to Macrobius's category of the *somnium* (the normal Latin word for 'dream'). Few are willing to dismiss their dreams as totally meaningless, though one recent theory has it that the function of sleep is to enable the brain, that great computer, to carry out programme revision and clearance processes, and that our dreams, being merely fragmentary glimpses of rejected programmes, have no meaning in themselves.[14] Most people cling instinctively to the notion that dreams are composed in a language which is intelligible in principle, though it requires interpretation, and there may be much disagreement as to the appropriate means of interpreting it – is the language of dreams communal and permanent, or has each dreamer his own personal symbolism? As we shall see, medieval dream-poems possess to some extent a common symbolic language, though, once an interest developed in the psychological basis of dreams, they also began to be used for the exploration of personal dilemmas. The precise terms used by Macrobius about the *somnium* are of special interest in implying that such dreams are 'natural' equivalents to the artifice of allegory, and thereby explaining why allegorical fictions so often came to be set in dreams. Unlike Freud, he does not suggest any reason why dreams should conceal their true meaning and need interpretation.

The *visio* is less widely credited now than in the Middle Ages, though the possibility that dreams are precognitive is still the subject of scientific experiment, and, in J. W. Dunne's *An Experiment with Time*, has been made the basis of a complete metaphysical theory. Since Macrobius goes on to explain that Scipio's dream was a *visio* in that it showed him 'the regions of his abode after death and his future condition' (p. 90), it appears that any dream of the other world might count as prophetic. Of Macrobius's five types, the *oraculum* alone now seems completely obsolete, and it will be worth pausing for a moment to consider why this should be so. It is perhaps true that in our times few people have dreams in which an authoritative figure such as a parent or priest gives advice; and yet Macrobius saw this as a recognizable category of dream, and it is one to which many literary dreams of classical and medieval times belong. One might suppose that this category was merely a literary convention, a convenient way of dressing up didacticism to make it more interesting and convincing. But there is also the possibility that dreams do not follow a constant pattern throughout the ages, and that this may be a respect in which dreaming-habits have changed. The anthropologist J. S. Lincoln has argued that, in addition to the anxiety and wish-fulfilment dreams that are common to all mankind, there are also dreams whose shape and content are determined by local culture-patterns, and which cease to occur when those culture-patterns are broken down (for example, when the way of life of a primitive tribe is transformed through its contact with civilization). This suggestion is taken further by E. R. Dodds, who proposes that the *oraculum* may be an example of a culture-pattern dream: it may be that people really did have dreams of that kind in patriarchal, authoritarian societies, identifying the authoritative figure as an ancestor, an angel, or God, according to the predominant culture-pattern; whereas we, in a society in which authority is less personal, have ceased to have such dreams.[15] If this is so, it would help to explain the persistence of the *oraculum* as a medieval dream-type, a persistence so powerful that it made possible such 'anti-*oracula*' as *The House of Fame* (in which a 'man of gret auctorite' appears only for the poem to break off) and *Pearl* (in which, by what is felt to be a shocking reversal of the natural order of things, the person giving information and advice in the dream is not the dreamer's parent but his child).

Scriptural and Christian visions

So far we have been examining the classical, pagan antecedents of the medieval dream-poem. But beside this classical tradition, there is also an even more powerful Judaeo-Christian stream of influence upon medieval literature, and in this, visionary experience appears still more prominently, and is openly admitted as such, not disguised as heroic adventure. For the Middle Ages, the explicitly visionary element in Scripture must have provided a major justification for a literature of dreams and visions. In the Book of Numbers, for example, God speaks as follows to Aaron and Miriam:

> If there be among you a prophet of the Lord, I will appear to him in a vision, or I will speak to him in a dream.
> But it is not so with my servant Moses who is most faithful in all my house.
> For I speak to him mouth to mouth, and plainly: and not by riddles and figures doth he see the Lord. (Numbers 12: 6–8)[16]

This distinction between two ways in which God speaks, either 'in a vision,... in a dream' (*in visione,...per somnium*) or, very occasionally, 'mouth to mouth' (*ore ad os*) and 'not by riddles and figures' (*non per aenigmata et figuras*), was to be of great importance when the Fathers of the Church came to discuss mystical experience as one kind of dream or vision: it is emphasised, for example, by St Augustine in his *De Genesi ad Litteram*. Again, the supreme significance of dreams is asserted by Elihu in the Book of Job:

> By a dream in a vision by night, when deep sleep falleth upon men, and they are sleeping in their beds:
> Then he openeth the ears of men, and teaching instructeth them in what they are to learn. (Job 33: 15–16)

There are many examples in Scripture of divinely inspired visions. In the Old Testament, for instance, there are the dreams of Pharaoh, Joseph, and Nebuchadnezzar, referred to by Chaucer and Langland, all of which could be interpreted as foretelling the future. There is the Book of Ezechiel, which begins (giving a precise date, like many medieval dream-poems): 'Now it came to pass, in the thirtieth year, in the fourth month, on the fifth day of the month, when I was in the midst of the captives by the river Chobar, the heavens were opened, and I saw the visions of God' – and the whole book consists of a record of his visions. In the New Testament, an important reference occurs in St Paul's second Epistle to the Corinthians, where the context makes it clear that Paul is speaking of his own experiences:

> I will come to visions and revelations of the Lord.
> I know a man in Christ; above fourteen years ago (whether in the body, I know not, or out of the body, I know not; God knoweth), such a one caught up to the third heaven.
> And I know such a man (whether in the body, or out of the body, I know not; God knoweth);
> That he was caught up into paradise, and heard secret words which it is not granted to man to utter. (II Corinthians 12: 1–4)

And perhaps the most powerful and influential of all the visions in Scripture is that of St John the Divine, in his Apocalypse or Revelation. Here, after an introductory section, we are told:

After these things, I looked; and, behold a door was opened in heaven. And the first voice which I heard, as it were of a trumpet speaking with me, said: Come up hither and I will show thee the things which must be done hereafter. And immediately I was in the spirit... (Apocalypse 4: 1-2)

In his vision, along with much fantastic symbolism (the beasts, the red dragon, the great whore, and so on), St John sees heaven, with God in the form both of the Father and of the Lamb. The future of the world is revealed to him, down to the end of all things and the resurrection of the dead, and finally he sees the heavenly Jerusalem, a jewelled city full of brilliant light. These two visions, of St Paul and St John, were to be taken as types of mystical experience by theological writers such as St Augustine and St Gregory, and we shall find frequent allusions to them in medieval dream-poems.

The early centuries of Christianity, and indeed the whole period down to and including the Middle Ages, saw the growth of religious vision-literature on a large scale – so large that it is impossible to do more here than to give a few examples of the kind of work that may have been known, directly or indirectly, to medieval writers. The first of these is a work which was certainly known to Dante, Chaucer, and other poets: the *Apocalypse of St Paul*.[17] This dates from the third century A.D.; it was translated from Greek into Latin by the sixth century, and the many surviving manuscripts indicate that it was widely read. It derives from St Paul's brief account of his visionary experience, mentioned above, and it purports to be an account of what he saw when he was 'caught up into paradise'. Right down to the fourteenth century it was widely accepted as an authentic part of Scripture. What Paul saw in the other world, according to this document, was a strange mixture of paradisal and apocalyptic scenes, greatly influenced by both Genesis and St John's Apocalypse. He sees too what happens to the souls of the good and the wicked. The sinners are being tormented in various ways, reminiscent of the underworld as seen by Odysseus and Aeneas: those who mocked at God's word are now gnawing their own tongues, fast-breakers are tormented like Tantalus by being hung over water and fruit they cannot reach, and so on. Some of the blessed souls inhabit a beautiful land seven times brighter than silver, with rivers and fruit-trees; others are in a city called the city of Christ and Jerusalem, which is made of gold and encompassed by four rivers. This work, derivative and absurd as it is in itself, was a most important influence on medieval visions of the world beyond death, and it was seen by Dante, for example, as forming part of a unified Classical and Scriptural tradition of spiritual adventure. At the very beginning of the *Divine Comedy*, Virgil tells Dante of the journey through Hell and Purgatory that lies before him, and Dante draws back in fear, exclaiming, 'Io non Enea, io non Paolo sono' (*Inferno* II. 32) (I am not Aeneas, I am not Paul). For him, clearly, whatever we may think of the infinite distance between them in literary value, the *Aeneid* and the *Apocalypse of St Paul* were works to be mentioned in the same breath.

My second example of a Christian vision comes from several centuries later, but, like the *Apocalypse of St Paul*, it deals with that always fascinating topic, the fate awaiting human souls after death. The work in question was written in Latin by Hincmar, who was a ninth-century archbishop of Rheims, an astute politician, and a bad poet. This work concerns the vision granted to a certain priest called Bernoldus.[18] He had been lying seriously ill for four days, in a kind of trance and apparently at the point of death, or even dead. But he recovered at last, and explained to his confessor that he had had a vision of the other world. (In this early vision-literature, the vision of the world after death is commonly granted to someone actually on the brink of death.) Hincmar evidently intended his work as a contribution to a contemporary theological controversy: its aim is to prove that the dead can be assisted by the prayers of the living, and a single pattern of action is repeated several times in Bernoldus's story. This pattern is as follows. Bernoldus meets in the other world some person he recognizes, who is being tormented for his sins; this person begs Bernoldus to ask his friends to pray for him; Bernoldus is returned to this world to carry out the errand; and finally he is carried back to the other world, to find the person who was formerly in torment already released from his pains through his friends' prayers. The doctrinal implication is obvious; but the work also contains propaganda of a more specific kind. One of the persons Bernoldus sees in agony is Charles the Bald, King of France, whom he finds being eaten by worms, so that there was little left of him but bones and sinews. The King explains that he is suffering in this way because, when he was alive, he had failed to follow the good advice of those who loved him – including, of course, Archbishop Hincmar.

This use of the other-world vision for theological and political polemic is to be found later in the *Divine Comedy*, where Dante is sometimes as personal as Hincmar in the way he consigns his enemies to torment. Even in *Pearl* we can recognize a similar underlying structure: there too a man is carried in spirit to the other world, meets there a dead person whom he knew in this world, and is instructed by that person, from a position of unassailable authority, on an important doctrinal issue (the salvation of the innocent and the equality of heavenly rewards). In every other respect, *Pearl* is totally unlike the *Visio Bernoldi*; but even the most subtle and sophisticated of later dream-poems owes something to the early tradition of visions. Hincmar himself, like the later dream-poets, is conscious of writing in a tradition to which he refers as authentication for his own work. At the end of his account, he explains that, though he did not receive the story from Bernoldus himself, it is worthy of belief because one can read elsewhere of similar revelations granted through visions. He mentions a large number of them: those recounted in the *Dialogues* of St Gregory (including the famous vision of St Benedict), in Bede's *Ecclesiastical History*, in the writings of St Boniface, and, in his own days, in a work by Walafrid Strabo which put Charlemagne in hell.

My final example of Christian vision-literature is among those mentioned by Hincmar: the vision of Dryhthelm, described by Bede in the *Ecclesiastical History* v. 12. Dryhthelm, like Bernoldus, was ill and appeared to be dead, but he then revived and described the spiritual experience he had had. He was accompanied in his vision by 'a handsome man in a shining robe', who led him to the north-east, where he saw first the souls of men who had repented only on their death-beds, being tormented in flames and ice, and afterwards the mouth of hell itself, where damned souls were being dragged by devils into everlasting agony. Next he was led by his guide to the south-east, and

as he led me forwards in bright light, I saw before us a tremendous wall which seemed to be of infinite length and height in all directions. As I could see no gate, window, or entrance in it, I began to wonder why we went up to the wall. But when we reached it, all at once – I know not by what means – we were on top of it. Within lay a very broad and pleasant meadow, so filled with the scent of spring flowers that its wonderful fragrance quickly dispelled all the stench of the gloomy furnace that had overcome me. Such was the light flooding all this place that it seemed greater than the brightness of daylight or of the sun's rays at noon. In this meadow were innumerable companies of men in white robes, and many parties of happy people were sitting together. And as my guide led me through these crowds of happy citizens, I began to wonder whether this was the Kingdom of Heaven, of which I had heard so often.[19]

However, his guide explains to him that this is only the waiting place for those who led lives that were good, but not good enough to deserve heaven itself immediately. Lastly, Dryhthelm is given just a glimpse of the true kingdom of heaven, where he sees a wonderful light, hears a 'sweet sound of people singing', and smells a scent of 'surpassing fragrance'; but then his guide leads him away again. One last detail is worth mentioning as a further example of the unified tradition to which visions of this kind belong. When describing the approach to hell, the Christian author Bede quotes words used by the pagan Virgil to describe the approach to the underworld in *Aeneid* VI. 268: *sola sub nocte per umbras* (through the shades of the lone night).

Visions of place

The tradition I have been describing is, among other things, a tradition of visions of a certain place, or group of places: the other world, the world after death, conceived from Classical times as divided into a place of punishment and a place of reward, and then later, as Catholic conceptions of the afterlife crystallized, as a threefold place, hell, purgatory and heaven. This is the setting of *The Divine Comedy* and of Deguileville's *Pelerinage de la Vie Humaine*. The majority of English dream-poems show nothing of purgatory, and their treatment of hell is usually subordinate and often oblique.[20] *Piers Plowman*, it is true, does include a vision of hell as it is harrowed by Christ, even though the setting of the poem as a whole is not the other world. But in *The Book of the Duchess*, for example, a version of hell occurs only in the description of the cave of Morpheus, which was 'as derk/ As helle-pit overal aboute' (170–1), and, in the dream itself, still more obliquely, as part of the misery of the Black Knight, who has 'more sorowe than Tantale' (709). In *The Parliament of Fowls*, Dante's hell has become a vision of unhappy love, conceived as a state of barrenness and sterility,

> Ther nevere tre shal fruyt ne leves bere;
> This strem yow ledeth to the sorweful were
> There as the fish in prysoun is al drye;
> Th'eschewyng is only the remedye! (137–40)
> *were* weir, trap

Hell may be thought of in this way as a prison; alternatively, by way of contrast with the enclosed garden of paradise, it may be seen as 'a desert with no boundaries at all'.[21] There is a vision of this kind in *The House of Fame*, where once more a displacement has occurred, and the sterility is perhaps that of a love-poet's lack of inspiration:

> Then sawgh I but a large feld,
> As fer as that I myghte see,
> Withouten toun, or hous, or tree,
> Or bush, or grass, or eryd lond;
> For al the feld nas but of sond

As smal as man may se yet lye
In the desert of Lybye;
Ne no maner creature
That ys yformed be Nature
Ne sawgh I, me to rede or wisse. (482–91)
eryd ploughed; *nas but* was only; *rede* advise; *wisse* guide

In the anonymous fifteenth-century *Court of Sapience* the displacement
is taken still further, and a 'place desert' is identified as 'dredeful
worldly occupacioun'.[22] In Douglas's *Palice of Honour*, still later, the
dream begins with a superb description of a landscape of unnatural
sterility, where a river like 'Cochyte the river infernall' (138) is running
blood-red between bare banks.[23] Here the meaning of the landscape
remains to be discussed.

By contrast with this varying treatment of hell, medieval dream-poems
regularly employ a heavenly setting of a constant kind. The fact that
the poets' heavens are almost invariably places of the same type may
be seen simply as a matter of a powerful literary tradition, but the power
of the tradition must itself have some deeper explanation. We seem to
be dealing with a place of the mind, a universal psychic archetype. The
sources of medieval visions of heaven are partly Scriptural: the description of the Garden of Eden, or earthly paradise, in Genesis, that of the
heavenly paradise, partly based on Genesis, in the Apocalypse, and the
symbolic garden of the Song of Songs, the *hortus conclusus*: 'My sister,
my spouse, is a garden enclosed, a garden enclosed, a fountain sealed
up' (Song of Songs 4:12). The sources are also partly classical. E. R.
Curtius has shown how a particular tradition of description of an ideal
landscape, originating with classical poets such as Homer, Theocritus
and Virgil, was imitated by minor writers and codified in rhetorical
textbooks, and so was passed on to the writers of Late Antiquity and
the Middle Ages as an established convention.[24] The *locus amoenus* or
'beautiful place', which became the heavenly landscape of literary visions
and dreams, is basically a Mediterranean landscape, an ideal originating
in Greece, Italy, and Palestine. It is typically set in bright southern
sunlight (perhaps augmented by or transformed into the jewelled brilliance of the Apocalypse), but it also provides shade against the sun, and
is therefore furnished with a tree or trees, often fruit-trees. The trees
will be in a flowery meadow, which will provide fragrance as well as bright
colours, and there will probably be birds singing in them (though in some
cases the place of birds is taken by human or angelic song). In the
meadow there is almost invariably a spring or brook, often rising from
a fountain, and there will usually be a breeze, both features being

necessities for comfort in a hot country. It is perhaps somewhat surprising that this Mediterranean ideal should have been taken over so readily into the literature of northern Europe, where water and breezes might be thought commoner and less desirable. But taken over it is, spreading gradually north-west as far as Scotland, where in the early sixteenth century Douglas is still describing a supposedly Scottish scene which includes grapes and olives. This heavenly landscape occurs often enough outside dreams in medieval literature, but it is a particularly common feature of dream-poems. The fact that we shall encounter it so frequently later in the discussion of specific poems makes it unnecessary for me to illustrate it here.

Visions of the other world, then, and the dream-poems which derive from them, frequently give access to a special place; but, as we have partly seen already, they normally also give access to some form of information or teaching. The visionary goes to the other world in order to learn something: that is the usual pattern, and it is an important feature of medieval dream-poems. Nothing could be further from the truth than to suppose that medieval people expected a literary dream to provide *simply* escape from the tedious and no doubt frequently squalid realities of their lives into a more ideal world, an imagined paradise. Medieval religion and courtly culture directed themselves towards ideals, which could be realized in poetic dreams more fully than in the waking reality of earthly life; and the glimpses of such realizations given in dream-poems might well help to sustain the orientation of medieval life towards the ideals themselves. But even apart from this, as we have learned from Macrobius, it was expected that something could be learned from real dreams, and hence from literary dreams: advice or warnings about the future, or philosophical truths which it would be important to know in waking life. This is a role which real dreams have played in many cultures, and it was a common role for medieval literary dreams. My last two examples of the visionary writings out of which medieval dream-poems developed will be more strongly and explicitly doctrinal visions.

Doctrinal visions

The first of these is the highly influential *De Consolatione Philosophiae* of Boethius, which was translated from Latin by two major dream-poets: into French by Jean de Meun and into English by Chaucer. It is not an explicitly visionary work, though the events it describes could not occur literally in normal waking life, but might naturally find their place in a Macrobian *oraculum*. (Boethius probably knew the *Somnium Scipionis*.)

The authoritative figure who appears to the author is in this case Philosophy, who comes to Boethius's bedside when he is sick with despair. She is an ancient lady who is yet youthful in appearance, and whose height varies from the normal human size to higher than the sky. Boethius quickly identifies her as a personification of philosophy; and such personification-allegory is common in subsequent dream-poems. Allegory of this kind is not usually intended to be obscure, in the way that real dream-symbolism sometimes is. Some of the details of Philosophy's appearance are symbolic, it is true: her aged yet youthful appearance is meant to remind us of the subject-matter of philosophy – ancient problems which are always relevant to the present – while her varying height indicates that philosophy deals with topics of varying importance, from mundane matters of conduct to the supreme questions of metaphysics. Similarly, on her robe are embroidered the Greek letters Pi and Theta, standing for practical and contemplative philosophy. None of this symbolism was esoteric when the work was written (in the sixth century), and it was probably meant to be interpreted without difficulty. But the great bulk of the work is not susceptible of allegorical interpretation at all, except in so far as a conversation between Boethius and Philosophy can be seen to correspond to a process of thought within Boethius himself. This is important, because it implies that the Boethius who is undergoing the conflict represented in the fiction both is and is not the same person as the Boethius who created the fiction, and who had presumably resolved the problems he depicts. We shall find a similar deliberate doubleness of effect in many dream-poems, where the dreamer both is and is not the same as the writer who names him as 'I' in the poem.

In the case of the *De Consolatione*, the whole work is a dialogue, in imitation of the dialogues of Plato, in which Boethius asks questions about the ordering of the universe, and Philosophy answers them, and gradually brings him round to an acceptance of his situation. He is writing in prison, having fallen suddenly from a high position as minister to the Emperor Theodoric to being arrested and condemned, and eventually, after he had written the book, tortured and executed. The conversation touches on the disparity between God's orderly rule of Nature and the disorder he permits in human affairs; on Fortune (this section being a major source for many medieval treatments of change and chance in human life); on the nature of happiness, nobility, and the good; on providence; and on predestination and freewill. These are all matters which were later discussed in medieval dream-poems, often by personified figures. A reading of Boethius would prevent us from being surprised either to find serious doctrinal matter framed in a dream, or to find personifications introduced into a dream in order to utter doctrine rather than to take part in some symbolic action which then requires further interpretation. Medieval writers seem regularly to have associated personification with dream (though each can, of course, be found separately). Personified abstractions could not engage in dialogue and homily in the objective world, but they could well do so in the world of the mind, to which dreams give access; and indeed some modern dream-interpretation, particularly of a Jungian kind, comes close to identifying dream-figures as personifications.

One other element of the *De Consolatione* which became an important influence on medieval dream-poems was a passage early in book IV in which Philosophy promises Boethius to 'fycchen fetheris in thi thought',[25] and goes on to describe a journey of the mind through the heavens towards God. The sensation of flying is common in real dreams, and many literary dreams, by Chaucer, Douglas, and Lindsay, were later to represent such flights as mental journeys.

My second example of doctrinal vision is the *De Planctu Naturae* of Alanus de Insulis, a French theologian of the twelfth century. In some ways this work can be seen as bridging the gap between Boethius and the dream-poem proper. Its form – alternating sections of prose and verse – imitates that of the *De Consolatione Philosophiae*, and, like Boethius's work, it begins with the appearance to the author of an impressive female personification, Nature, dressed in symbolic clothing. But the appearance is now placed in a supernaturally inspired dream, as the conclusion of the *De Planctu* makes clear: 'With the mirror of this visionary sight taken away, the previous view of the mystic apparition left me, who had been fired by ecstasy [*ab extasi excitatum*], in sleep' (pr. IX. 249–52).[26] The visionary, however, is not adequate to the content of his vision: he swoons as Nature descends from her chariot, and does not recognize who she is. In this he himself exemplifies the human imperfection she has come to lament,[27] and becomes the forerunner of many medieval dreamers who fall below the level of their dreams. Moreover, the doctrine which the work contains is now not that of philosophy in general, but that of sexual love considered in the context of general philosophy. This is the characteristic subject-matter of courtly dream-poetry in French and English, and the *De Planctu Naturae* had an important direct influence on the *Roman de la Rose*. It is presumably not by accident that sexual love should so frequently form the subject-matter of medieval dream-poems, since the content of dreams themselves is so often sexual. Alanus was a monk, not a courtier, and, though his work uses some courtly terminology, it is not chiefly concerned with the 'art of love' (like the poems in the tradition derived from the *Roman de la Rose*) but with the offence against nature involved in sexual perversion. His Nature's robe has depicted on it the 'parliament of the living creation' (pr. I. 217–18) – Chaucer was to recall this in *The Parliament of Fowls* – and her tunic, coloured like the earth, shows the different species of animals, including man, who 'laid aside the idleness of sensuality, and by the direct guidance of reason penetrated the secrets of the heavens' (pr. I. 344–6). But this part of her tunic is torn, indicating the imperfection into which man has fallen, just as in Boethius Philosophy's robe had been torn, to indicate the contentions of the different schools of philosophers.

It is the imperfection of man that Nature has come to lament, an imperfection which shows itself especially in sexual perversion. She describes, in a manner reminiscent of Boethius, how all the rest of the created world is obedient to her commands: the sea does not encroach on the earth nor the earth on the sea, and so on. 'Man alone,' she continues, 'rejects the music of my harp, and raves under the lyre of frenzied Orpheus. For the human race, derogate from its high birth, commits monstrous acts in its union of genders, and perverts the rules of love by a practice of extreme and abnormal irregularity' (pr. IV. 87–92). The peculiar grammatical metaphor in this passage, which recurs throughout the work, is connected with the characterization of the visionary as a writer (an element of great importance in dream-poems later). Nature deplores homosexuality not simply because it is irregular, but because it is an offence against the natural duty of sexual reproduction. She explains that God, in order to ensure the continuity of species despite the mortality of individuals, appointed her as his *vicaria* (deputy), and she in turn appointed Venus as her *subvicaria*, to be assisted by her husband Hymen and her son Cupid, to 'weave together the line of the human race in unwearied continuation' (pr. IV. 383–4). Nature provided Venus with hammers and anvils, 'with a command that she should apply these same hammers to the anvils, and faithfully give herself up to the forming of things, not permitting the hammers to leave their proper work, and become strangers to the anvils' (pr. V. 44–8). Nature also supplied Venus with an 'especially potent reed-pen' (pr. V. 50), which, like the hammers and anvils, is a sexual symbol, and which is also connected with the recurrent grammatical imaginery. But eventually Venus became tired with the repetitiousness of her work. She was unfaithful to Hymen (the god of weddings), committed adultery with Antigamus, and produced the bastard son Jocus (mirth), who is contrasted at length with her true son Cupid.

Thus we arrive at an explanation of the present state of things, in which sexual perversion is rife. But it has become clear that Alanus, despite a possibly prurient interest in sexual perversion itself, is considering it not as an independent phenomenon, but as a particularly striking and destructive type of a more general perversion of human nature. At an early stage in the *De Planctu*, Nature turns from homosexuality to mention examples of other kinds of perverse love, other ways in which man has deformed his original beauty with lust – Helen (adultery), Pasiphaë (bestiality), Myrrha (incest), Medea (infanticide), and Narcissus (self-love). Later, she broadens her field still more, by turning from sexual love, considered as a form of idolatry, to all the other false loves which lie at the root of the sins: the love of food and drink, the love of money, the various forms of pride, envy and flattery. After Nature has spoken of these various idolatries in which human evil consists, a number of other allegorical figures begin to appear. First comes Hymen, accompanied by silent musicians and wearing clothes on which pictures symbolizing marriage have largely faded. Afterwards there arrive in order Chastity, Temperance, Generosity, and Humility. Nature says that she knows they have come because men 'are endeavouring to disinherit you from your patrimony of an earthly habitation, and are seizing all power on earth, and forcing you to repair to your celestial home' (pr. VIII. 247–50). From this we gather that the scene of the poem's action, like that of other visions we have considered, is imagined as being a heavenly other world.

Nature adds that she will send Hymen with a letter to Genius, asking his help in anathematizing those who persist in the offences mentioned in the work. Who Genius is has been the subject of some discussion. The Roman encyclopaedist Varro, according to St Augustine, had described him as the god in charge of 'the generation of all things';[28] and Alanus's older contemporary William of Conches wrote that *genius est naturalis concupiscentia* (Genius is natural desire).[29] These definitions will apply well enough to Alanus's Genius, but he is also the *genius* in another sense of Nature herself – her *alter ego*, in whom she recognizes herself 'as in a mirror'. He is, as one scholar has argued, 'man's link with Paradise, the element in his nature which, albeit subliminally, recalls and seeks to regain his original perfection'.[30] As we might expect, therefore, Genius tells Nature that he is glad to give her his support. He dresses in priestly robes, and pronounces anathema against any who 'turn awry the lawful course of love' or pursue any of the other vices Nature has lamented. All the onlookers agree, and, with this, the vision ends.

The *De Planctu Naturae*, beyond its interest as a learned visionary work from just before the rise of the courtly dream-poem, was highly influential, partly through being read itself (as by Chaucer), and partly indirectly, through its influence on Jean de Meun's part of the *Roman de la Rose*. One of its interests for our purposes is that it makes explicit the link between human love, that central concern of medieval dream-poetry, and the larger philosophical conception of Nature – a link which in later medieval works is often assumed without being stated. It is important, however, not to misunderstand the bases of Alanus's thought. He has traditionally been described as a 'naturalist' and as a member of the 'school of Chartres', among the poets of which school, as C. S. Lewis puts it, 'Nature appears, not to be corrected by Grace, but as the goddess and the *vicaria* of God, herself correcting the unnatural'.[31] Recent scholarly work indicates that the importance of the 'school of Chartres', considered as a distinct philosophical and literary movement, may have been exaggerated;[32] and a sober reading of the *De Planctu* shows that Alanus's 'naturalism' is of a strictly limited kind. In the *De Consolatione*, Boethius deals only with philosophical considerations, and leaves out theological matters, because what he is writing about is the consolation of *philosophy* – which does not imply that he thinks theology false or irrelevant. Similarly, in the *De Planctu*, Alanus largely confines himself to the natural order, but that does not mean that he thinks there is nothing beyond it. On the contrary, for him, as for other medieval Christians, the natural order is subordinate to the supernatural, and Nature does indeed require to be completed, if not corrected, by Grace. When Nature first appears, in her chariot, we are told that 'a man who towered above the head of the virgin and the chariot, and whose countenance breathed not the commonness of earth, but rather the mystery of godship, aided the weakness of the womanly nature and guided the approach of the chariot in a well-regulated course' (pr. II. 17–22). Alanus is implying that even the daily course of nature cannot be fully regulated by Nature alone, but requires divine guidance. And later Nature herself insists that she is subordinate to God: 'man by my working is born, by the might of God is born again. Through me he is called from not being into being; through Him he is led from being on into a better being. For through me man is begotten unto death; through Him he is created unto life again' (pr. III. 225–30). Thus Nature herself asserts the Pauline conception of man's second birth in the order of Grace.

Alanus, then, cannot be called a 'naturalist' in the full sense; still less, finally, is he a believer that sexuality ought to be the driving force of human existence, even in the natural order. Nature, though she contrasts Cupid (sexual normality) with Jocus (sexual abnormality), is also highly critical of Cupid. She lays great emphasis on the violence and other forms of evil to which he has given rise – this too will be a theme of *The Parliament of Fowls* – and she apologises, with some embarrassment, for the fact that she has included 'slight signs of blame' – a considerable understatement – in her description of him, 'although he is allied to me by the connection of own blood-relationship' (pr. v. 5–7), on the ground that, though love is honourable in moderation, in excess it must be restrained. The *De Planctu Naturae* includes both the fantasies of sexual abnormality which are a common part of the content of real dreams, and a largely orthodox intellectual framework within which they are contained and judged.

The 'Roman de la Rose': Guillaume de Lorris

I now turn to dream-poems proper – those written in French, which were a major influence on the English courtly poetry of the fourteenth and fifteenth centuries. I consider first the most influential of all medieval dream-poems, the *Roman de la Rose*. This is a work of great length – over 20,000 lines – and one which achieved more popularity than any other medieval dream-poem: over two hundred manuscripts of it survive, many of them beautifully illuminated. A work on such a scale demands a whole book to itself, and indeed has received more than one.[33] To consider it briefly, as I must in a book concerned chiefly with English poems, is embarrassingly difficult, nor is it a poem which can easily be considered selectively, because its intellectual and tonal sequences are often highly intricate. In one way, it is a great advantage for readers of medieval English literature that we have a Middle English translation of two substantial parts of the *Roman de la Rose*, consisting of the first 5,000 lines or so (of which about a third was probably translated by Chaucer) and of a passage around lines 10,000 to 12,000. But in another way this has been a misfortune, because it has encouraged a selective reading of the *Roman* by English readers, and has helped to give currency to the view that the work as a whole is incoherently digressive. Certainly, by far the commonest view has been that there is little connection between the poem's two parts: part I, down to line 4028, written by Guillaume de Lorris in the second quarter of the thirteenth century, and part II, a continuation of some 18,000 lines more, written about forty years later by Jean de Meun. It has been common to assert that Guillaume was a delicate courtly allegorist, who wrote idealistically and sympathetically of the progress of that experience called *fin amor*

24

in the Middle Ages, while Jean de Meun was a bourgeois writer, who cared nothing for allegory, wrote a sprawling encyclopaedic work which treats *fin amor* and many other things satirically, and was himself a naturalist, a misogynist, and a believer in free love. More recent scholarly work has attempted, with varying degrees of success, to defend the unity of the poem, or its Christian orthodoxy, or both. I shall begin by considering Guillaume's opening to the poem, and shall then turn to look at some parts of Jean's continuation and at various issues they raise concerning the nature of the poem as a whole.

The *Roman de la Rose* is the first work I have considered which begins by presenting itself straightforwardly as a dream. With a reference to Macrobius's commentary on the *Somnium Scipionis*, Guillaume claims that dreams sometimes foretell the future. The implication, plainly, is that this dream is one such, a *visio*:

> Aucunes genz dient qu'en songes
> n'a se fables non et mençonges;
> mes l'en puet tex songes songier
> qui ne sont mie mençongier,
> ainz sont aprés bien aparant,
> si en puis bien traire a garant
> un auctor qui ot non Macrobes,
> qui ne tint pas songes a lobes,
> ançois escrit l'avision
> qui avint au roi Scypion.
> Qui c'onques cuit ne qui que die
> qu'il est folor et musardie
> de croire que songes aviegne,
> qui se voudra, por fol m'en teigne,
> quar endroit moi ai ge fiance
> que songes est senefiance
> des biens as genz et des anuiz,
> que li plusor songent de nuiz
> maintes choses covertement
> que l'en voit puis apertement. (1–20)

(Many men say that there is nothing in dreams but fables and lies, but one may have dreams which are not deceitful, whose import becomes quite clear afterward. We may take as witness an author named Macrobius, who did not take dreams as trifles, for he wrote of the vision which came to King Scipio. Whoever thinks or says that to believe in a dream's coming true is folly and stupidity may, if he wishes, think me a fool; but, for my part, I am convinced that a dream signifies the good and evil that come to men, for most men at night dream many things in a hidden way which may afterward be seen openly.)[34]

That opening, with its discussion of the validity of dreams – some say they are fables and lies, others that they tell the truth – provides the model for what will become a regular element in the dream-poem of the fourteenth century. When Guillaume takes us into the dream itself, which he says happened in May, five years ago, when he was about twenty, it looks at first very like one of the otherworld visions previously discussed. Inside the dream, as at the moment when the Dreamer fell asleep, it is springtime, the season of love: a May morning, when leaves are green and birds singing. The Dreamer walks among branches covered with blossoms and singing birds, washes his face in a river, and stroll through a meadow which runs alongside it. Then, suddenly, he comes upon a garden, surrounded by apparently impenetrable high walls. One is reminded of Bede's vision of Dryhthelm; not that that is a direct source of the *Roman*, but the experience involved seems to correspond exactly to what can be found in such religious visions. In Dryhthelm's vision there were two paradisal landscapes, the second even more beautiful than the first. Dryhthelm heard sweet voices singing from inside the second of his paradises – the truly heavenly one – and just so in the *Roman de la Rose* the Dreamer, as he stands disconsolately outside the walled garden and longs to get in, hears the sweet song of many birds coming from behind the wall. The wall is decorated with carved and painted figures of allegorical personages: Hate, Crime, Churlishness, Covetousness, Avarice, Envy, Sorrow, Old Age, Hypocrisy, and Poverty. These represent the qualities which are excluded from the inner paradise of the dream; and here we begin to see that the *Roman de la Rose* cannot be simply a religious vision, though it may be a courtly transmutation or even parody of such a vision. The personifications fall into two groups. Some are qualities which would be excluded from a Christian heaven, but others, such as Sorrow, Old Age and Poverty, are certainly not sins by Christian standards, and it seems clear that the value-system which could reject them, while it might overlap with Christianity to some extent, must be essentially not Christian but worldly. The personified figures on the garden wall are those attributes which exclude one from the courtly pursuit of earthly love.

The Dreamer at last finds a little gate in the wall. He knocks on it, and is admitted by a young woman called Oiseuse (Idleness) – another essential quality for the courtier and lover – who tells him that the lord of the garden is Deduit (Delight). Inside, it becomes clear that the small dream-world of the garden, like the larger dream-world outside, borrows its main characteristics from religious visions. The Dreamer remarks that

> je cuidai estre
> por voir em paradis terrestre:
> tant estoit li leus delitables,

> qu'i sembloit estre esperitables;
> car, si come lors m'ert avis,
> il ne fet en nul paradis
> si bon estre com il fessoit
> el vergier, qui tant me plesoit. (633–40)

(I thought that I was truly in the earthly paradise. So delightful was the place that it seemed to me to belong to the world of the spirit, for, as it seemed to me then, there was no paradise where existence was so good as it was in that garden which so pleased me.)

The very birds 'chantoient un chant autel / con fussent angre esperituel' (661–2) (sang a song as though they were heavenly angels), and the garden contains a dancing company of people who 'sembloient / tot por voir angres empenez' (722–3) (seemed, in absolute truth, winged angels). Finally, the Dreamer sees among the dancers the God of Love himself, a figure of terrifying beauty and magnificence, of whom he says that

> Il sembloit que ce fust uns angres
> qui fust tot droit venuz dou ciel. (902–3)

(It seemed that he was an angel come straight from heaven.)

Perhaps, after all this, we shall not be surprised to find at the centre of the garden secular versions of the Tree of Life and the River of Life. These are a pine-tree and the fountain of Narcissus (the one in which Narcissus gazed at his own reflection and was drowned). The Dreamer looks into it, and sees at the bottom two crystal stones which have the marvellous property of reflecting the whole garden: what he notices especially in them is the reflection of a rose-bush. This is perhaps the only obscure part of the allegory. C. S. Lewis suggested that these stones symbolized the eyes of the lady with whom the Dreamer was about to fall in love; but if this is the fountain of Narcissus they ought surely to be his own eyes, and this would carry the suggestion that his subsequent love of the rose is a form of self-love.[35] He turns to the rose-bush itself, is deeply attracted by one particular rose-bud, and, as he is looking at it, is pierced by an arrow shot by the God of Love. This is the beginning of his complicated love-affair. Here there is no space to follow it out in detail, but I must mention one other incident from Guillaume's part of the *Roman*. When the Dreamer submits himself to the God of Love (thereby becoming the Lover), he receives a set of commandments from him. There is the same effect of religious parody here as with the qualities excluded from the garden. There are ten commandments, of course, and several of them correspond to Christian ethics – avoid slander, avoid avarice, avoid pride – but others are courtly in their tendency: honour women, be entertaining and amusing by whatever accomplishments you can, and make sure you wash frequently.

The question raised by these elements of religious parody in the *Roman de la Rose* is, what attitude towards love and religion do they imply on Guillaume's part? – a question raised by much medieval courtly literature. Is this 'religion of love' something wholeheartedly adopted by the poet, as a kind of Christian heresy? Is it an elborate joke? A satiric parody, intended to expose the cult of romantic love as a heresy? Or something different again? It seems clear, at least, that a major reason for the use of the setting of the religious vision, and of all the other details taken from religion, is that it is intended to correspond to and convey the intensity of the actual experience of falling in love. In the Middle Ages, the only language of absolute value was the language of religion, and therefore that was the obvious language to convey the fascinating and consciousness-transforming experience of falling in love. It is more like undergoing a religious experience than it is like anything else. That at least is how it feels from the inside; but here we come upon one of the great advantages of the dream-poem for such a subject. The dream may, in itself, have the force of a religious vision; but the turning of the dream into a poem provides for the possibility of a separation between inside and outside – between the Dreamer, who is absorbed in his own experience (which, like all dreams, is in the present tense), and the poet, who is repeating the story five years afterwards, in the past tense, 'si come lors m'ert avis' (637) (as it seemed to me then). The Dreamer and the poet are both 'I', but 'I' as poet does not necessarily endorse his reactions as Dreamer to the dream-experience of five years back.

This separability of poet from Dreamer is something we are made aware of, in sometimes paradoxical ways, throughout the poem. In these early stages, for example, there are points at which the 'I' of the poem has to tell us as poet about something of which, as Dreamer, he was unaware. The God of Love begins secretly to prepare his arrows to shoot at the Dreamer:

> Li dex d'Amors tantost de loing
> me prist a sivre l'arc ou poing.
> Or me gart Dex de mortel plaie,
> se tant avient qu'il a moi traie!
> Je, cui de ce ne fu noient,
> m'alai adez esbanoiant
> par le vergier tot a delivre,
> et cil pensa tost de moi sivre. (1311–18)

(Straightway the God of Love began to follow me, bow in hand, from a distance. Now may God protect me from a mortal wound if he goes so far as to shoot at me! Knowing nothing of all this, always enjoying myself, I went along quite freely through the garden, while the God of Love set his intent on following me.)

It is the poet, not the Dreamer, who sees the pursuit of the God of Love, and the poet, not the Dreamer, who appeals to 'Dex' (expanded in the Middle English translation to 'God, that sitteth in Magesté') to preserve the Dreamer from the attacks of that other god, 'Li Dex d'Amors'. I do not mean to suggest that the poet and the Dreamer are rigidly separated all the time, as they might be by a novelist such as James or Conrad, strongly conscious of 'point of view'. It is rather that they are *separable*: from time to time a gap can open up between them, and we shall realize for a moment that the scale of values embodied in the dream-experience may not be taken for granted by the poet. Perhaps this happens in the case of yet another reference to paradise, when the Dreamer looks longingly at the company of lovers and exclaims,

> Dex! com menoient bone vie!
> Fox est qui n'a de tel envie!
> Qui autel vie avoir porroit,
> de meillor bien se soufreroit,
> qu'il n'est nus graindres paradis
> d'avoir amie a son devis. (1293–8)

(God! what a good life they led! He who does not long for such a life is a fool. He who could have such a life might dispense with a greater good, since there is no greater paradise than to have one's beloved at one's desire.)

In the context of the past-tense narration as a whole, the Dreamer's fervent commitment to a paradisal view of romantic love becomes at least questionable. Chaucer in particular learned much from the *Roman de la Rose* about the possibilities the dream-form offered for subtle interplay between identification and separation of poet and Dreamer.

Even in Guillaume's part of the poem, however, we do not have to rely solely on the poet, as opposed to the Dreamer, for suggesting the possibility of a view of the religion of love from the outside. It is not that this religion is a mere fraud. Dedication to the God of Love is by no means the same as dedication to selfish enjoyment: the God himself insists that it is a discipline involving 'poine et fais' (1939) (pain and burden) as well as delight. Here is another religious parallel: the service of Amors is a kind of *ascesis*, analogous to Christian self-mortification. But there is another voice besides the Dreamer's and the God's to tell us what being in love is like, and that is Reason's. It is part of the psychological significance of the poem's allegory that Reason should speak to the Dreamer after he has had his first rebuff from Dangiers (Resistance), his first setback in the love-affair; but Reason is described as something higher than the commonsense that might well step in at such a stage in any young man's life. She is introduced, with no previous mention or explanation, as

la dame de la haute engarde,
qui de sa tor aval esgarde (2957–8)

(the lady of the high observation-point, who looks down from her tower).

When she sees the Dreamer, almost mad with frustration, she comes
down to him from her tower, and we are told,

A son semblant et a son vis
part qu'el fu fete ou paravis,
car Nature ne seüst pas
ovre fere de tel compas.
Sachiez, se la letre ne ment,
que Dex la fist ou firmament
a sa semblance et a s'image. (2969–75)

(By her appearance and her face it seemed that she was made in paradise, for
Nature would not have known how to make a work of such regularity. Know,
if the letter does not lie,[36] that God made her in the skies in his likeness and in
his image.)

Reason, then, is the image of God in the human soul; the Dreamer thinks
she was made in paradise, and, though he may not at this stage be able
to tell paradise itself from an earthly imitation, the meaning of his
contrast with Nature is clear. The Nature mentioned here is evidently
the same as Alanus's Nature, set below God; this was recognized by the
Middle English translator when he introduced into these lines a
reference to Nature's 'forge' and even a contrast between Nature and
Grace such as Lewis said was not to be found among the poets of the
'school of Chartres':

Nature hadde nevere such a gras,
To forge a werk of such compas. (3207–8)

The limited power of Nature as compared with Reason might make
us wish to look again at some earlier parts of the vision. For example,
when the Dreamer was about to choose 'his' rose from among all the
others, we were told that it was 'si vermeille et si fine/con Nature le pot
plus faire' (1658–9) (as red and as pure as the best that Nature can
produce). In retrospect, this seems to imply a limitation as much as a
superlative. The context concerned the transience of roses, and in the
eyes of Reason roses, however beautiful, are corruptible earthly goods.
Reason in her address to the Dreamer reproves him for his whole course
of action so far, from the moment he entered the garden. She advises
him to forget the God of Love, and to put aside 'li maus qui amors a
non' (3025) (that sickness [or evil] called love). But it is too late; the
Dreamer has already become Love's man, and he tells Reason that he
is only annoyed by anyone who attempts to correct him. When Reason
hears this, with an effect of telling simplicity and reticence, she departs.

The Dreamer's encounter with Reason has established a moral frame-work for the poem, which is assumed by Jean de Meun quite as much as by Guillaume de Lorris, though, as we shall see, it may well be that Jean accepted it in a different spirit. It is the framework of medieval religious orthodoxy; and while, up to this point, we may have been encouraged to sympathize with the Dreamer in his exciting and confus-ing experience of the early stages of romantic love, from now on the tone of the poem becomes more detached, comic, and satirical, and the Dreamer himself, as he devotes himself more and more single-mindedly to the sole object of possession of the rose, becomes more and more corrupt. It is important to recognize that this change begins, not at the point at which Jean de Meun took over the work, but towards the end of Guillaume's part.

The 'Roman de la Rose': Jean de Meun

The 'story' of the remainder of the poem tells of the various setbacks the Dreamer receives in his pursuit of the rose. The rose is guarded by personifications such as Dangiers, Honte (Shame) and Peor (Fear), while the Dreamer and his master, the God of Love, have as their allies other allegorical and mythological figures such as Bel Acueil (Fair Welcoming), Ami (Friend), Faus Semblant (False Seeming), Venus, Nature and Genius. Bel Acueil is imprisoned in a castle, but eventually the castle is stormed by Love's army, Bel Acueil is released, and the Dreamer obtains his rose. But the great bulk of the second part of the poem is made up not of actions but, like the *De Planctu Naturae*, of speeches by the various allegorical participants. These speeches are frequently called 'digressions', and, in the technical sense of medieval rhetoric, that is what they are. But one would no more be without them than without Chaucer's *Wife of Bath's Prologue*, or his Pardoner's 'digression' on his methods of preaching. Indeed, both these parts of Chaucer's work are derived from speeches in the *Roman de la Rose*, the first from that of La Vielle, the old woman who is Bel Acueil's guardian, and the second from that of Faus Semblant, who is a friar. And in a more fundamental way such speeches *are* the substance of the poem, which essentially consists of an intricately interlinked structure of attitudes towards love and human nature. Though they may seem rambling in themselves as well as digressive in relation to the story-line, they are in fact carefully constructed, with an intricate interweaving of themes and images for which perhaps music offers the best analogy. There is a 'music of ideas' in the *Roman*, which cannot be appreciated unless one reads the poem as a whole, so that one can see how some particular passage comes as the culmination of a whole series of earlier hints, or refers back, despite appearances, to a passage much earlier in the poem. It is possible that Jean de Meun, and later Langland too, learned how to create musical structures of this kind, symphonies of discourse, from medieval sermons and works on the art of preaching, but it is worth noting, too, how appropriate such structures are to dream-poems. Superficially, there is little that is dreamlike about the *Roman de la Rose*; but dreams too, digressive and disconnected though they may appear, abound in hidden connections when we come to examine them closely.

It is of crucial importance to realize that the speeches in Jean de Meun's *Roman* express the views of their speakers, not necessarily those of Jean himself. The commonsense rule about how to read literary fictions was laid down long ago by John Milton:

We should consider not so much what the poet says, as who in the poem says it. Various figures appear, some good, some bad, some wise, some foolish, each speaking not the poet's opinions but what is appropriate for each person.[37]

Nevertheless, the *Roman* has frequently been treated as though the various personifications were merely excuses for the poet to let loose his own opinions. In that case, there would be little justification for the use of personification-allegory at all, and the poet would appear to be muddled and self-indulgent. But in fact, just as, when Reason speaks, she says what Reason would say, which might well not correspond to what the poet would have said and done in real life, so characters such as Ami, La Vielle, Nature and Genius express characteristic opinions and attitudes, moulded and limited by the conceptions embodied in their speakers, and by no means necessarily to be identified with those of Jean de Meun. Indeed, as the poem proceeds, we seem to know less and less of what Jean de Meun really thought about love and human nature. At bottom, no doubt, he accepted the Christian orthodoxy of his time, just as Chaucer accepted the views expressed in the Retractions to the *Canterbury Tales*. A modern critic has written, 'Whether we share Chaucer's Christian conformity or not, we should recognize what an admirable source of detachment it is to him'.[38] So with Jean de Meun, what his Christian orthodoxy (if that is what it was) gave him for literary purposes was not so much the impetus to a positive expression of religious views, as a source of detachment from all earthly views, so that any human attitude could be the object of satire or irony. We may not know where Jean himself is to be found, but at least we know a number of positions which he is able to define with incomparable vigour and fulness precisely because he is not to be found in them. Jean's method takes its rise from that potentiality of the dream-poem which is already present in Guillaume's part of the work – a growing sense of the poet's detachment from his Dreamer, confirmed by the introduction of Reason and the Dreamer's rejection of her. But Jean develops this detachment to an extent that Guillaume can scarcely have envisaged, until he arrives at what seems like a detachment from all the values to which his characters commit themselves. The digressive form of his poem can be seen as a natural consequence of this method.

This point may be clarified by a comparison with other artistic phenomena of the thirteenth century. Professor Eugène Vinaver has compared the structure of the great polyphonic romance cycles of the period with that of the characteristic 'interlace' ornament of Romanesque art. He finds in both 'the same seemingly impossible combination of *acentricity* and *cohesion*', and in both an expansiveness which

is not, as in classical ornament, a movement towards or away from a real or imaginary centre – since there is no centre – but towards potential infinity. The artist, like the author of a fully interlaced cyclic composition, has the entire development in mind, knows where the point of departure is for each ramification – or digression – and how to take us back, if necessary, to the line or curve we previously followed. At the same time both the artist and the cyclic romance writer see in their mind's eye endless possibilities of further growth... everything we see or read about is part of a wider canvas, of a work still unwritten, of a design still unfulfilled.[39]

The conceptions of acentricity of design in Romanesque ornament and of narrative acentricity in polyphonic romance offer helpful analogies to the idea of discursive acentricity in the *Roman de la Rose*. The only resting-place of Jean de Meun's thought seems to be a Christian orthodoxy which is purely theoretical in the sense that it receives no positive emphasis in his work; but it is precisely this absence of a centre that gives his work its extraordinary freedom to elaborate a whole range of possible attitudes towards fundamental human issues.

Here it will be possible to discuss briefly only a few examples of Jean's method. One of the *Roman*'s most striking digressive speeches, and one which itself encloses a further digressive speech, is that of Ami (lines 7216–9969), the friend to whom the Dreamer turns for help after Reason has paid him a second visit, and has once more been rejected. Ami begins by telling the Dreamer that hypocritical politeness towards the rose's guardians, together with various fraudulent tricks, will be the best way of winning her – as long as he is not found out. The Dreamer, still something of an idealist, is rather shocked by this unscrupulousness, and asks whether there is no other means by which he could succeed. Ami admits that large gifts of money would have the same effect; but since the Dreamer is not wealthy, he will have to confine himself to small presents. Ami goes on to describe the Golden Age, when love and *seignurie* (lordship) were not companions, and then recounts the imagined speech of a jealous husband (Li Jaloux), who attempts – wrongly, according to Ami – to impose his control on his wife. Li Jaloux delivers a long misogynistic diatribe, based upon various traditional sources of clerical antifeminism. In it, among other things, he asks why husbands take wives without trying them out first, as men try out horses before buying them; he objects to his wife's complicated dress because it not only cost him good money but gets in the way when he wants to make love to her; and he concludes that all women are whores and all husbands cuckolds. From this it has frequently been concluded that Jean de Meun was himself a misogynist, and indeed this is a view repeated by the poem's most recent editor, who writes: 'Jean de Meun...makes himself the champion of a frantic antifeminism, whose violence, and sometimes grossness, are carried as far as caricature'.[40] But there is no reason at all to suppose that these are Jean de Meun's views: the situation is more complicated. These words are spoken not by Jean, but by Li Jaloux, a character invented by a character whom Jean has invented.[41] So far as Ami is concerned, the views of Li Jaloux are a scandalous example of the intolerable abuse that beautiful ladies have to endure. But there is no reason to suppose that *that* represents Jean's opinion either; on the contrary, as Ami's other advice shows, he too really thinks that all women are whores, though he does not think it right to say so. They are right, according to him, to look for love outside marriage, because

> il covient amors morir,
> quant amant veulent seignorir.
> Amor ne peut durer ne vivre,
> s'el n'est en queur franc et delivre. (9409–12)

(Love must die when lovers desire lordship. Love cannot endure or live if it is not free and active in the heart.)

(We shall be familiar with such views from Chaucer's Franklin, and familiar too with the assumption that they must be Chaucer's own.) It was not so in the Golden Age; and thus, by a delightfully unexpected route, we are brought back from a *digressio* to the almost-forgotten original *materia*. In the Golden Age men and women were truly free; but Ami goes on to show what misery and chaos that state of freedom led to, and how *seignurie* was introduced as a necessary remedy for it.

Ami, then, unknown both to himself and to the Dreamer, is trapped in a self-contradiction; we can be sure that Jean de Meun was aware of this, but it is much more difficult, and hardly necessary, to be sure what he really thought about the matter; for it is only a dream.

A similar digressive monologue, forming a companion piece to that of Ami, is the speech by La Vielle (lines 12710–4516). Ami gives advice to men on how to get what they want from women; La Vielle gives advice to women on how to get what they want from men. Bel Acueil, La Vielle's prisoner, is personified as male, but it is appropriate that the advice should be given to him, because what he represents is an attribute of the rose – the lady's welcoming attitude towards her lover. La Vielle tells Bel Acueil that the God of Love's commandments are good, except for the last two, which are to be generous and to be faithful to a single sweetheart. On the contrary, she asserts, a woman must gain as much as she can by her attractions, and she must play off one lover against another. The chief end of 'love' – a word which by this stage of the poem is beginning to need to be permanently enclosed in quotation marks – is material gain, and women must pluck their lovers down to the last feather. By Nature, she says, women and men too are 'free' – free to mate with whom they please. Nature knows nothing of personal loves, because to her all men are simply males and all women simply females. Their natural desire is to couple promiscuously, as La Vielle says she well knows from the way men used to stare at her in the street when she was young and beautiful; and Nature cannot be prevented from having her own way. La Vielle ends her speech with some useful miscellaneous advice: simultaneous orgasm is a good thing; love-potions do not work, though fear is a powerful aphrodisiac; nuns are too risky and too expensive. This speech too has been read as giving Jean's own views, and he has thus been described, like Alanus, as a 'naturalist'. A thirteenth-century literary theorist, Boncompagno of Signa, explains that we can recognize an ironic speech, if we are in the speaker's presence, by his gestures (*gestus* being a recognized part of medieval rhetoric). If, however (like twentieth-century readers of Jean de Meun), we cannot see his gestures, we shall detect an ironic intention by the presence in what he says of *manifestum delictum et immunda conscientia* (manifest evil and impure belief).[42] I suppose that many of La Vielle's views would come under this heading, almost as obviously as the arguments in Swift's pamphlets for the abolition of Christianity or the eating of babies; and perhaps, as with Swift, the implied argument is that if you behave as certain people habitually do behave, then it would be logical to suppose that you adhere to the corresponding doctrines, and are an atheist or a cannibal or a 'naturalist'. The most likely interpretation of La Vielle's speech is, I believe, that through her Jean is expressing, with great relish and plausibility, an utterly debased view of human nature, one that omits all that is distinctively human, and leaves only 'nature'.

The poem's sequence of thought demands that eventually Nature herself should appear and deliver a monologue of her own. She does so; and Jean de Meun's Nature clearly derives from the Nature of the *De Planctu Naturae*. She is introduced in her forge, where she is busy creating individuals so as to preserve the species against death. Once more, Genius is her priest, and she confesses herself to him in a long speech (lines 16699–9375), in which she describes with unflagging vivacity the whole natural world, from planets down to stones, over which she rules. Into it she inserts a statement about the difference between 'nobility of ancestry' and 'nobility of true worth' (that is, based on virtuous behaviour), which derives from Boethius and was in turn highly influential on later poets such as Chaucer. Everything in the created world performs its duty as it should, except only man, who acts towards Nature worse than a wolf. God, she says, went so far as to take on human flesh – 'San moi, car je ne sai conmant' (19125) (without me, for I do not know how) – yet nothing could satisfy man. 'Si m'aïst Dex li crucefis,' she exclaims, 'mout me repant don home fis' (19179–80) (So help me God on the cross, I repent very much of having made man). When man comes to be judged by God, he will be tortured like Ixion, Tantalus, Sisyphus, or Tityus (and here we may remember the earlier visions of judgment, from Homer to the *Apocalypse of St Paul*). Nature says that she leaves man's punishment to God, but urges Genius to tell the God of Love

> que la vos anvoi
> por touz ceus esconmenier
> qui nous veulent contrarier,
> et por assoldre les vaillanz
> qui de bon queur sunt travaillanz
> au regles droitemant ansivre
> qui sunt escrites an mon livre. (19348–54)

(that I send you there to excommunicate all those who want to work against us, and that I send you to absolve the valiant ones who work with good heart to follow strictly the rules that are written in my book.)

To follow Nature's rules means above all to reproduce one's kind; but once again we need not suppose that Jean himself saw energetic copulation as the remedy for all ills. Nature can be used effectively as a standpoint from which to criticize the defects of civilization, but for all that she is limited in what she can see and understand – and more emphatically limited for Jean than for Alanus. In her forge she meditates on the 'choses / qui sunt desouz le ciel ancloses' (15863–4) (things that are enclosed beneath the heavens): by the very fact of being Nature she is precluded from understanding the supernatural, though she knows of its existence. She gives men freedom (as La Vielle previously claimed), but God gives them reason,

> qui les fet, tant est sage et bone,
> semblables a Dieu et aus anges,
> se mort nes an feïst estranges (18846–8)

(that is so wise and good that it makes them like God and the angels, if it were not that death made them different).

For Nature, death is the only enemy, and the only weapon against death which comes within her scope is generation. She has vague intimations of some higher order, but the only order which is tangible to her is 'Let copulation thrive!' It is important to grasp that this comes to us from Jean de Meun not as a recommendation but as a dramatized description: this is *Nature*'s remedy against death, and we have only to look at the world around us, or into our own instincts, to see it at work.

Like his Nature, Jean's Genius is taken over from Alanus but modified. After Nature's confession, the only penance Genius imposes on her is to continue to labour in her forge until God shall intruct her otherwise. He then takes off his priestly dress, flies away in mufti to the God of Love's army, and is dressed by the God as a bishop and has placed in his hands by Venus 'un ardant cierge, / qui n'estoit pas de cire vierge' (19459–60) (a burning torch, not of virgin wax). Genius proceeds to preach a sermon to the army, in which he curses all those who 'les oustiz osent foïr / que Diex de sa main antailla' (19546–7) (dare to flee from the tools that God shaped with his hand). The tools in question he describes variously as pens, hammers and ploughshares – all metaphors borrowed from Alanus. But whereas for Alanus homosexuality was chosen to stand for all the other sins because it was a conspicuous example of love idolatrously misdirected, for Jean's Genius homosexuality is wrong for exactly the same reason as chastity: it hinders Nature in her work of reproduction. Genius's doctrine is that the sexual 'tools' are to be used as vigorously as possible; and so it must be, for that is what Genius means – generation. He promises the army that if they keep at it, 'le dieu celestre / que Nature reclaime a mestre' (19865–6) (the heavenly God whom Nature calls her master) will save them, and they will never be prevented

d'antrer ou parc du champ joli,
ou les berbiz conduit o li,
saillant devant par les herbiz,
li filz de la Vierge berbiz (19905–8)

(from entering the park of the lovely field where the son of the virgin ewe leads his flock with him, leaping over the grass).

He goes on to describe this heavenly park, using all the traditional imagery of visions of paradise, and he even contrasts it with the garden of the rose. The park is truth, the garden fable; from the park are shut out not just uncourtly qualities, but everything earthly; inside the garden everything is transient and corruptible, inside the park are 'granz joies / et pardurables et veroies' (20349–50) (great joys, eternal and true). Above all, whereas the garden had in it 'la fonteine perilleuse' (20379) that killed Narcissus and caused the Dreamer pain, the park has the fountain of life and immortality, flowing (in an allegory of the Trinity) from three springs which are yet one: 'cele les vis de mort anivre, / mes ceste fet les morz revivre' (20595–6) (the other makes the living drunk with death, while this fountain makes the dead live again).

We may well wonder what we are intended to make of all this. One answer has been to claim that Genius is expressing Jean de Meun's own convictions, and that he really believed that the heavenly paradise was God's chosen reward for diligent sexual activity. One scholar, indeed, has named this doctrine 'Christian phallicism'.[43] History has shown what a wide range of doctrines may be brought under the capacious umbrella of Christianity, but it is surely no more likely that a man of the thirteenth century was a Christian phallicist than that Swift was a Christian cannibal. It is more probable that we have here the most dazzling and daring of Jean de Meun's ironies. He includes in the poem, to complete the parodic treatment of the religious vision which we found at the beginning, a contrast between the parody and the reality, the artificial and the real paradise; but he puts it in the mouth of the god of generation, who, dressed as a bishop, here inaugurates a new religion, and claims that it will not be through any opposition on his part if eager copulators fail to get to heaven. Here the delusions of transcendence which lie at the root of the cult of romantic love receive their apotheosis; here it is finally confirmed that sex gives entrance to the highest paradise. Jean could evidently rely on his readers to relish this daring joke, and to recognize in Genius's doctrine not truth but truth perverted. One of his readers, after all, was to be Geoffrey Chaucer; and in his *Prologue* to *The Legend of Good Women* the Dreamer is bitterly accused by the God of Love of having translated a work which 'is an heresye ayeins my lawe, / And

makest wise folk fro me withdrawe' (F 330–1). The work is 'the Romaunce of the Rose' (329); from which we may judge that Chaucer, at
any rate, did not see Jean de Meun as a sincere Christian phallicist. It
has remained for nineteenth- and twentieth-century scholars to make
earnest of Jean's savagely ironic game; just as we may expect the
scholars of six hundred years hence to be reading *1984* as a pious
account of how Winston Smith arrived at a true love of Big Brother.

Genius ends his sermon by throwing down his candle and vanishing.
The God of Love's army prepares to assault the castle, and Venus
carefully fires a flaming arrow through 'une petitete archiere' (20762)
(a tiny narrow aperture) placed by Nature between two pillars, at a
sanctuary more fragrant than pomander – that is, the lady's sexual
desires are now aroused. The remainder of the story is a hilarious
account, in ingenious symbolic terms, of how the Dreamer achieves the
possession of his rose. The allegory is not only obscene but blasphemous.
A leading image is that of the Dreamer as a pilgrim, whose goal is a
shrine; the shrine is the narrow aperture mentioned above, and the
pilgrim is somewhat hindered by having to carry with him the traditional
attributes of scrip (or wallet) and staff, the scrip being a sack with two
hammers in it, and the staff being 'roide et fort' (21324) (stiff and strong).
It is perhaps worth mentioning that this, like the blasphemous parody
which is to be found elsewhere in medieval literature, is not necessarily
irreligious.[44] It was precisely because the values implied in pilgrimage
had a real meaning for the poet and his audience that the profane
parody, with its identification of things that ought to be contrasted, was
worth elaborating.

Some of what I have been saying about the *Roman de la Rose* has not
related directly to its nature as a dream-poem, though the general point
has been implied throughout that Jean has used the fact that his work
purports to be no more than a dream as the excuse for an apparent
irresponsibility which actually points always towards the absent centre
– the Christian orthodoxy which is associated with the dream as religious
vision. I end with some remarks that more specifically concern the *Roman*
as a dream-poem.

The first derives from what I wrote earlier about the separability of
Dreamer from poet. I suspect that the dream-poem made an especially
favourable matrix for the development of a *persona* separable from the
author of a poem, simply because, in remembering and writing down
a dream, one cannot help feeling that one's dreaming self has been
separate at times from one's waking self. In the *Roman de la Rose* this
separability leads both to quiet ironies and to spectacular paradoxes. As

an example of quiet irony – one among many in the poem – one might mention the moment at which the God of Love asks the Dreamer if he has kept all his commandments, and the Dreamer answers that he has done his best, and that he wishes that he may die in the very act of love; then his friends will be able to say,

> bien iert ceste mort convenable
> a la vie que tu menoies
> quant l'ame avec ce cors tenoies (10352–4)

(this death is indeed suitable to the life that you led when you kept your soul together with this body).

The word *convenable* speaks volumes, with its implication that a squalid death is the appropriate reward for that kind of love. Soon after this comes an example of elaborate paradox, deriving from the same source. The God of Love laments the death of great love poets such as Catullus and Ovid, regrets that Guillaume de Lorris is going to die (this is in Jean de Meun's part of the poem), and looks forward to the birth of Jean de Meun, who will be such a wise man that he will pay no attention to Reason. And yet who is the Dreamer–Lover, if not first Guillaume and then Jean, who have not yet been born? We have the fantastic situation of Jean de Meun dreaming of a God of Love who hopes that Jean de Meun will be born in order that he can grow up to dream of a God of Love. It is like one of those paradoxes involving time-travel in science fiction stories; and indeed this is only one of a number of ways in which the nearest modern equivalent to dream-poetry is to be found in science fiction. More important, for our purposes, is the fact that a moment such as this forces us to realize that it is a work of fiction we are reading, and that the very existence of fiction as an imitation of reality involves fundamental paradoxes.

My final point concerns the nature of the dream itself. We have seen that Guillaume begins the poem by claiming that some dreams, including this one, do convey truths; that the early stages of the poem take us into a world which is a secular version of the religious vision of paradise; and that it becomes steadily more apparent, until it is eventually made explicit by Genius, of all people, that this secular heaven is only an imitation, not the real thing. The last line of the poem is 'Atant fu jorz, et je m'esveille' (Straightway it was day, and I awoke); and perhaps this completes the transformation of the dream from a vision of truth to a mere fantasy, from a *visio* (in Macrobius's terms) to an *insomnium*. If so, the *Roman de la Rose* treats the dream differently from any other dream-poem discussed in this book; but it is also the first to make deliberate use of the ambiguity of the concept of 'dream', which will come to be of great importance in later dream-poems. Nature, in her monologue, has classed dreams along with distorting mirrors and glasses, as means by which people are deceived about reality, and she has included the dream of Scipio along with the other deceptions (but then, that is what Nature would be expected to think about a supernatural experience). It is perhaps the last of the poem's ironies, that what began by claiming to give true insight into the future ends with an awakening from fantasy into reality.

Fourteenth-century French dream-poems

I now turn to the French dream-poetry that follows the *Roman de la Rose* but precedes Chaucer and is made use of by him in his dream-poems. I must emphasize that I am not attempting a comprehensive study of French dream-poetry in the fourteenth century. I have simply chosen a few poems by Watriquet de Couvin, Guillaume de Machaut and Jean Froissart, as samples of what developments were taking place in the French dream-poem. Much of this poetry, especially in the earlier fourteenth century, is heavily influenced by the *Roman de la Rose*, and offers little more than an echo of its courtly and secular version of the religious vision. In Machaut's earliest poem, the *Dit dou Vergier*, the narrator wakes up one fine April morning, walks along a path to an orchard, enters it, and finds it full of singing birds and of flowers and flowering trees. He remarks,

> Je ne say que ce pooit estre,
> Fors que le paradis terrestre (65–6)[45]
(I do not know what it could be if not the earthly paradise).

But the orchard gives him no pleasure, because he is suffering from love-sickness; and in his misery he falls into a swoon, in which there comes to him a *vision* (149). In it he sees the God of Love, who explains his own attributes, identifies his large company of allegorical followers, and expounds the course of an allegorical love-affair. The Dreamer begs for assistance, but the God only commends loyalty and secrecy to him, and with that the vision comes to an end, and the narrator vows to be true to his lady for ever. In Watriquet de Couvin's *Dis des Quatre Sieges*, the narrator is 'ravis...en une avision' (18–19),[46] is carried by an angel to the 'paradis celestre' (47), and sees the state of blessed souls after death. Vast numbers of them are enthroned, but four extra large thrones are left vacant in the highest place. The Dreamer is informed that these are kept reserved for four great contemporary noblemen, among them the poet's patron; and with this he wakes. Here indeed the vision of judgment has hardly been secularized after the fashion of the *Roman de la Rose*, except that the poet represents himself as having his dream while lying in bed with his mistress.

As the century proceeded, there was a tendency for allegory to move into the background, to be replaced by persons and scenes taken from real life, whose function is no longer merely illustrative, as it is in the *Roman de la Rose*. This movement towards a kind of realism, at least of surface, is typical of the later medieval arts in general, and it is of great importance for the development of the dream-poem, involving a new interest in the realities of sleep and dreaming, in the poet-dreamer's real life, and in his personality and social status. But before I illustrate this development, I must explain that some of it takes place in poems which are not dream-poems, but are better called *dits amoreux*.[47] Poems such as Machaut's *Jugement dou Roy de Behaigne* and *Jugement dou Roy de Navarre* and Froissart's *Espinette Amoureuse* are, like the dream-poems of the same writers, first-person narratives of personal experience (whether real or fictional), though they lack the dream-setting. But the dream-poem, which cannot be anything but a first-person narrative of personal experience, is the ideal form for such narratives, and, as we shall see, in Chaucer's work the dream-form enriches and justifies the artistic organization developed in the French *dit amoreux*. It is significant, certainly, that in borrowing from the three poems mentioned Chaucer imposes the dream-form on their material, and that all his *dits amoreux* of any substance are dream-poems. From the point of view of the present study, then, the French *dit amoreux* must be part of the history of the English dream-poem.

The new interest in sleep and dreams as real-life phenomena, and not just as metaphors for religious or pseudo-religious vision, can already be found in the *Dis des Quatre Sieges* and the *Dit dou Vergier*. In the former, as I have mentioned, the narrator falls asleep in his mistress's arms, and is surprised to find himself alone when he wakes. In the latter there is an example of what later becomes a regular element in the dream-poem: the dreamer is awakened by some sensory disturbance within his dream. In the *Dit dou Vergier*, when the God of Love flies away, he makes the bushes shake:

> Si qu'adont la froide rousée
> Est seur mon visage avalée,
> Que li dieus y fist dechëoir
> Par la force de son mouvoir.
> Et quant je senti la froidure

Qui chut de dessus la verdure,
Elle me fist tout tressaillir,
Si qu'a moy me fist revenir
Et mist hors dou transissement
Ou j'avoie esté longuement. (1201–10)

(So that the cold dew, which the god caused to fall by the force of his movement, dropped on to my face. And when I felt the cold which fell from the foliage, it made me tremble all over, so that it made me come back to myself and thrust me out of the trance in which I had long been.)

In Froissart's dream-poem, the *Paradys d'Amours,* there is a similar effect, conveyed by means of an allegorical joke. In his dream, the lady whom the Dreamer has been wooing invites him to take a walk with her, and he is struck with pleasure. But in allegorical terms to be struck with pleasure is to receive a blow from Plaisance; the blow awakens him, and he feels his bed to find out where he is. A similar interest begins to be shown in the beginning of sleep. In the same poem, the poet does not simply fall asleep, but is suffering from insomnia caused by love-sickness, prays to the god of sleep for help, and only after that achieves sleep and a dream in which he gains the God of Love's support in wooing his lady. The motif of insomnia defeated by a prayer to the god of sleep is borrowed by Chaucer in *The Book of the Duchess,* and in Froissart's poem we detect the beginning of that psychological link between the content of the dream and the dreamer's waking state of mind which becomes so important in Chaucer's dream-poetry. The dream in the *Paradys d'Amours* seems to be a clear example of that wish-fulfilment which Freud and others have seen as the normal shaper of dreams.

More important is the development of an interest in the real life and personality of the poem's narrator. Though Jean de Meun had supplied the names of the authors of the *Roman de la Rose,* one narrator had served for both: a dreamer referred to by the generic name of Amant, and having few noticeable psychological traits other than naivety. But the narrator of a dream-poem or *dit amoreux* by Machaut or Froissart frequently has the poet's own name and some parts at least of the poet's biography. The *Jugement dou Roy de Behaigne* includes among its characters the King of Bohemia who was really Machaut's patron; the *Jugement dou Roy de Navarre* begins with a historically accurate account of the plague year 1348–9 and goes on to allude to the unfavourable reception given by certain ladies to the decision in the previous *Jugement* and to describe the reversal of that decision by the newly-crowned King of Navarre, Charles the Bad. Froissart's *Espinette Amoureuse* begins with a charming account of the poet's boyhood and goes on to represent what was probably a real love-affair with a lady called Marguerite, and also

43

one of Froissart's visits to England. In such poems, we cannot rely on every detail to be biographically accurate, but the narrator is clearly intended as a fictional representative of the poet as he really was. Similarly, in the English dream-poems which derive from this tradition, Chaucer will allude to his real patrons John of Gaunt and Anne of Bohemia and will be addressed as 'Geoffrey', Langland will be called 'Will', and Skelton will introduce the real Countess of Surrey and her attendants.

A tendency is already developing, too, for narrators, however individualized, to share in a kind of common dream-personality. In real dreams, it is normal for the dreamer to feel that he is not in control of the events which are unfolding and in which he is an involuntary participant. Hence the dreamer's role cannot be very dignified, and we see this lack of dignity amusingly represented in Froissart's *Paradys d'Amours*. In his dream he sings a *complainte* against the cruelty of love, and sits down in stunned misery. But then he hears a noise, and, fearing he has been overheard,

> Lors des arbrisseaus me couvri
> Et un petit mes yex ouvri
> A savoir que ce pooit estre. (233-5)[48]

(Then I covered myself in the shrubs and opened my eyes a little to see what it might be.)

At once two ladies come along, talking angrily about him; he wishes he could run away, but since this is impossible decides to appease them, throws himself to his knees, and makes a pretty speech. There is a parallel between the position of the Dreamer, comically at the mercy of events inside his dream, and the position of the fourteenth-century poet (or at least the position he must assume), comically deferential to his noble patrons. This real or assumed social inferiority of the poet is also taken up by Machaut: for example, in the *Jugement dou Roy de Navarre* he represents himself as being accused by his lady of giving offence by the verdict delivered in the *Jugement dou Roy de Behaigne* – that a lady whose lover has died suffers less than a knight whose lady has been untrue to him. He is brought before the King of Navarre for judgment, and is sentenced to compose a lay, a song and a balade. We shall find this double inferiority of the dreamer-poet assuming a central importance in Chaucer's dream-poems. It appears that the dream-poem was of use, among other things, as a literary solution to a social problem of the court culture of the later Middle Ages: how can the socially inferior poet address himself to his aristocratic audience?

But in such a situation the comic indignity of the dreamer may well begin to have an effect too on the superior figures whom he meets in his dream. The dream-poem is potentially one 'version of pastoral', in which the simplicity of the dreamer encourages us to think critically about the validity of the authorities he encounters in his dream; and all the more so because the dreamer is also the reporter of the encounters. The narrator of the *Jugement dou Roy de Navarre* is represented as socially inferior to the great lady who objects to the verdict of his previous poem, and it is inevitable that her objection will be sustained; but all the same, the vehemence with which she embraces the opposing view is meant to seem comic:

> Aroit cils aussi grief com celle?
> Nennil! Il ne puet avenir;
> Cils poins ne se puet soustenir.
> Dont j'ay fait, et fais, et vueil faire
> Protestation dou contraire. (1540–4)

(Will he [the knight] suffer as much as she [the lady]? Not at all! It cannot happen; this point cannot be sustained. Thus I have made, and make, and will make affirmation of the contrary.)

It seems likely, too, that a humorously critical attitude was at least implied towards the authority encountered in the dream in the *Dit dou Vergier*. There, it will be remembered, the Dreamer was suffering from love-sickness, and when he meets the God of Love in his dream, he naturally begs him to reward his sufferings. But the God interrupts, saying that he will answer in due time and place, but that he first wishes to explain the 'signefiance' of himself and his followers. He proceeds to do so, to the length of some six hundred lines, and then concludes, with great self-satisfaction, that he has told the Dreamer everything, concealing nothing. What he has not told him, of course, is the one thing he wishes to know: what reward will he receive for his sufferings? The God's only advice is that he must be loyal and secret, and the Dreamer is left, when the God flies away, no further forward in his quest for fulfilment. From one point of view, this courtly *oraculum* serves to demonstrate the God's grandeur and the insignificance of the Dreamer; but, once the Dreamer has been individualized, we cannot help seeing the experience through his eyes too. The dream-poem has already taken a first step towards the situation in *The House of Fame*, in which the Dreamer is bodily seized by his authority and carried with him to the heavens, sulkily protesting that he does not wish for the information he is so liberally being given.

The treatment of the dreamer as a real person, based on the poet himself, inevitably implies that the dreamer shares the poet's profession

as a writer of poems; and in this he is quite unlike the Amant of the
Roman de la Rose, or earlier visionaries.[49] The *Jugement dou Roy de
Navarre*, as we have seen, functions as an apology for Machaut's earlier
Jugement dou Roy de Behaigne, which it is assumed the audience will know.
The recantation is also a form of self-advertisement: for example, when
the lady tells the narrator that his offence lies in something he has
written, he begs her to identify the particular piece, for he has written
many poems, 'de pluseurs manieres, / De moult de diverses matieres'
(885–6) (in several manners, on many different subjects). Machaut's
punishment is to compose further poems: he ends this one by naming
himself, adding his surname to the Christian name by which he has been
addressed earlier in the poem. The next poem in the manuscript
collection of his work is the first of those he has been sentenced to
compose. Froissart has the habit of demonstrating his virtuosity as a
writer by incorporating lyrical pieces in his *dits amoreux*, and he does so
with no pretence of being anything other than a writer. In his *Paradys
d'Amours*, the Dreamer is led by two allegorical ladies to the paradise
of the God of Love. With a dreamer's characteristic inadequacy, he does
not know what to say to the God, but one of the ladies advises him to
write a lay, because he is in the habit of writing poems. He answers that
it would take him all day to write a new one, but that he just happens
to be carrying one about with him, in case it should be needed. He
proceeds to repeat it: it is a piece of 276 lines, in twelve different
metrical forms, which could certainly not have been composed im-
promptu, and which may perhaps have been known to the poem's
audience as an existing work of Froissart's. From one point of view, the
whole dream-poem exists as a setting for this elaborate composition,
justifying its delivery and providing it obliquely with suitable praise. The
God is deeply moved by it, though the modern reader will probably
prefer the frame to the picture, for the lay itself is thin and tedious, an
exclamatory tissue of commonplaces, decked out in threadbare classical
mythology. Later in the dream, the Dreamer meets his own lady, who
asks him 'Avés vous riens fait de nouvel?' (1602) (Have you written
anything new?), and he answers that he has composed a balade 'de
sentement' (1604) (based on personal feeling), which he proceeds to
recite. The lady comments that it is very good, and she crowns him in
tribute with a chaplet of the flowers which share her own name, Marguerite. Thus the Dreamer is represented as a lover who is also a poet,
and whose love is the inspiration of his poetry; and the crowning with
the chaplet is at once a gesture of love and a tribute to his poetic skill.
The poem moves back and forth most ingeniously between fiction and

reality: it is all only a dream, but a dream 'Où nulle riens n'a de mençonge' (1711) (where there is nothing at all of deceit); and yet the dream is itself a poem, a product of the very skill it praises. The *Paradys d'Amours* celebrates not only love but the paradoxical existence of poetic fiction, and in this it is the forerunner of many of the greatest English dream-poems.

2

CHAUCER

My chief purpose in this chapter will be to offer detailed studies of each of Chaucer's four dream-poems, but I begin with some brief general remarks about Chaucer as a dream-poet. The first is that, being widely read, he was familiar with many of the visionary works, dream-poems, and *dits amoreux* already mentioned. He had certainly read the *Aeneid*, the *Somnium Scipionis* with Macrobius's commentary, the *De Consolatione Philosophiae*, the Biblical and apocryphal visions, Alanus, the *Roman de la Rose*, several of the poems of Machaut and Froissart, and, after the middle 1370s, Dante. Some, though not all, of this wide reading is likely to have been shared by his own readers and listeners.

Second, Chaucer wrote a comparatively large number of dream-poems. Though he may be thought of nowadays chiefly as the poet of *The Canterbury Tales* and *Troilus and Criseyde* (and I do not dispute that these remain his major works), he also wrote four dream-poems, or five, if we include his translation of the *Roman de la Rose*. Only Dunbar, whose poems are very much shorter, has more dream-poems attributed to him than that. Part of my argument will be that, although each of these poems has an independent existence as a work of art, they also form an intelligible sequence, in which certain leading themes are carried from one poem to another, and are not merely repeated but developed. The existence of this series of related dream-poems is of great help in our understanding of any one of them, because each throws light on the others. Although there is no reason to suppose that the poems reflect a real series of Chaucer's dreams, they are like dreams in being the most personal and intimate of his works, and it may be that a series of dream-poems gives the literary critic the same kind of advantage as a series of dreams gives the dream-analyst. The point has been made by Jung:

Every interpretation is hypothetical, for it is a mere attempt to read an unfamiliar text. An obscure dream, taken by itself, can rarely be interpreted with any certainty, so that I attach little importance to the interpretation of single dreams. With a series of dreams we can have more confidence in our interpretations, for the later dreams correct the mistakes we have made in handling those that went before. We are also better able, in a dream series, to recognize the important contents and basic themes...[1]

Jung is of course aware of the analogy between dream-interpretation and literary interpretation, as his reference to reading an unfamiliar text makes clear.

Third, Chaucer, more than any other dream-poet known to me, was interested in dreams as they really are. The existence of four dream-poems is only part of the evidence for this: he includes dreams and their interpretations in several of his other poems, and also several elaborate discussions of the significance and validity of dreams. One such is the sceptical statement about the validity of dreams made by Pandarus in book v of *Troilus and Criseyde*, followed shortly by Cassandra's serious interpretation of one of Troilus's dreams.[2] Another is the comically solemn discussion between Chauntecleer and Pertelote in *The Nun's Priest's Tale* about the significance of Chauntecleer's dream of the fox. In looking at Chaucer's dream-poems, we shall see again and again that he is making use of his understanding of real dreams, in producing works which are dreamlike, not only in superficial details, but in matters of method and structure.

'The Book of the Duchess'

Chaucer's earliest dream-poem, *The Book of the Duchess*, in one way looks like another example of a type of work already familiar to us. It is apparently a vision of the other world, in which the visionary not only visits another place, but learns a truth from an authoritative person whom he meets and questions there. The narrator falls asleep, and dreams that he wakes up in his bed on a May morning. He has been awakened by birds, singing 'the moste solempne servise' (302), as harmoniously as if 'hyt had be a thyng of heven' (308). This is the paradisal world we have come to expect in religious visions and their courtly imitations; and there is the usual reference back to a literary tradition of visions when the Dreamer tells us that the walls of his dream-bedroom were painted with 'al the Romaunce of the Rose' (334). When he goes outside, he finds the sun shining, but it is neither too hot nor too cold – this avoidance of extremes of temperature is another common feature of medieval conceptions of paradise. He hears and sees men hunting, and follows them into the forest; they lose track of the hart they are pursuing; then a little puppy comes up to him in a friendly way, and he follows it deeper into the forest, along a path which is still paradisal, for it has as many flowers

As thogh the erthe envye wolde
To be gayer than the heven. (406-7)
envye desire

There are also the usual shady trees, and many living creatures running about beneath them. Suddenly, beneath one tree, the Dreamer sees sitting a 'man in blak' (445), a knightly figure in a state of profound melancholy. They have a long conversation, a major theme of which recalls Boethius's *De Consolatione*: the power of Fortune over human life, and the attitude men should adopt towards it. The Black Knight explains that he has played at chess with Fortune, and she has captured his queen; the Dreamer begs him to

Remembre yow of Socrates,
For he ne counted nat thre strees
Of noght that Fortune koude doo. (717-19)
strees straws

The Dreamer fails to understand the metaphor of the game of chess, and the knight has to tell him the story of his love for a beautiful lady, herself an almost heavenly being, a 'goddesse' (1040). The Dreamer persists in trying to find the cause of the knight's depression; it finally emerges that it is that his lady is dead. With this the dream ends, and the Dreamer finds himself lying once more in his bed. All this seems thoroughly familiar; and if one is startled at first, as one is probably meant to be, by the appearance of mourning and death in the midst of an earthly paradise, one may reflect that it is perfectly usual, from Homer onwards, for otherworld visions to bring news of the dead.

But two aspects of this courtly vision demand further comment. The first is that *The Book of the Duchess* appears to be written for an occasion, and to allude to an event in real life. Most scholars would agree that the 'man in blak' in the dream represents John of Gaunt, Duke of Lancaster, and that the lady he has lost, whom he calls 'goode faire White' (948), represents his first wife Blanche, who died in 1369. We know that from 1374 onwards Chaucer received a pension from John of Gaunt, for services which may have included the writing of this poem. Chaucer himself refers to the poem as 'the Deeth of Blaunche the Duchesse' in the *Prologue* to *The Legend of Good Women*, and the odd name 'White' is obviously an anglicized version of Blanche. Towards the end of the poem, there are also certain cryptographic allusions to John of Gaunt: within two lines we find a 'long castel' (Lancaster), a 'ryche hil' (Richmond, of which John was Earl), and 'seynt Johan' (1318-19). There is widespread agreement that the poem was written to commemorate the death of Blanche and to console her husband, though some would deny that the Black Knight is to be identified with the Duke. One scholar, for example, sees the whole poem as having a Boethian meaning, and takes the Black Knight to represent unreasonable grief and the Dreamer to stand for reason.[3] This seems unlikely, because, in view of the cryptograms and the real-life situation, the courtly circle which formed the poem's original public could hardly have failed to identify the Black Knight with the bereaved Duke; and it is hard to believe that Chaucer was in a position to lecture him on the unreasonable nature of his grief. Besides, it would be highly abnormal in a medieval dream-poem for the dreamer and not an authority he meets in his dream to be the source of doctrine. An interpretation in terms of historical allegory seems the obvious one, though the transmutation of the Duke and Duchess into 'man in blak' and 'goode faire White', as if they were pieces in Fortune's game of chess, gives them a generality of significance beyond their historical identities. Where the poem differs from the tradition of otherworld visions is in the fact that the Dreamer sees not the dead person living a life after death, whether of reward or punishment, but the bereaved survivor. The dead lady is brought back to life in imagination only, through the knight's mere words in recalling the course of his devotion to her and the happiness it brought him. The dream brings no supernatural revelation: what the Dreamer learns is not the state of the lady's soul after death, but the bare fact that 'She ys ded' (1309). Once the knight has admitted that, there is no more to say: he can ride 'homwardes' (1315) to a castle where a bell marks the completion of a phase of experience by striking 'houres twelve' (1323), and the vision can come to an end. We shall see that a fundamental theme of Chaucer's later dream-poems is the validity and limitations of poetic imagination, frequently symbolized by the dream itself. Already in the dream of *The Book of the Duchess*, it is imagination – the knight's imagination, and the 'sorwful ymagynacioun' (14) of the poet who created the knight – that brings the dead back to life, and that only momentarily: the poem offers no assurance of any other life after death.

The second aspect of *The Book of the Duchess*, considered as a traditional vision, which demands further comment is that the actual dream forms only part of the poem. The *Book* has 1333 lines,[4] but it is not until line 291 that the narrator falls asleep. In the long introduction to the dream, the narrator begins by explaining that he is suffering from insomnia. This has been caused by a mysterious sickness, referred to in such a way that most readers (especially if aware of such precedents as the love-

sickness of the narrator at the beginning of Machaut's *Dit dou Vergier*)
gather that love-sickness is meant. There is but one physician who could
heal him,

> but that is don.
> Passe we over untill eft;
> That wil not be mot nede be left. (40–2)

eft later

If the sickness is love-sickness, the one physician is presumably the lady
who refuses to respond to his love. Some scholars see the sickness rather
as spiritual, and the physician as God;[5] but in that case why is the
narrator so sure that the physician will not heal him? Moreover, as we
shall see later, love-sickness would help to provide a psychological
explanation for certain aspects of the dream which follows. In any case,
the narrator takes a book one night to read himself asleep, a collection
of pagan stories written 'While men loved the lawe of kinde' (56), and
in it he finds the story of Ceyx and Alcyone. These details identify the
book as Ovid's *Metamorphoses*, but Chaucer never mentions its author;
and indeed he followed what was to be a common practice in his poetry
by comparing different versions of the same story, taking as his source
not only Ovid's version but a retelling of it by Machaut in his *Dit de la
Fonteinne Amoreuse*. The story is repeated, of how King Ceyx was
drowned at sea, and how his wife Alcyone bitterly mourned his absence,
and prayed to Juno to send her in a dream definite information about
his fate. We learn how Juno responded by sending a messenger to
Morpheus, the god of sleep, to order him to convey a dream-image of
Ceyx to Alcyone. The messenger had difficulty in waking Morpheus and
his assistant deities – naturally enough, they were sleeping – but eventually he succeeded by blowing his horn loudly, and the necessary dream
was sent to Alcyone, who almost at once died of grief. Here Chaucer
cuts the story short, with the favourite excuse that 'Hyt were to longe
for to dwelle' (217). But the abridgment is a matter of the poet's design
rather than his audience's convenience, because it means that he silently
omits the metamorphosis in Ovid's version, which has both husband and
wife transformed into seabirds and thus reunited beyond death. Instead,
the narrator explains that from the story he got the idea of praying to
Morpheus, Juno, 'Or som wight elles, I ne roghte who' (244) (or some
other being, I did not care who) – he does not really believe in these
pagan gods – and vowing that he will give him a magnificent feather-bed
if he will send him to sleep. No sooner has he pronounced this vow than
sleep descends on him, and he dreams a dream so 'wonderful' (277) that
it could not be interpreted by either Joseph or Macrobius. The rest of

the poem, except for the last eleven lines, describing his awakening, consists of the dream itself.

What is to be made of this highly elaborate introduction to the dream? I believe that interpretations of a number of different kinds are possible, and, because they are on different planes, they do not necessarily clash. One thing they have in common, though, is that they see the function of the preliminary material as an extension or support of the dream itself; it is not by accident that Chaucer has brought together in the same poem (and, as we shall see, in his later dream-poems too) a dream and an elaborate introduction. The most general kind of interpretation would relate the introduction to late-medieval aesthetic principles, and it would apply as much to *dits amoreux* (such as Machaut's *Jugement dou Roy de Navarre*, with its long introductory account of the events of 1348–9) as to dream-poems proper. Much recent work on Chaucer makes us aware that it is not enough to think of him simply as a medieval poet; he is more specifically a late-medieval poet, who reflects in his work many tendencies of style and structure found in other arts of the late Middle Ages. The *Roman de la Rose* belongs to an earlier phase of medieval style, in which a basically simple outline is still visible beneath the elaborately acentric surface. But already in Chaucer's earliest poetry, as in the French poetry of the mid-fourteenth century, we can recognize at least the outward signs of what Huizinga sensationally called 'the Waning of the Middle Ages'. Wolfgang Clemen was among the first to recognize this, and he writes, in connection with *The Book of the Duchess*, that 'The liking for an indirect method of presentation, for shrouding the theme in exuberant ornament and disguise, corresponds to the *gout des complications* illustrated in the flamboyant style of late Gothic art'.[6]

A more recent art-historian, George Henderson, finds a tendency towards ambivalence in late-Gothic architecture, which provides a suggestive parallel to the introductory technique of *The Book of the Duchess*:

The ambivalence of late-Gothic architecture is immediately obvious in the silhouette of buildings. Long since conditioned not to commit themselves to any formal accent unless they can balance it by its opposite, Gothic architects even attempted a fantastic and ingenious compromise between the two poles of being and non-being. A Gothic building cannot simply stop, it has to fade away. Hence the familiar flurry of curves and spikes, by which the physical presence is gradually withdrawn and the dense material mass is dissolved into the empty air.[7]

Henderson speaks of the building as 'dissolving' rather than 'stopping'; one might equally reverse the image, and speak of it as 'condensing' rather than 'starting'. It would then apply well to *The Book of the Duchess*: the introduction gets the poem started almost imperceptibly, as if it were condensing out of the empty air; it forms that 'familiar flurry of curves and spikes' with which late-medieval artists felt it necessary to mediate between the everyday world and the work of art. It can now be seen that the setting of the poem in a dream is, from one point of view, a means to the same end, for the dream is neither being nor non-being, but a compromise between the two. And from the same point of view, the first part of the contents of the dream serves the same purpose of meditation between everyday reality and the world of imagination. The Dreamer leaves his dream-bedroom, goes first into a field and then into a forest, and penetrates to the very depths of the forest before he finally comes to the true subject of his poem, the encounter with the Black Knight. Thus the dream-poem, as developed in fourteenth-century France and England, is an ideal expression of late-Gothic taste.

Secondly, this very process of elaborate introduction can be seen to relate to the poem's specific social occasion. The encounter between the Dreamer and the Black Knight appears to represent, in symbolic form, an imaginary encounter between Chaucer and the Duke of Lancaster. But these two were persons of very different social standing. The poet was a wine-merchant's son who had married into the aristocracy, and who was making his way in courtly circles by his own gifts and skills. The Duke was King Edward III's fourth son, and was one of the wealthiest and most powerful men of his time. We should not exaggerate the rigidity of the class-system in fourteenth-century England, but surely the only setting in which these two could chat together on such a delicate subject, even in fiction, was one made studiously remote from everyday reality. Now the sense of remoteness is given partly, of course, by the dream-setting itself. Things can happen in dreams which cannot happen in real life; but some things cannot happen even in dreams unless they are translated into a symbolic form – put into code, as Freud sees it, in order to deceive the internal censor. It was presumably something analogous to this – a social rather than psychological censorship – which made it impossible for Chaucer to begin his poem more directly by saying that he, Geoffrey Chaucer, met the Duke of Lancaster and had a chat with him about his recent sad bereavement. I am not suggesting that *The Book of the Duchess* would have been a better poem if Chaucer had felt able to write in that way. On the contrary, the translation into symbolic form has a generalizing and enriching effect, and is indeed creative. Similarly, much post-Freudian work on dreams, beginning with Jung, has insisted that the symbolism of dreams cannot be simply interpreted away, but has its own validity as being the best way of expressing something that could not be fully expressed in other terms.[8] The introduction to the dream has a similar effect. The preliminary section of the poem gives the feeling of passing through one anteroom after another until we reach the work's inner sanctum. And that inner sanctum is, for the Duke, a place of intimate feeling – the feeling of bereavement, loss, desolation, even though within this is encapsulated the recollection of the happy past. This is not to imply that the poem necessarily articulates the Duke's, or indeed Chaucer's, real feelings at Blanche's death. We have no means of knowing what those were. It is rather that *The Book of the Duchess*, like other public elegies of the Middle Ages or the Renaissance, expresses the feeling appropriate to a death. Such feelings are made both more special and more tolerable when they are set within an elaborate fiction which enacts its own remoteness from the mundane and the quotidian.

Thirdly, and for our purposes most importantly, the introductory part of *The Book of the Duchess* serves to provide a psychological explanation for the dream that follows; and this is where Chaucer's originality as a dream-poet shows itself most strikingly. Throughout the introductory section there is a clear linkage of cause and effect on the psychological plane. Because the narrator is sick, he cannot sleep; because he cannot sleep, he reads a book; because the book tells a story of a sleep brought on by a vow to a god, he makes a similar vow; because of this he falls asleep; and, above all, because of the state of mind he was in and the effect on his mind of the contents of the book he read, he has a dream of a certain kind. The content of the dream, that is, can be accounted for not only externally, as the reflection of a real-life situation, but also internally, as a reflection of the Dreamer's psychological state. There is nothing similar to this psychological causation in the poem's French sources, and I must now digress somewhat in order to explain the theories underlying it.

We have seen that, according to Macrobius, there are two basic types of dream – those with natural and those with supernatural causes – which are then divided into a number of sub-types. Dream-classifications of this kind went on being made throughout the Middle Ages, and, though they differed considerably in detail, often according to the special interests of the classifier as a theologian, doctor, astrologer, or whatever he might be, they usually went back to Macrobius, and retained a similar basic distinction. W. C. Curry, for example, has shown how physicians, with their greater interest in the natural than in the supernatural, tended towards a threefold classification into *somnia naturalia*, *somnia animalia*, and *somnia coelestia*.[9] There is no evidence that Chaucer knew this specific terminology, but he certainly shows a knowledge of these three categories of dream, and they prove to be convenient for discussion of his dream-poetry. The *somnium naturale* is the dream of purely physical origin. According to medieval physiology, the most fundamental cause of illness is a disturbance of the balance of the four bodily humours – blood, phlegm, choler and melancholy – and this disturbance will tend to be reflected in the image-making part of the patient's mind in the form of a dream. Because the content of the dream will indicate the nature of the disturbance giving rise to it, *somnia naturalia* can be used by doctors for diagnostic purposes. Chaucer shows his knowledge of this category of dream in *The Nun's Priest's Tale*. There Pertelote explains to Chauntecleer that when people have an excess of choler (which is red) in their bodies, they dream of red things; when they have an excess of melancholy (which is black), they dream of black things; Chauntecleer has dreamed of a red doglike creature with black tips to its tail and ears, therefore he has an excess of both humours, and needs to 'taak som laxatyf'. The *somnium animale*, the second category, is the dream of mental origin, caused by the preoccupations of the waking mind, and reflecting these in its content. This is the type described by Chaucer in a passage in *The Parliament of Fowls* (lines 99–105) where the hunter is said to dream of hunting, the knight of fighting, the lover of success in love, and so on. The third category, the *somnium coeleste*, comes from outside the mind, being produced, as the theologians see it, by God or by angels or devils, or, as astrologers see it, indirectly through planetary influences. The doctors naturally have little to say about the *somnium coeleste*, because it is the speciality of experts in other fields. Chaucer shows his knowledge of it when he makes Pandarus, the sceptical pagan, describe it as the speciality of priests:

> For prestes of the temple tellen this,
> That dremes ben the revelaciouns
> Of goddes, and as wel they telle, ywis,
> That they ben infernals illusiouns.
>
> (*Troilus and Criseyde* v. 365–8)

In the same passage, Pandarus goes on to summarize the other types of dream I have been listing, describing each as the product of the thought of particular groups of men: doctors see dreams as caused by physical disease, others see them as resulting from mental preoccupations, others again as varying according to the seasons of the year and phases of the moon.

Similar kinds of dream-classification, often using different terminology, can be found in many medieval writers. Some of the sources used by Curry to illustrate medieval dreamlore are later than Chaucer's time, but I add one further illustration of the kind of discussion that Chaucer himself could have read. In the *Liber de Modo Bene Vivendi*, which in Chaucer's time was wrongly attributed to St Bernard, we find:

Certain dreams occur through eating too much or too little;...certain again arise from preceding thought [*ex proposita cogitatione*], for often we meet again during the night the things we have been thinking of during the day; many dreams occur through the illusions of impure spirits...; sometimes however there occur visions in the true sense of the word, that is, visions concerning the mystery of revelation...And sometimes there occur visions of a mixed kind...[10]

As it happens, this particular classification would have been available to Chaucer and his audience in English, because this section of the *Liber* had been translated, with certain modifications, by Richard Rolle in his widely-read treatise, *The Form of Living*.[11] But Chaucer's interest in dreams no doubt led him to read widely about them in Latin and French as well as English, and I am not trying to identify specific sources, but to illustrate the range of ideas about the causes of dreams that was available in Chaucer's time.

Having glanced at this range of ideas, we can form a clearer picture of the links between the waking section at the beginning of *The Book of the Duchess* and the dream itself. With remarkable ingenuity, Chaucer has made it possible to see the dream as linked to the narrator's waking life in all three of the ways indicated as alternatives in the theories we have been considering. The dream can be seen as a *somnium naturale* or a *somnium animale* or a *somnium coeleste*. Chauntecleer's dream as seen by his wife offers a clear analogy to the view of the *Book of the Duchess* dream as a *somnium naturale*. An excess of melancholy causes one to dream of black things; the narrator at the beginning of the *Book* is plainly dominated by the humour of melancholy, and indeed tells us that 'melancolye / And drede I have for to dye' (23–4); it is therefore natural that his sickness should cause him to dream of a 'man in blak'. It is also suggested, though it is not clear how seriously we should take the suggestion, that the dream could be seen as a *somnium coeleste*. The dream sent to Alcyone in the tale from Ovid, as a result of her prayer to Juno, is a vision of supernatural origin which discloses a truth to her. The narrator is stimulated by this story to make his own prayer to the gods, even though he does not really believe in them; what he prays for is sleep, and sleep is immediately granted to him. Perhaps his dream too may come from some supernatural source, pagan or Christian? Certainly, in just the same way as Alcyone's dream, it discloses the truth that someone is dead; and, in introducing the narrative of the dream, the narrator compares it with two celestial visions, one scriptural and one pagan – the dreams of Pharaoh interpreted by Joseph, and Scipio's dream. But there is an ambiguity here: the story of Alcyone's dream can be taken, from one viewpoint, as providing authoritative 'proof' that dreams give access to truth, but from another viewpoint it could be said that the fact of reading this story was itself the psychological cause of the following dream, which was in fact a *somnium animale*.

The *somnium animale* explanation is worth more detailed comment, for the poem's introductory section provides two separate elements of psychological causation for the dream, which, taken together, supply psychological links of a complexity commensurate with the richness and suggestiveness of the dream itself. The two elements are the Dreamer's predominant thoughts, and his reading of the story from Ovid. I take the latter first. The *somnium animale* is the category of dream in which the psycho-analysts have been particularly interested, and indeed they have tended to see all dreams as belonging to that category – a professional prejudice which would not have surprised Pandarus. Freud assures us that 'in every dream it is possible to find a point of contact with the experiences of the previous day', and he adds that that 'point of contact' is to be found in the manifest content of the dream as opposed to its latent content (which, in Freud's theory, will derive from childhood experiences).[12] Now Chaucer's major innovation in the tradition of medieval dream-poetry was to identify this point of contact in the experiences of the previous day with the reading of a book. There are one or two examples of the reading of a book in fourteenth-century French poems (Machaut's *Voir Dit* and Froissart's *Espinette Amoureuse*), but there is never that detailed connection between the contents of the book and the contents of a following dream which we find not only in *The Book of the Duchess* but in *The Parliament of Fowls* and in some dream-poems influenced by Chaucer.[13] In *The Book of the Duchess* the connection is ingenious and psychologically plausible. The narrator reads a story of a wife's loss of her husband by death, and in his dream the same situation reappears, but in a mirror-image: now it is the husband who has lost his wife by death. And Chaucer has been careful to make the story and the dream fit each other exactly. The purpose of the dream is not to offer the Black Knight the promise of a reunion beyond death, but to encourage him to adjust himself to the fact of the lady's death, and in doing so to celebrate her life. Hence Chaucer omits the part of the Ovidian story which has the couple reunited as seabirds, so that it will correspond more exactly to the dream it is to motivate. There are other, smaller reflections of the book in the dream, too; for example, the horn blown by Juno's messenger to awaken the sleeping Morpheus reappears in the dream as the horns blown by the huntsmen. The effect of such parallels is not only to gain psychological plausibility (for dreams do reflect details from our lives and reading in just such strange ways), but to achieve an artistic ordering of the poem's diverse material. Such diversity had been present in a merely sectional way in the French poems which lie behind Chaucer's, but now Chaucer, through his interest in dream-psychology, has begun to find a way of linking together the separate parts of the poem by the recurrence and development of certain themes and images.

The other element of psychological causation is the Dreamer's general state of mind. His 'sicknesse' (36) has psychological as well as purely physical symptoms; if, as seems likely, it is love-sickness, then it is natural that in his dream his troubled mind should frame the image of a melancholy lover. Thus the Black Knight has a double significance. From an external point of view, he stands for John of Gaunt; but from an internal point of view he is a projection of the narrator himself, though of course on a far grander and more aristocratic scale.[14] It need not surprise us to find the central figure of a dream thus possessing two distinct meanings. Freud explains that 'the dream-work is under some kind of necessity to combine all the sources which have acted as stimuli for the dream into a single unity in the dream itself'. This necessary element in the work carried out by dreams he calls 'condensation', and he shows, with numerous examples, that 'The construction of collective and composite figures is one of the chief methods by which condensation operates in dreams'.[15] There are many parallels between the narrator and the Black Knight. For example, the narrator tells us at the beginning of the poem that it is a wonder he is still alive,

> For Nature wolde nat suffyse
> To noon erthly creature
> Nat longe tyme to endure
> Withoute slep and be in sorwe. (18–21)
> *suffyse* permit

When he meets the Black Knight, his first thought is of a very similar kind:

> Hit was gret wonder that Nature
> Myght suffre any creature
> To have such sorwe, and be not ded. (467–9)

Again, the narrator hints that his sickness can be cured by one doctor only (presumably the lady who scorns him); and similarly the Black

Knight describes his lady as 'my lyves leche' (920) and later says that when he first saw her she cured him of all his grief (1104). Admittedly such parallels are somewhat conventional in content, but they still serve to bring the two figures close together.

Moreover, the implicit contradiction between the two meanings of the Black Knight seems to move towards explicitness within the poem. Inasmuch as the dream is a *somnium coeleste*, which in symbolic form reveals a truth to the Dreamer and to us, it has an autonomous existence, independent of the Dreamer and perhaps outside his previous range of experience. This reflects a situation in which, as the poem tactfully implies, Gaunt has known a true cause for noble grief, but Geoffrey Chaucer has not: his petty sorrow can be brushed aside with a 'Passe we over untill eft'. But inasmuch as the dream is a *somnium animale*, it must reflect the Dreamer's own experiences and preoccupations, which he naturally tends to impose on the figure in his dream. This is to be seen in the central question of the cause of the Black Knight's sorrow. This is precisely what the Dreamer is trying to find out as he questions the knight, and he evidently begins from the assumption that the cause must be the same as that of his own sorrow – rejection by the lady he loves. For this reason, he persistently fails to grasp the point of the knight's statements; this has the effect of drawing out the knight still further, in the effort to convey his meaning to the Dreamer; and it is not until almost the end of the poem that the Dreamer makes explicit his initial assumption, and is thus able to learn the truth. The Dreamer is eager to know how the knight made his love known to his lady, perhaps in the hope of getting a hint about how to approach his own unresponsive mistress. Then he naively goes on to ask what it is that the knight has lost and, if it is the lady herself, what he did to offend her:

> 'But wolde ye tel me the manere
> To hire which was your firste speche,
> Therof I wolde yow beseche;
> And how she knewe first your thoght,
> Whether ye loved hir or noght.
> And telleth me eke what ye have lore,
> I herde yow telle herebefore.'
> 'Yee!' seyde he, 'thow nost what thow menest;
> I have lost more than thou wenest.'
> 'What los ys that?' quod I thoo;
> 'Nyl she not love yow? ys hyt soo?
> Or have ye oght doon amys,
> That she hath left yow? ys hyt this?
> For Goddes love, telle me al.' (1130–43)
> *lore* lost; *nost* knowest not; *thoo* then

In response to this, the knight tells how when he first declared his love his lady rejected him, but then later he tried again and was more successful. Once more the Dreamer interposes a question based on his own self-reflecting assumption, and now at last he hears and grasps the truth: 'She ys ded'. The nakedness of the statement, coming after so much amplifying description of the lady's beauty and virtue, is irresistibly touching; and so is the simplicity of the Dreamer's response, as the truth at last breaks through his self-projection:

> 'Sir,' quod I, 'where is she now?'
> 'Now?' quod he, and stynte anoon.
> Therwith he wax as ded as stoon,
> And seyde, 'Allas, that I was bore!
> That was the los that here-before
> I tolde the that I hadde lorn.
> Bethenke how I seyde here-beforn,
> "Thow wost ful lytel what thow menest;
> I have lost more than thow wenest" –
> God wot, allas! ryght that was she!'
> 'Allas, sir, how? what may that be?'
> 'She ys ded!' 'Nay!' 'Yis, be my trouthe!'
> 'Is that youre los? Be God, hyt ys routhe!' (1298–310)
>
> *stynte anoon* ceased at once; *wax* became; *bore* born; *routhe* a pity

The dream in *The Book of the Duchess*, then, could be classified as a *somnium naturale*, a *somnium animale*, or a *somnium coeleste*. One significance of this uncertainty as to how it should be classified is that it is part of the tact with which it fulfils its social function. Seen in one way, the dream is a heavenly vision, conveying the truth in a symbolic form: Blanche is dead, and death is a fact which can only be accepted. But on the other hand, who is Chaucer to claim visionary powers, which would seem to place him in a superior role, priestly or prophetic, in relation to his patron? Surely it would be better for the poet to hedge his bets, by hinting at the visionary possibilities of the dream, but claiming explicitly no more than that it is 'wonderful' and hard to interpret? In this way he could leave open the possibility that the dream was merely one of the 'fantasies' (28) in the head of a melancholiac, or the product of mental indigestion caused by too much reading in pagan books. At the same time, the merely psychological explanation of the dream would provide suggestions for the organization of the dream-poem as an intricate late-medieval work of art. In later dream-poems Chaucer will make these issues explicit and generalize them, so that the uncertainty about the status of dreams can be used as a way of discussing the status of the poem as such. For the moment, in *The Book of the*

Duchess, he is only feeling his way towards this, and the importance of the treatment of the dream as a *somnium animale* lies chiefly in the model it provides for a new kind of poetic structure.

Many people, both in the Middle Ages and now, have seen dreams as incoherent fantasies. One of the commonest medieval sayings about dreams is *somnia ne cures*, or, as Pertelote translates it, 'Ne do no fors of dremes' (*Nun's Priest's Tale* 2941). More recently, James Winny has written that 'We should now regard a dream, with its curious linking together of seemingly unrelated ideas, as differing fundamentally from the creative activity of imagination', while George Kane has said of dream-poems that 'the reported dream must surpass any actual dream in organization, coherence, and circumstantial character'.[16] Chaucer from time to time made use of this low view of dreams in his poems (as in the case of Pandarus), but I do not believe that it was his own view, nor do I believe that it is a correct view. Freud frequently calls attention to the similarity between the 'dream work' and the methods by which literature shapes experience, and he points out in particular that, just as dreams demand a multiple interpretation if they are to be fully understood, so 'all genuinely creative writings are the product of more than a single motive and more than a single impulse in the poet's mind, and are open to more than a single interpretation'.[17] There is an obvious parallel, for example, between the unity which the imagination attempts to impose on all the component parts of a poem and the unity which dreams seek to achieve by 'condensation'. A standard Freudian work on dreams claims that 'the dream is the matrix from which art is developed', and draws many parallels between the stylistic devices of literature and the methods of communication (which, in the Freudian view, are also methods of concealment) used by dreams.[18] Jung, too, is much aware of this parallel, and argues that Freud gives insufficient weight to the genuinely creative and exploratory nature of dream-symbolism.[19] Dreams surely *are* works of art, though, since they are inescapably private experiences, they can never be fully open to criticism. Perhaps they are the only kind of work of art which most of us go on producing throughout our lives. All children can draw and paint, and, given the materials, do; most of us stop doing these things when we grow up, but we go on dreaming. I believe that one of Chaucer's greatest achievements in his early poems was to make use in consciously contrived works of literature of the creative and constructive methods employed by the unconscious mind to make dreams. This does not mean, of course, that his dream-poems are surrealist productions, the direct expressions of his unconscious mind. Nor does it mean that they are always dreamlike in their surface effect (though they sometimes are).[20] The dream-poems *make use* of the methods of dreams. One of the most striking character-istics of dreams is that on a superficial level (that of their 'manifest content') they are mysteriously disordered and often unintelligible, and in particular that they involve abrupt transitions from one sequence of events to another, with a lack of any connecting links. And yet on a deeper level (that of their 'latent content') they can be shown to be intricately ordered and fully intelligible. This characteristic is shared by the dream in *The Book of the Duchess*, as I hope to show.

The narrator of the *Book* finds himself, in his dream, in bed, where he has apparently been awakened by birdsong. As he lies there, he hears another noise, a horn blowing, and then others still, all indicative of a hunt going on outside. Men are talking of hunting the hart; at this, the Dreamer is glad, and he immediately takes his horse and leaves his bedroom. The horse, we must suppose, was in his bedroom – a typical makeshift device of the kind used by real dreams to cover a transition from one setting or sequence to another. He overtakes the huntsmen, learns from one of them that it is 'th'emperour Octovyen' (368) who is going hunting, and himself joins the hunt. Who is the emperor Octavian?[21] Why should the Dreamer take it upon himself to join his hunt uninvited? Is he suitably dressed for hunting? (He told us that he was 'in my bed al naked' (293), and he has said nothing about putting his clothes on, unlike the narrator of the *Roman de la Rose*, who carefully washes and dresses before walking out into his dream-world.) If we pause for a reply to such questions, we are likely to pause for a long time. In dreams, such questions do not arise, and this is surely a part of the poem which is thoroughly dreamlike in its effect. The hunt finds the hart, then loses it again, and the Dreamer is left by himself. But a puppy comes up to him and makes itself pleasant, in a charmingly doglike way –

> Hyt com and crepte to me as lowe
> Ryght as hyt hadde me yknowe,
> Helde doun hys hed and joyned his eres,
> And leyde al smothe doun hys heres. (391–4)

The puppy leads the Dreamer deeper into the forest, and there, quite suddenly, he notices the 'man in blak' sitting with his back to a huge oak. He observes how pale and melancholy he is, overhears him speaking a lay in which he laments that his lady is dead, and finally goes right up to him. At first the knight fails to notice him, but eventually the Dreamer strikes up conversation, and the rest of the poem consists of their conversation, which begins at line 519 and ends only 24 lines before the end of the poem.

It is an obvious question to ask why the scenes of the hunt and the puppy are in the poem at all. One kind of answer to this question would relate them to the late-medieval aesthetic of transitions, of 'fading' in and out, discussed earlier. Another kind of answer, somewhat more specific, would say that hunting was a characteristic pastime of the medieval aristocracy, and one which is habitually described in terms of joy and energy. Its place in the poem would then be to establish a contrast between the present melancholy of the Black Knight and the gaiety and vitality of the mode of existence which would be normal for him, but which he is wearily allowing to pass him by. And a third kind of answer, more specific still, would suggest a metaphoric relationship between the hunt and the encounter with the Black Knight. Once the literal hunt has disappeared, its place is taken by a metaphorical hunt, and the transition between them is provided by the scene with the puppy.[22] The puppy is a kind of miniature hunting hound, and he leads the Dreamer on a quest into the forest, where he comes upon an unexpected quarry, the Black Knight, whom the Dreamer 'stalks' (this is the very word used in line 458) before addressing him. The ensuing dialogue with the knight takes the form of a psychological hunt, in which the Dreamer's questions press him to disclose more and more of what lies at his heart, until he eventually admits that his lady is dead. At this point the hunt is over; and, to confirm the metaphoric relationship, the moment we learn that 'She ys ded' we are told that the literal huntsmen sound the call for returning home (*strake forth*), because their hart-hunting is finished:

> 'She ys ded!' 'Nay!' 'Yis, be my trouthe!'
> 'Is that youre los? Be God, hyt ys routhe!'
> And with that word ryght anoon
> They gan to strake forth; al was doon,
> For that tyme, the hert-huntyng. (1309–13)

We may even take the equivalence between the two hunts a little further, because, if the huntsmen are in pursuit of a *hart*, so the Dreamer, as metaphorical huntsman, has the *heart* of the Black Knight as his quarry. It is no accident that the word *hert*, which means both 'hart' and 'heart', occurs nearly thirty times in the poem, sometimes referring to the animal, sometimes to the organ of the body, sometimes (as a term of endearment) to the lady, sometimes to the knight's feelings for her. One of the first things the Dreamer notices about the knight is the pallor of his face, and he explains at some length that all the blood had rushed to comfort his injured heart.[23]

It must be added that a medieval audience would have been prepared to see a poetic hunt as metaphorical even if it did not occur in a dream. In *Sir Gawain and the Green Knight*, just as in Chaucer's poem, there are hunting scenes which frame scenes of conversation, in such a way that we understand that what is happening in Gawain's bedroom is also a kind of hunt, perhaps to the death. In both poems, scenes of hunting and of conversation are superficially contrasted but at a deeper level parallel. In *Sir Gawain*, however, the relationship between the hunting and bedroom scenes is conveyed by a threefold repetition of the same formal pattern (hunt begins, bedroom scene, hunt ends); in *The Book of the Duchess* the aesthetic patterning is less marked and has more of the obscurity of a dream. Freud points out that if dreams form a language, it is a language without a syntax, that is to say without any explicit means of indicating the relationships among its juxtaposed elements. It may be impossible for the dream to represent directly 'those parts of speech which indicate thought-relations, e.g. "because," "therefore," "but," and so on', but instead

...the dream-work succeeds in expressing much of the content of the latent thoughts by means of peculiarities in the *form* of the manifest dream, by its distinctness or obscurity, its division into various parts, etc. The number of parts into which a dream is divided corresponds as a rule with the number of its main themes, the successive trains of thought in the latent dream; a short preliminary dream often stands in an introductory or causal relation to the subsequent detailed main dream; whilst a subordinate dream-thought is represented by the interpolation into the manifest dream of a change of scene, and so on. The form of dreams, then, is by no means unimportant in itself, and itself demands interpretation.[24]

This doctrine can of course be applied to poems generally: Freud's work on dreams represents a major contribution to literary criticism. For Chaucer, it seems likely that the study of dreams suggested ways of giving unity and richness of meaning to structures which in his literary models were merely sectional and episodic. In *The Book of the Duchess*, the formal juxtaposition of hunt and human encounter is a way of indicating the link in meaning between those two elements. Moreover, Freud's theories even provide for the pun on *hert*, as an example of that central principle of the dream-work, condensation, which we also found in the double meaning of the Black Knight. As Freud puts it, 'the dream-work... strives to condense two different thoughts by selecting, after the manner of wit, an ambiguous word which can suggest both thoughts'.[25]

I must now mention another way in which *The Book of the Duchess* organizes its meaning by using the methods of dreams. The *Book* is a poem about death, but it is also a poem about sleep, and it persistently works in such a way as to identify these two similar states. It is surprising, the narrator remarks at the beginning, that he can remain alive despite his sleeplessness. Insomnia has 'sleyn my spirit of quyknesse' (26), and 'melancolye / And drede I have for to dye' (23-4). In the story from Ovid, after Alcyone has prayed to Juno, she is seized by 'the dede slep' (127), and in her sleep she dreams of death. In Morpheus's dark valley, streams falling from the cliffs make 'a dedly slepynge soun' (162). After all this, we ought not to be surprised that when the narrator himself falls asleep, he does not thereby merely escape from the death he fears, but comes upon death in a different form – that of a knight, dressed in black, who looks as if he were about to die of grief, and whose grief is caused by the death of his lady. 'She is dead' is a message being delivered by the poem long before it reaches its end. This repetition of the same message in different forms is strongly characteristic of dreams: 'A dream will state and restate the same theme until the solution is reached'[26] – the 'solution' in *The Book of the Duchess* being an acknowledgment of the unchangeable fact of death.

It is interesting that recent work on the structure of myths has indicated that they too work in this way, repeating certain motifs which are their means of conveying latent significances. Moreover, in at least some myths there is a tendency for the manifest meaning to come gradually closer and closer to the latent meaning as the latter is repeated, until eventually the two are identified. Claude Lévi-Strauss, for example, writes of a Canadian Indian myth: 'Everything seems to suggest that, as it draws to its close, the obvious narrative...tends to approach the latent content of the myth...; a convergence which is not unlike that which the listener discovers in the final chords of a symphony'.[27] *The Book of the Duchess*, at once like a dream and like a myth, conforms to this pattern: the final 'She is dead', understood at last by both participants in the encounter, comes as the confirmation of a whole series of earlier hints, in the form of metaphor, analogy, and half-understood statement.

I now turn from the structure of *The Book of the Duchess* to consider another aspect, which is closely connected with its nature as a dream-poem, and which raises some important general issues about medieval literature. This is the role in the poem of the character called 'I', who is first the narrator and then, once asleep, the Dreamer. Many medieval poems, not only dream-poems, include figures of this kind, but they are of special importance in dream-poems, because a dream can only be a

66

first-person experience. There has been much discussion of the part
played in medieval poems by such first-person dreamer–narrators. The
simplest view of the matter would be that, being 'I', the Dreamer is
identical with the writer of the poem. Even if we rejected the naive
supposition that Chaucer really had the dream described in his poem,
there would still be the fact that the poem itself asserts by its conclusion
that the narrator is in some sense the same as the poet. The narrator
wakes from his dream, to find himself in bed, with the book containing
the story of Ceyx and Alcyone in his hand:

> Thoghte I, 'Thys ys so queynte a sweven
> That I wol, be processe of tyme,
> Fonde to put this sweven in ryme
> As I kan best, and that anoon.'
> This was my sweven; now hit ys doon. (1330–4)
>
> *queynte* strange; *sweven* dream; *Fonde* attempt

And so the poem ends. Yet on the other hand the narrator is represented
in the poem as something of a simpleton. He is extremely kind-hearted,
it is true: when he merely reads of Alcyone's sorrow, his sympathy flows
as freely as a child's:

> Such sorowe this lady to her tok,
> That trewly I, which made this book,
> Had such pittee and such rowthe
> To rede hir sorwe that, by my trowthe,
> I ferde the worse al the morwe
> Aftir, to thenken on hir sorwe. (95–100)
>
> *ferde* fared

The same reaction occurs when he dreams of the Black Knight's sorrow;
and he seems anxious to give him what comfort he can, as when he tells
him,

> Me thynketh in gret sorowe I yow see.
> But certes, sire, yif that yee
> Wolde ought discure me youre woo,
> I wolde, as wys God helpe me soo,
> Amende hyt, yif I kan or may. (547–51)
>
> *ought...me* reveal to me anything of; *as...soo* as sure as God may help me

Yet he apparently fails to grasp much of what the knight says. He does
not understand the extended metaphor by which he speaks of his loss
as that of a queen in a game of chess with Fortune; he makes lukewarm
comments which are bound to seem inadequate to the bereaved lover;
and, above all, he reports that before addressing the knight he overheard
him speaking a lay in which he disclosed that his lady was dead – and

yet, once the conversation has started, he appears not to have understood this, or to have forgotten it. Surely this stupid Dreamer cannot be the real Chaucer? The point was made many years ago by G. L. Kittredge. The Dreamer, he wrote, is 'a purely imaginary figure, to whom certain purely imaginary things happen, in a purely imaginary dream'. And he went on:

This childlike Dreamer, who never reasons, but only feels and gets impressions, who never knows what anything means until he is told in the plainest language, is not Geoffrey Chaucer, the humorist and man of the world. He is a creature of the imagination, and his childlikeness is part of his dramatic character.[28]

The essential question for our purposes is not whether the Dreamer is the real Chaucer (because 'the real Chaucer' can be no more than a hypothesis); the essential question is how, and how far, is the Dreamer characterized? We have seen that fourteenth-century French poets, whose works formed the main sources of *The Book of the Duchess*, had developed the convention of a narrator who was in some sense identified with the poet, but who was characterized as naive and socially inferior. It seems likely enough that Chaucer should have adopted a similar literary solution to a similar social problem. But how consistently does he characterize himself as narrator and Dreamer? L. D. Benson has suggested that it was the existence of the dream-poem convention which made possible the development in fourteenth-century poems of 'a fully developed and consistently maintained personal, dramatic point of view'. This may be an exaggeration, because a growing interest in 'point of view' can be observed in the fourteenth-century arts generally – for example, in the development of perspective in painting. But at least the existence of the dream-poem convention must have made it easier for fourteenth-century poets to explore the possibilities of a 'personal, dramatic point of view'; and that was surely one reason for the continuing interest in dream-poetry. Benson goes on to contrast the dream-poem with the romance:

A romance always takes place in some remote past, and its narrator is always a clerk, depending on written authority and transmitting, ostensibly unchanged, the ancient story 'as the book tells'. The dream or vision, on the other hand, is always a contemporary event, a personal experience related by a narrator who, so he asserts, saw everything with his own eyes. Such a narrator is necessarily naïve rather than omniscient, for the 'eyewitness' convention requires that he report only what he has personally seen or heard.[29]

There may be some exaggeration here, too, in respect of the 'eyewitness convention'. We have seen that in the *Roman de la Rose* there are occasions when the narrator has to tell us about something of which, as Dreamer, he was unaware. There are similar moments in Machaut's *dits amoreux*, though he has begun to be more conscious of problems of point of view.[30] Perhaps the situation for Chaucer about 1370 was that, while the dream-poem exerted a distinct pull towards a 'personal, dramatic point of view', it did not yet demand that such a point of view should be maintained with complete consistency.

Kittredge and others have seen the Dreamer of the *Book* as child-like; but a different school of commentators has seen him quite differently.[31] They find it difficult to believe in a Dreamer so dull-witted that he fails to understand the lay which he himself reports the Black Knight as speaking, and they argue that he is not really childlike, but displays a sophisticated tact. He does not really fail to understand the knight's statement that 'my lady bryght...Is fro me ded and ys agoon' (477–9); he only pretends not to have overheard it. His whole purpose is to encourage the knight to relieve his sorrow by giving utterance to it, and that is why he pretends not to know its cause and not to understand the chess metaphor, and why he makes remarks which can only have the effect of arousing the knight's indignation and thus inciting him to recall the past more fully:

> 'By oure Lord,' quod I, 'y trowe yow wel!
> Hardely, your love was wel beset!
> I not how ye myghte have do bet!'
> 'Bet? ne no wyght so wel,' quod he.
> 'Y trowe hyt, sir,' quod I, 'parde!'
> 'Nay, leve hyt wel!' 'Sire, so do I;
> I leve yow wel, that trewely
> Yow thoghte that she was the beste,
> And to beholde the alderfayreste,
> Whoso had loked hir with your eyen!'
> 'With myn? nay, alle that hir seyen
> Seyde and sworen hyt was soo...' (1042–53)
>
> *Hardely* certainly; *beset* bestowed; *not* know not; *bet* better; *leve* believe; *Yow thoghte* it seemed to you; *alderfayreste* fairest of all; *Whoso* if one; *seyen* saw

And off he goes again, to explain in more detail just how he would have loved his lady whoever he had been, and what it was that made her so irresistibly loveable. The Dreamer, after all, having no religious conso-lation to offer, can do no better than to encourage the knight to come to terms with his earthly situation, both his past happiness and his present bereavement.

Yet a tactful Dreamer may be more difficult to believe in than a naive Dreamer, and it is possible that those who have seen him as tactful have confused the nature of the Dreamer with the nature of the poem. *The*

Book of the Duchess is certainly a supremely tactful poem. It is not a private poem; delivering it must have been a public act. It would not do for Chaucer to lecture his noble patron on what his attitude should be towards his wife's death, still less to promise a heavenly reunion – for all we know, Gaunt may have been planning his second marriage by the time the poem was read. It would be better to contrive some way in which Gaunt himself would be the central figure of the poem, noble and glamorous in the depth of his grief, and the dead lady would live on only in his memory. Even in the licensed setting of a dream, Chaucer would surely be tactful not by presenting *himself* as tactful, managing his patron and drawing him out with admirable skill, but by establishing a contrast between his patron's transcendent grief and his own clumsy and uncomprehending attempts to grasp its nature. The Black Knight is thoroughly at home in the ideal world of Chaucer's dream; it is Chaucer himself who is ill at ease in it, and fails to understand what would be obvious to any 'gentil herte'. The Dreamer is kind-hearted but slow on the uptake, innocent and inexperienced, because he, unlike the knight, knows nothing of the fulfilled love which is, in courtly theory, the peculiar property of the truly noble.[32] On the other hand, we do not have to believe that he is so stupid as not to understand the knight's lay when he hears it. The lay must be in the poem so that we, the audience, shall know all along what is the cause of the knight's sorrow, and shall thus be able to feel with him more deeply than the Dreamer does, and to recognize the full extent of the Dreamer's failure to gauge the depth of his sorrow. But the convention of the dream-poem does not demand that we should be *conscious* of the Dreamer as the witness of every event in his dream. We have to imagine ourselves among the original listeners to the poem, when it was first read aloud to a courtly circle. In those circumstances, we should inevitably always be aware of the *poet*, as narrator of everything in the poem; but we should only be aware of the poet *as Dreamer* when Chaucer gave him something of a noticeably personal kind to say.

Through quite large sections of the poem, we have no reason to be conscious of the Dreamer at all. For example, when the Black Knight is delivering one of his longer speeches, the speech itself is conveyed directly, and insofar as the poet is doing any dramatic impersonation in his reading, it must be of the knight, not of the Dreamer listening to him. Our attention will be focused on what the knight himself is saying, and it would only be in pursuit of a theory, not in response to the words of the poem, or any imaginable recitation of them, that we could be thinking of it as being transmitted to us through the consciousness of the Dreamer. This is not to apply to *The Book of the Duchess* McLuhan's remark that 'The "I" of medieval narrative did not provide a point of view so much as immediacy of effect.'[33] That is too sweeping: what I want to suggest is that the 'I' of this narrative provides a point of view only intermittently, and that there are times when the poet employs the ambiguity or instability of his 'I' to allow the Dreamer as such to fade away. There would be an obvious parallel in the visual arts of Chaucer's time, where there is a growing interest in the perspective effects that derive from Italian painting, but, as yet, no conviction that the whole of a picture must form a single three-dimensional space, seen from a single point of view. Perspective is still a local, partial effect, in competition with older methods of organizing a picture; and so it is with Chaucer's poem. This helps to explain what happens in the case of the knight's lay. Its words are presented to us immediately, in the form of direct, not reported, speech; it is on them that we concentrate, and for the moment we cease to be aware of the Dreamer at all. We hear them without noticing that, theoretically, he must be hearing them too.

I end with a brief consideration of the effect of the narrator on the tone of *The Book of the Duchess*. Like most other aspects of the poem, this is one about which widely differing views have been held. C. S. Lewis, for example, wrote of 'comic effects which are disastrous, and which were certainly not intended', while P. M. Kean has described the poem as 'Chaucer's longest and most successful essay in pure urbanity'.[34] Certainly in the dream itself there is a recurrent comedy which radiates from the Dreamer in his innocently clumsy attempts to understand something outside the range of his possible experience; and he in turn strikes comic sparks from the Black Knight. I suggested earlier that sometimes in French dream-poems and *dits amoreux* 'the simplicity of the dreamer encourages us to think critically about the validity of the authorities he encounters in his dream'. There is surely some sign of this in lines 1042–53 of *The Book of the Duchess* (quoted above), where the knight becomes indignant and even irritable to have his total idealization of the dead lady submitted to questioning and measurement, brought down to earth. This part of the dialogue brings us back to the question of point of view, for what the Dreamer is saying is that the lady was the best and fairest of all ladies if seen from the viewpoint of her lover – 'Whoso had loked hir with your eyen' – whereas the knight is asserting that she was the best and fairest from anyone's viewpoint – 'alle that hir seyen / Seyde and sworen hyt was soo'. The Dreamer is a relativist, the knight an absolutist. The dialogue between them articulates a contradiction latent at the heart of the dream-poem as a medieval

literary form. Insofar as the dream is a vision, a *somnium coeleste*, it claims
to convey absolute truth, unmodified by the personal consciousness of
the visionary; insofar as it is a psychological product, a *somnium animale*,
it must inevitably reflect the relativism of the dreamer's personal point
of view. As we shall see, fourteenth-century dream-poems show a strong
tendency to develop conflicts between absolutist and relativist conceptions of reality; and this ambivalent nature of the dream itself will be
treated more explicitly and more prominently in Chaucer's subsequent
dream-poems.

In *The Book of the Duchess* – and this is inevitable in view of the poem's
personal occasion – the balance is tilted in favour of the Black Knight's
absolute claims for his idealization of the lady herself and of his love
for her. Much of what he has to say is in the form of set-pieces for which
recipes could be found in textbooks of medieval rhetoric. Here I have
not discussed these parts of the poem; they would include the elaborate
description of the lady's appearance (816ff.), the extended paradox in
which he states that each of his qualities has been transformed by grief
into its opposite (599ff.), the description of the goddess Fortune in
similarly paradoxical terms (620ff.), and the passage in which he asserts
that he would still have loved the lady if he had been as beautiful as
Alcibiades, as strong as Hercules, as excellent as Alexander, and so on
(1056ff.). The Dreamer's interjections may express a natural human
unwillingness to believe that reality could truly correspond to such ideal
patterns, but, with him, we have eventually to be convinced that it could.
Perhaps, as twentieth-century readers, natural sceptics and relativists,
we cannot always be convinced, and we may well find some parts of the
knight's discourse tedious. But in most cases one is carried forward by
the poem's enthusiasm, and perhaps particularly by the knight's insistence that the lady did *not* always conform to what might be expected
of a courtly mistress. She did not deceive men, or play hard to get, or
set a suitor some impossible task as the test of his worthiness:

> And byd hym faste anoon that he
> Goo hoodles to the Drye Se
> And come hom by the Carrenar,
> And seye, 'Sir, be now ryght war
> That I may of yow here seyn
> Worshyp, or that ye come ageyn!'
> She ne used no suche knakkes smale. (1027–33)

faste anoon straight away; *Drye Se* Gobi Desert; *Carrenar* Black Lake; *war* careful;
here seyn hear spoken; *Worshyp* honour; *or that* before; *knakkes smale* petty tricks

There is no contradiction between the knight's joyful recollection of the past and the comedy associated with the Dreamer, for this is ultimately not a poem of mourning but of celebration. It is partly for this reason that elements of comedy are also introduced into the introductory section, so that in tone as well as content it will prepare the way for the main part. The narrator's love-sickness cannot be taken quite seriously, and his promise of a feather-bed to Morpheus if he will cure his insomnia displays just the literal-mindedness or materialism that is also part of his character as Dreamer. Even the sad tale of Ceyx and Alcyone is enlivened by the vigorous action of Juno's messenger in waking the inhabitants of the cave of Morpheus by blowing his horn 'ryght in here eere' (182), and by the way that even then the god of sleep can get only one eye open. We may find it difficult to adjust ourselves to the flexibility of tone of *The Book of the Duchess*, but I believe that that is as much under Chaucer's control as the poem's complex associative structure.

'The House of Fame'

The date of *The House of Fame* is uncertain, but it was probably written in the middle or late 1370s, and is thus Chaucer's second dream-poem. It is the most boldly experimental of his dream-poems, and this, added to the fact that it has come down to us in an unfinished form, makes it peculiarly resistant to interpretation and analysis. Most readers would agree that, though its energy and vivacity make it inexhaustibly interesting, it is not a perfect work, in the sense that Chaucer's underlying intentions are not fully embodied in the poem as it stands. Some of the creative work is left for us to do; and this was no doubt part of the attraction the *House* had for subsequent poets such as Lydgate, Skelton and Douglas. Skelton and Douglas at least wrote poems which do not merely imitate it but rework the material Chaucer left to create new poetic wholes. This is what Chaucer's poem seems to demand, and the commentator who is not a poet approaches this do-it-yourself poem-kit at his peril. In what follows I have tried not to rewrite *The House of Fame*, but I have found it impossible to pin down for rational analysis a work which seems ready to fly apart when touched, but in which also everything comes to seem connected with everything else. I have had to content myself with a series of approaches to the poem from different angles, none of them complete in itself.

The House of Fame begins with a proem of 65 lines, which consists largely of a discussion of the causes and validity of dreams. This comes closer to raising explicitly questions of a kind that were only hinted at in *The Book of the Duchess*. Discussions of the fundamental issue of the relationship between dream and truth come to form a regular part of the medieval English dream-poem, and the case of *The House of Fame* makes it particularly clear why this should be so. We have seen that the Middle Ages possessed a variety of elaborate methods of classifying dreams according to their causes and their value or lack of value as guides to truth. These systems of classification were highly ingenious, but they had one fundamental drawback: there was almost never any way of telling from a dream itself which category it belonged to. It might look and feel like a true vision of the future caused by divine or planetary influence, when really it was a mere fantasy caused by indigestion or drunkenness or melancholy or the influence of books or even by diabolic means. Only subsequent events would tell whether or not it was really prophetic. This drawback was much to be lamented by doctors or theologians, but for poets it could prove a distinct advantage. Dreams and poems are both types of fiction; and one thing that was lacking to medieval culture, whose intellectual roots were theological, was an adequate theory of fiction, and particularly a way of allowing some intrinsic value to the works of the human imagination. A fiction might be seen as an allegory or parable, in which case it could be said to convey the truth in a veiled form; a favourite medieval image for this is that of the sweet kernel of truth hidden inside the worthless shell of the fable. But nutshells, once cracked, are thrown away, and so this is not really a defence of fiction. Or again a fiction might claim to be a true history, an account of what really happened as set down in authentic sources. But there was no way of saying that a fiction possessed an imaginative truth or validity even though it did not correspond to any literal truth; in that case it was merely a lie, and there was no way of justifying its delightfulness. In these circumstances, to present a literary fiction as a dream – one imaginative product as an analogue or metaphor for another imaginative product – offered a medieval poet an extremely useful way out of his dilemma.[35] Precisely because it was almost impossible to tell from any individual dream whether it was a reflection of a truth outside itself, the dream in general was felt to be a highly ambivalent phenomenon. There is an amusing image of this situation in *The Nun's Priest's Tale*, where Chauntecleer thinks his dream must foretell the future because he believes that all dreams are 'significaciouns' of what is to come, while Pertelote thinks the same dream is 'vanitee' because she believes that all dreams are the product of bodily disorders.

Some scholars have argued that the main use of the dream-framework was to provide an assurance of authenticity: 'It is perhaps hard today to think of the dream framework as an authenticating device, but... For much of the past it served to suspend disbelief and to obtain credence. The dream may be fantastic, but it really happened.'[36] One purpose of the dream-framework is no doubt to define an area within which the poem, as it were, 'has permission to exist', a purpose which can be seen at its simplest in the closing line of *The Book of the Duchess*: 'This was my sweven; now hit ys doon'. But within this area the medieval reader or listener was not necessarily called on to suspend his disbelief. The use of the dream-framework is frequently to evade the whole question of authenticity, of belief or disbelief. What the dream-poet implicitly says is not, 'This is true – I know, because I dreamed it – and therefore you must believe it'. It is, 'I truly dreamed it; but there can be no guarantee that a dream corresponds to the truth. You had better give it whatever credence you usually give to dreams.' This is precisely the implication of the opening proem of *The House of Fame*. It begins by praying, 'God turne us every drem to goode!' – not 'May all our dreams come true', but 'May God make every dream profitable for us'. And it goes on at once to say that to the narrator it is a wonder what causes dreams and why some come true but others do not. He then lists the elaborate technical terminology of medieval dreamlore – *avisioun, revelacioun, drem, sweven, fantome, oracle* – not defining the terms, but saying that he does not know why dreams belong to these categories. Next, at greater length, and with enormous relish, he goes through all the possible causes of dreams: the bodily humours, or illness, or hardship, or overwork, or melancholy, or religious devotion, or the hopes and fears of lovers, or spirits, or the prophetic powers of the soul itself. Finally, when we are burning with impatience to learn which of all these is the true cause, he concludes with a teasing profession of ignorance:

> But why the cause is, noght wot I.
> Wel worthe, of this thyng, grete clerkys,
> That trete of this and other werkes;
> For I of noon opinion
> Nyl as now make mensyon,
> But oonly that the holy roode
> Turne us every drem to goode! (51–7)

> *Wel worthe...clerkys* Let great scholars concern themselves with this matter;
> *Nyl* will not

And that leaves us exactly where we started. All he will say about the dream which follows, and which contains the rest of the poem, is that it is 'wonderful' (62), which is what the narrator said about the dream in *The Book of the Duchess*: not true, or false, but wonderful. The dream is indeed full of wonders, which Chaucer describes with fine energy, though, as many readers have felt, with a bewildering uncertainty of direction. We saw, from the opening stages of the *Book of the Duchess* dream, that one possibility of the dream-framework for Chaucer was that, like a real dream, it could liberate the mind from the demands of causal and rational coherence, so as to open creative opportunities of a different kind. It is conceivable that in *The House of Fame* he experimentally pushed still further in that direction, but was unable to develop alternative principles of structure.

If we stand far enough back from the wonders seen by the Dreamer, we can easily recognize in *The House of Fame* the outlines of a *somnium coeleste*. I set aside for the moment book I, in which the Dreamer finds himself in a temple of Venus decorated with a pictorial version of the *Aeneid*; but from the moment a great eagle swoops down from the heavens at the end of book I, he seems embarked on a religious vision. The eagle itself is derived most immediately from Dante's *Purgatorio* IX, one of the few parts of the *Divine Comedy* which is explicitly in the form of a dream or vision. Dante falls asleep, and has a dream in the morning, the time when, as he says, 'la mente nostra...alle sue vision quasi è divina' (IX. 16–18) (our mind is almost divine in its power of vision). He dreams of being carried by a golden eagle up to the sun, and there consumed. The eagle was often used in the Middle Ages as a symbol of the flight of contemplation or of thought.[37] Indeed, when the Dreamer is in mid-flight, he remembers a passage from the *De Consolatione*, which we noted earlier, and which seems to confirm that this is the significance of the eagle here:

> And thoo thoughte y upon Boece,
> That writ, 'A thought may flee so hye,
> Wyth fetheres of Philosophye,
> To passen everych element;
> And whan he hath so fer ywent,
> Than may be seen, byhynde hys bak,
> Cloude'... (972–8)
> *Boece* Boethius; *flee* fly

Philosophy had told Boethius,

I have...swifte fetheris that surmounten the heighte of the hevene. Whanne the swifte thoght hath clothid itself in tho fetheris, it despiseth the hateful erthes, and surmounteth the rowndnesse of the gret ayr; and it seth the clowdes byhynde his bak... (IV, m. I. 1–6)

The eagle, then, is a personification of philosophical thought itself, carrying the Dreamer on a journey through the heavens, a vantage point from which 'al the world, as to myn yë, / No more semed than a prikke [point]' (906–7); or, as Philosophy puts it to Boethius, 'al the envyroun-ynge of the erthe aboute ne halt but the resoun of a prykke at regard of the gretnesse of hevene' (II, pr. 7. 24–6) (the whole surface of the earth is of no more consideration than a point in comparison with the greatness of heaven). It is all very like a real dream, both in the common dream-sensation of flying, and in the transformation of Boethius's metaphor of feathers into the dream-reality of an eagle.

There are numerous other indications that the dream is a *visio* or *somnium coeleste*. The eagle explains that he has been sent by Jupiter of 'his grace' (661, 2007) (the eagle being Jupiter's bird in classical myth-ology), to reward the Dreamer for his 'great humblesse, / And vertu eke' (630–1); and the Jupiter of a dream could no doubt stand for the Christian God. He tells the Dreamer that he is being carried higher than

> Daun Scipio,
> That saw in drem, at poynt devys,
> Helle and erthe and paradys. (916–18)
>
> *at poynt devys* with exactitude

The Dreamer even repeats on his own part some of the words of St Paul which allude to his vision of paradise, and which came to suggest the *Apocalypse of St Paul* and to be considered typical of mystical experience:

> Thoo gan y wexen in a were,
> And seyde, 'Y wot wel y am here;
> But wher in body or in gost
> I not, ywys; but God, thou wost!' (979–82)
>
> *wexen in a were* fall into doubt; *wher* whether; *not* know not

And although, as we shall see, the goddess Fame is a somewhat dubious theme for a *somnium coeleste*, she is compared with what St John saw in his vision –

> For as feele eyen hadde she
> As fetheres upon foules be,
> Or weren on the bestes foure
> That Goddis trone gunne honoure
> As John writ in th'Apocalips (1381–5)
>
> *feele* many; *gunne honoure* honoured

– and, like Boethius's Philosophy, she sometimes seems small and some-times to touch the heavens. Finally, at the point where the poem breaks off, it appears about to declare itself as a Macrobian *oraculum*, in which one who 'semed for to be / A man of gret auctorite' (2157–8) is going to deliver some important doctrine to the Dreamer – the 'tydynges' that he has been promised as the goal of his vision.

We can discern then, in *The House of Fame*, the outline of a *somnium*

77

coeleste, and the more convincingly, perhaps, because the whole poem, except for the introductory sections to each book, is included in the dream. It has the same basic structural divisions as *The Book of the Duchess*: first a section which repeats a story from a classical poet, second a journey in which the Dreamer has an animal as his guide, and third the arrival at what appears to be the main subject of the poem, a section in which the Dreamer is searching for some piece of information. But in the *Book* the classical story (from Ovid) is read by the narrator before he falls asleep, and thus becomes a likely influence on his dream, considered as a *somnium animale*; while in the *House* the classical story (from Virgil) is itself part of the dream, and no natural cause of the dream is suggested. When we look at the *House* more closely, however, the conception of it as a *somnium coeleste* has to be modified. One kind of modification is already familiar to us from the *Roman de la Rose* and its tradition. The religious vision is secularized and applied to the purposes of human love. The eagle tells the Dreamer that his vision comes as a reward for his services not to Jupiter himself but to 'Hys blynde nevew Cupido, / And faire Venus also' (617–18). Like the narrator of the *Book*, the Dreamer here has had no success in the practice of love, but that has not stopped him from writing poems 'in reverence / Of Love, and of hys servantes eke' (624–5). He is so devoted to his books that he has 'no tydynges / Of Loves folk yf they be glade' (644–5), and his reward will be to be carried where he can learn 'of Loves folk moo tydynges' (675). The theme of love helps us to see the relevance of book I to the remainder of the poem. The Dreamer recognizes the temple in which he finds himself as being dedicated to Venus, and in it he sees carved or engraved the opening lines of the *Aeneid*, followed by the rest of the story in pictures. A retelling of the story through a description of the pictures makes up the substance of book I, and it is a retelling which, in the medieval way, presents it as centring in the love-affair of Aeneas and Dido. It is Venus who commands Aeneas, her son, to flee from Troy, who implores Jupiter to save his ship in the storm, who appears in order to comfort him when he lands at Carthage, and who

> made Eneas so in grace
> Of Dido, quene of that contree,
> That, shortly for to tellen, she
> Becam hys love, and let him doo
> Al that weddynge longeth too. (240–4)
>
> *weddynge. . . too* appertains to marriage

The love-affair itself is recounted at length, with great emphasis on Dido's sufferings, and at the end of the story the part played by Venus

is once more stressed and is related to the lives of the poet and his
audience:

> For Jupiter took of hym cure
> At the prayer of Venus, –
> The whiche I preye alwey save us,
> And us ay of oure sorwes lyghte! (464–7)
>
> *cure* care; *lyghte* relieve

But the expectations that may have been aroused by book I and by
the eagle's promises in book II, that the poem will be a secular *visio* of
love, are not fulfilled by the remainder. Much of book II consists of an
exposition by the eagle of the theory of sound, in explanation of how
all that men say is transmitted to the house of Fame.[38] And when the
Dreamer reaches his destination, he finds in book III little that corresponds to the love-tidings he has been promised as his reward. There
are entertainers, but 'love-daunces' (1235) are only one of the pleasures
they offer. There are poets, but only one of them, 'Venus clerk, Ovide'
(1487), is a love-poet. There are many groups of suppliants to the
goddess for renown or oblivion, but only 'the sexte companye' (1727)
refer specifically to love in their requests, asking that they may be
reputed to be great lovers though they are not so really. The Dreamer
himself begins to be dissatisfied with the lack of what he has been led
to expect, and when an unnamed person asks if he has come there to
gain fame himself, he answers that he has not, that he has been promised
'Tydynges, other this or that, / Of love, or suche thynges glade' (1888–9),
but that 'these be no suche tydynges' (1894). His interlocutor therefore
invites him to go elsewhere to find 'What thou desirest for to here' (1911),
and leads him to the house of Rumour instead. There he once more
finds the eagle, who repeats Jupiter's wish that the Dreamer should be
rewarded for his sufferings, though now those sufferings are not explicitly associated with love, nor are the tidings which are to be his reward.
There is a scene of violent confusion, as various tidings struggle to get
out of the windows and make their way to Fame. At last the Dreamer
hears a great noise 'In a corner of the halle, / Ther men of love-tydynges
tolde' (2142–3). He sees the man of 'gret auctorite' amid the bustle, and
it seems that his and our expectations are to be fulfilled at last – but at
this point the poem breaks off. Various suggestions have been made as
to what the man might have said: perhaps, for example, he was going
to deliver a 'love-tiding' that related to some court love-affair, and for
that very reason the end of the poem has been suppressed. But there
is absolutely no evidence for this, and in any case it is impossible to
imagine any 'love-tiding' that could by now make the poem cohere as

a love-vision. If that is its intended purpose, it has long ago begun to disintegrate, and we must agree with Muscatine that *The House of Fame* has 'the elaborateness and pointlessness' of much poetry of the following century, and that it belongs to the 'decadence of late Gothic art'.[39]

Chaucer himself called his poem 'the book of Fame' (*Canterbury Tales* x. 1085), but we have not yet seen how far fame can be defined as the true theme of the vision. Certainly it could be argued that Fame has almost as good a claim as Venus to be the presiding goddess of book I. Dido laments that every man would have three wives if he could, for 'of oon he wolde have fame / In magnyfinge of hys name' (305–6), and she later invokes Fame herself, as she apostrophizes the absent Aeneas:

> For thorgh yow is my name lorn,
> And alle myn actes red and songe
> Over al thys lond, on every tonge.
> O wikke Fame! for ther nys
> Nothing so swift, lo, as she is!
> O, soth ys, every thing ys wyst,
> Though hit be kevered with the myst. (346–52)

name lorn reputation lost; *wyst* known; *kevered* covered

This passage suggests a way in which the whole conception of book I is relevant to the theme of fame, for it was by means of Virgil's poem that Dido's acts were 'red and songe', and came to be known in Chaucer's time. Further, as we discover from book III, there is a special unreliability about Fame, exemplified in the case of those who have the reputation of being great lovers and even prefer the name to the reality: 'Sufficeth that we han the fame' (1762). In retrospect, then, it would be possible to see the lengthy complaints of Dido and the Dreamer about the deceptiveness of men as illustrating this aspect of fame: the 'apparence' (265) which may be the very opposite of the reality of things. In retrospect, too, we shall notice perhaps that Aeolus, the 'god of wyndes' (203), who plays a part in the story of Aeneas by blowing up the storm which endangers the Trojan ships, reappears in book III as the messenger of Fame, with two trumpets called 'Clere Laude' (noble praise) and 'Sklaundre' (1575–80). And if fame, whether good or bad, is 'Bot wind inflat in uther mennis eiris',[40] then we can also see the relevance to this theme of the Dreamer's journey through the heavens in book II, and the eagle's discourse on sound.[41] We begin to recognize in the poem just that dreamlike recurrence and development of themes and images that we found in *The Book of the Duchess*, though here it is still further removed from the claims of logical discourse.

The central idea of book III, the imaginative evocation of the nature of an abstract conception such as 'Fame' by means of a description of the palace or house which the personified abstraction is said to inhabit, is thoroughly traditional. An ultimate source is Ovid's description of Fame's dwelling in *Metamorphoses* XII; more immediate sources are probably the descriptions of the dwelling of Fortune in two French dream-poems, the *Roman de la Rose* and Nicole de Margival's *Panthère d'Amours*. The similarity between Fame and Fortune is noted by the Dreamer when he says that Fame treats her suppliants arbitrarily, 'Ryght as her suster, dame Fortune' (1547); and it seems likely that Chaucer's picture of Fame was influenced by the depiction of 'Fortune as arbiter of Fame'[42] in the *Mirour de l'Omme* of his friend John Gower. Many of the details of the description in Chaucer's poem are symbolic, though none obscurely so. The placing of Fame's castle on a rock of ice illustrates the time-honoured idea that the ascent to fame is slippery and insecure; at the same time, the fact that some of the names written in the ice have melted away, while others are still fresh and legible, indicates the arbitrariness with which some people are remembered and others forgotten. Further, the castle itself has walls of beryl, a precious stone which is said to have a magnifying effect: they

> made wel more than hit was
> To semen every thing, ywis,
> As kynde thyng of Fames is. (1290–2)
> *kynde thyng* natural attribute

Thus, as in dreams, thoughts are translated into images; moreover, the whole description of Fame's dwelling is not presented as a formal set-piece, as in Ovid, but is conveyed bit by bit, as seen through the eyes of the Dreamer as he moves about, noticing first one thing and then another.[43] In *The House of Fame*, far more than in *The Book of the Duchess*, we feel the effect of that pull towards the 'personal, dramatic point of view' which is characteristic of dream-poetry. Always at the centre of the poem is the figure of the Dreamer, bewildered by the strange experiences of his dream.

We have already seen, in Watriquet de Couvin's *Dis des Quatre Sieges*, an example of the adaptation of the religious vision to claim glory in heaven for those who have achieved fame on earth. The vision is only pseudo-religious, in the sense that it presents heavenly glory as a mere reflection of earthly fame; but on the other hand the poem conceives of fame, whether early or heavenly, as genuine and deserved. In *The House of Fame*, however, the goddess is arbitrary and unreliable in her gifts. Some of her suppliants have done good, some evil, and some nothing at all; some seek fame, some oblivion; but she grants them good, bad or no reputation entirely according to her own whims, without regard to their deeds. Further, it emerges that Fame is dependent on Rumour: Rumour's enormous revolving house of twigs is full of tidings on every possible topic, which have to escape through the windows before Fame can decide what their fates shall be, and pass them on to Aeolus to be spread abroad. The whole atmosphere of book III is one of hilariously contradictory movement and noise, verging on hysteria, and far removed from that of religious vision, or the solemn seats of state in Watriquet's poem. Chaucer's poem, indeed, seems to embody a humorous critique or exposure of the notion of fame as a positive value. It may perhaps be significant that both the allusions to the *De Consolatione* noted above come from contexts which reflect unfavourably on earthly fame. The passage on the smallness of the earth compared with heaven occurs in the course of Philosophy's demonstration of the unimportance of that earthly fame that men strive for so eagerly: 'And ye thanne, that ben envyrouned and closed withynne the leeste prykke of thilke prykke, thynken ye to manyfesten or publisschen your renoun and doon yowr name for to be born forth?' (II, pr. 7. 41–5). Chaucer in his translation of this section uses the words *renoun, glorie,* and *fame* with little if any difference in meaning. And the passage on the feathers of philosophy comes immediately after a statement by Philosophy that in the kingdom of God 'blisfulnesses [blessings] comen alwey to goode folk, and infortune comith alwey to wikkide folk' (IV, pr. 1. 54–6). The order of the heavenly kingdom is thus described as the very opposite of the disorder of earthly affairs, ruled by the sisters Fortune and Fame. There is nothing heavenly about Fame's kingdom; and, just as the *Roman de la Rose* was, among other things, a mock-*visio* set in a pseudo-paradise, so *The House of Fame* might be seen as a mock-*oraculum*, setting forth the full meaninglessness of earthly renown and leading up to the non-delivery of doctrinal truth by one who only '*semed* for to be / A man of gret auctorite'. Fame's world is one of seeming, of *apparence*, where reality and truth are not to be found.

Such a view of the poem, though relating it intelligibly (as it demands to be related) to the complex tradition of visionary writing and dream-poetry, still over-simplifies it, in that it does not relate the theme of fame to that of love. I suggest that the link between the two is to be found in the Dreamer himself. We have seen that the Dreamer of *The House of Fame* is conceived not only as an unsuccessful lover but as a love-poet. In *The Book of the Duchess*, the Dreamer, as 'I, which made this book' (96), was a poet too, but merely in a formal sense; the *House* is the first

of Chaucer's poems in which the narrator is realized in the specific role
of poet. There is good reason why this could not have happened earlier
in Chaucer's work; it is surely not that 'The idea of making [the
narrator] a hopeful but untalented poet seems not to have occurred to
Chaucer until he came to write *The Hous of Fame*',[44] but that Chaucer
could not have presented himself as one who had done his incompetent
best to write poems 'in reverence / Of Love, and of hys servantes eke'
(624–5) until he was known as a love-poet to his audience. Once the
Dreamer is characterized at all, his biography must be based on that of
the poet. To be a poet, in the courtly circle for which Chaucer wrote,
was the same as to be a love-poet; it was taken for granted that love was
the inspiration of poetry, and that is why Chaucer, in the proem to book
II, invokes the aid of Venus (*Cipris*, 518) ahead of that of the Muses in
his poetic enterprise. But he is a poet quite without experience of the
main subject of his art, and thus, although he retells the *Aeneid* as a
love-story, when he comes to speak of the sexual relations between
Aeneas and Dido, he draws modestly back:

> What shulde I speke more queynte,
> And peyne me my wordes peynte
> To speke of love? Hyt wol not be;
> I kan not of that faculte. (245–8)

(Why should I speak more elaborately, labouring to decorate my words in
speaking of love? It cannot be; I know nothing of that branch of study.)

It is for this reason that he needs to be rewarded with tidings of love
in the house of Fame.

The connection between poetry and love, then, is clear, and we now
need to consider the connection between poetry and fame. They are
associated in more than one way. Poetry is a chief means by which fame
is conferred and transmitted: we saw that this was so in book I, in Dido's
prediction that her deeds would be 'red and songe', and indeed one
function of book I is to present the *Aeneid* as an example of this power
of poetry. In book III we learn that the permanent inhabitants of Fame's
palace are minstrels, harpers, musicians, magicians, poets, and his-
torians. With the exception of magicians, all these groups of people can
be seen as conveying fame through words. The greatest detail is given
in the case of poets: Statius, 'That bar of Thebes up the fame' (1461);
Homer, Dares, Dictys, Guido de Columpnis, Geoffrey of Monmouth,
and the mysterious 'Lollius' (the supposed source of *Troilus and Criseyde*), all of whom bore up the 'hevy...fame' (1473) of Troy; 'Venus
clerk, Ovide' (1487), who raised the fame of the God of Love; Virgil
(another link with book I); Lucan and other poets who 'writen of Romes

myghty werkes' (1504); and Claudian who in his *De Raptu Proserpinae* 'bar up al the fame of helle' (1510). For Chaucer, words were the chief means by which fame was created, and above all words in their most memorable and lasting form, as poetry; and in his list of poets he is naming many of the major sources of his own works, past and future. But to say this is to suggest another aspect of the matter; Chaucer as poet does not merely transmit fame, he is dependent upon fame for his subject-matter. As a modern writing about the classical past, he is inevitably stepping outside the bounds of his personal experience, and he has to rely on what has been written by others. And as a love-poet with no experience of love, he is in the same position, and can only pass on 'love-tydynges', whispers originating in rumour and half-heard amid the hubbub of Fame's palace. In book II we learn that such fame is 'noght but eyr ybroken' (765), and in book II we see how impossible it is to rely on any correspondence between fame and the reality of human experience. The narratorial method of *Troilus and Criseyde* is founded on Chaucer's sense of this dilemma for the poet: relying on the dubious 'Lollius' for his information about the Trojan war, and on what 'men say' for his understanding of love, how can he do anything but withdraw from judgment? His position is precisely that dramatized in book I of the *House*: a man seeing a story of profound historical and emotional significance not directly, but only through the images of art. This dependence on secondary sources is conveyed pervasively throughout the Dreamer's visit to the temple, by the constant repetitions of 'Ther saugh I...' and the relegation of the actual events of the story to subordinate clauses. The main verbs in book I belong to the Dreamer as he sees and tries to understand the 'queynte manere of figures / Of olde werk' (126–7). As he leaves the temple, it is still not the events themselves that hold his attention (for there is inevitably the barrier of art between him and them), but the artistic means by which they are conveyed, the 'noblesse / Of ymages' (471–2).

Thus it is the situation of the Dreamer as poet that lies at the heart of *The House of Fame*. The first proem, as we have seen, is concerned with the uncertainty of the relation between dreams and truth, and it will now be more apparent, perhaps, that this is a way of approaching the uncertainty of the relation between poetry and truth. Poetry can be inspired and prophetic, and in both the second and third proems Chaucer for the first time, under the impact of his reading of Dante and Boccaccio, indicates the possibility of this high role for the poet. In the second proem, after describing the dream confidently as a 'sely... avisyon' (513) (blessed vision) like that of Isaiah or Scipio, he invokes the aid of Venus and the Muses, and invites men to judge the 'engyn and myght' (528) (skill and power) of the 'Thought' (memory) (523) that fixed this vision in the treasury of his brain.[45] Thus he presents himself as the dedicated recorder of an inspired truth. And in the third proem he invokes the guidance of Apollo, the 'god of science [knowledge] and of lyght' (1091) and the 'devyne vertu' (1101), in expressing the 'sentence...That in myn hed ymarked ys' (1100–3) (meaning that is imprinted in my brain).[46] The dream has come to him on the tenth of December, a date which may have some astronomical significance, but which also suggests the sterility and deadness of winter, and hence the poet's need for some quickening inspiration. In the temple of Venus, the Dreamer confronts his own situation as poet: a mere onlooker, a tourist in the shrine of love, repeating a story that comes to him at second hand. When he leaves the temple, he finds himself in a landscape of terrifying desolation, related, as I suggested earlier, to the hell that forms part of traditional visions of the other world:

> Then sawgh I but a large feld,
> As fer as that I myghte see,
> Withouten toun, or hous, or tree,
> Or bush, or gras, or eryd lond;
> For al the feld nas but of sond
> As smal as man may se yet lye
> In the desert of Lybye;
> Ne no maner creature
> That ys yformed be Nature
> Ne sawgh I, me to rede or wisse.
> 'O Crist!' thoughte I, 'that art in blysse,
> Fro fantome and illusion
> Me save!' and with devocion
> Myn eyen to the hevene I caste. (482–95)
>
> eryd ploughed; rede advise; wisse guide

Thus, when the poet leaves his secondhand dealings with love, he finds himself in a state of frightening emptiness, with nothing whatever to say. Not for the last time, one senses a certain personal resonance in this passage: the landscape conveys a sense of the failure of creative power, reinforcing the wintry date of the dream. The poet needs heavenly inspiration to rescue him; and as he looks up, it appears to be coming, in the shape of the swooping eagle.

We have seen that the eagle can be a symbol of the flight of contemplation or philosophical thought; and in this context of secularized vision, in which the visionary has become a courtly poet of love, it is easily transformed into a symbol of poetic inspiration. Certainly, the whole experience the Dreamer now undergoes, of being 'carried away' by a force outside himself, seems to relate to that of inspiration, whether philosophical, religious, or poetic. We have seen that in the distant past these distinctions were not made, and the poet and the religious prophet were one and the same. But at the same time, the experience is irresistibly comic, in a way which is analogous to the encounter between Dreamer and Black Knight in *The Book of the Duchess*. The Dreamer remains earthbound in spirit, and does not wish to be carried to the heavens. First he faints and then he wriggles, and the eagle complains that he is 'noyous for to carye' (574). He fears that he is going to be 'stellified', turned into a star like the prophets and heroes of old, and he protests that

> I neyther am Ennok, ne Elye,
> Ne Romulus, ne Ganymede,
> That was ybore up, as men rede,
> To hevene with daun Jupiter,
> And mad the goddys botiller. (588–92)
> *Ennok* Enoch; *Elye* Elijah; *daun* lord

Since Chaucer's father had been the king's deputy butler, the court audience might recognize a personal reference here, and be amused at how firmly the Dreamer's thoughts were attached to earthly things. Well might he repeat in a lower key Dante's 'Io non Enea, io non Paolo sono', and with far greater truth: rather, he is a kind of J. Alfred Prufrock of the fourteenth century, who is not Prince Hamlet, nor was meant to be:

> Deferential, glad to be of use,
> Politic, cautious, and meticulous;
> Full of high sentence, but a bit obtuse;
> At times, indeed, almost ridiculous –
> Almost, at times, the Fool.[47]

He does not wish to take this unique opportunity of learning about the stars:

> 'Wilt thou lere of the sterres aught?'
> 'Nay, certeynly,' quod y, 'ryght naught'. (993–4)
> *aught* anything

He gives two reasons for this reluctance: first that he is too old, and second, most significantly, that he does not need this firsthand knowledge, because he believes what he reads in books:

> 'No fors,' quod y, 'hyt is no nede.
> I leve as wel, so God me spede,

Hem that write of this matere,
As though I knew her places here;
And eke they shynen here so bryghte,
Hyt shulde shenden al my syghte,
To loke on hem.' 'That may wel be,'
Quod he...(1011-17)
fors matter; *shenden* damage

The Dreamer is content with his books after all; he feels no need for reality, and is afraid it might shine so brightly as to hurt his eyes. The eagle, whose eye can gaze on the sun unharmed, sadly agrees, and immediately deposits him at Fame's dwelling, where he will be untroubled by direct experience, and will at best receive no more than 'tydynges' of love.

Chaucer's portrait of himself as a poet whose timidity makes him positively resistant to inspiration, and the use he makes of this portrait to explore the whole question of the relationship of art to experience, is a brilliant achievement, the more so in view of the fact that the poem in which it is conveyed is itself deeply indebted to literary tradition and yet generates a strong sense of the occasionally uneasy working out of a personal problem. Equally brilliant is the portrait of the eagle; and in *The House of Fame*, far more than in *The Book of the Duchess*, the comic treatment of the Dreamer infects the presentation of his dream-authority. The eagle does not hold the privileged position in the poem that must necessarily be granted to a figure representing Gaunt. He is no genuinely authoritative figure, whose words the Dreamer is too simple and inexperienced to understand, but rather a garrulous and complacent pedant, whom the Dreamer has good reason not to wish to understand. Hence the comedy is broader than in the earlier poem: on one side we find verbose self-congratulation, on the other monosyllabic sullenness. 'Have y not preved,' asks the eagle,

'Have y not preved thus symply,
Withoute any subtilite
Of speche, or gret prolixite
Of termes of philosophie,
Of figures of poetrie,
Or colours of rethorike?
Pardee, hit oughte the to lyke!
For hard langage and hard matere
Ys encombrous for to here
Attones; wost thou not wel this?'
And y answered and seyde, 'Yis.'
'A ha!' quod he, 'lo, so I can
Lewedly to a lewed man

87

Speke, and shewe hym swyche skiles
That he may shake hem by the biles,
So palpable they shulden be.' (854–69)

the to lyke to please you; *encombrous* burdensome; *Attones* at the same time; *Lewedly* unlearnedly; *skiles* arguments; *biles* beaks

The eagle, even at his most schoolmasterly, remains imprisoned within his avian nature, and thinks of even arguments as having beaks.

The poem is incomplete, almost certainly because Chaucer did not finish it, rather than because part has been lost in transmission.[48] It can plausibly be guessed that Chaucer was unable to complete it, not because it was 'pointless' (as Muscatine suggests), but because it had too painful a point, in its exploration of problems concerning Chaucer's own life as a poet, problems which he was unable to resolve. It seems to have been a matter of bearable pain, rather than of the unbalancing *Angst* from which more recent artists have suffered; and when the Dreamer is asked, near the end, whether he has come to Fame's house to seek fame for himself, he answers, with a nice blend of modesty and sturdy self-reliance,

I cam noght hyder, graunt mercy,
For no such cause, by my hed!
Sufficeth me, as I were ded,
That no wight have my name in honde.
I wot myself best how y stonde;
For what I drye, or what I thynke,
I wil myselven al hyt drynke,
Certeyn, for the more part,
As fer forth as I kan myn art. (1874–82)

as...ded i.e. by my life; *drye* suffer; *drynke* swallow; *fer forth* far; *kan* have knowledge of

Chaucer evidently felt, rightly, that he had inner resources that would enable him to move forward, even if at present he could not see exactly in what direction, and was therefore forced to leave his poem incomplete. It is rather unlikely that the incompleteness was a planned part of the poem's effect, and that Chaucer had intended all along that the 'man of gret auctorite' would have nothing to say. On the other hand, he evidently put it into circulation in its incomplete form, and, at least for subsequent readers, its incompleteness may make it all the more telling. I have suggested that this may have been part of its attraction for later medieval poets; and modern readers, with the benefit of hindsight, can see the final appearance of a bustling crowd including 'shipmen and pilgrimes' (2122) and 'pardoners' (2127) as pointing towards *The Canterbury Tales*,[49] where Chaucer was to find in the framed narrative a final solution to the problem of the validity of fiction. What is more, the artistic effect of *The House of Fame*, with its dynamic restlessness, is positively enhanced by incompleteness. Some words of Arnold Hauser about Gothic architecture might have been written with this poem in mind:

A Gothic church...seems to be in process of development, as if it were rising up before our very eyes; it expresses a process, not a result. The resolution of the whole mass into a number of forces, the dissolution of all that is rigid and at rest by means of a dialectic of functions and subordinations, this ebb and flood, circulation and transformation of energy, gives us the impression of a dramatic conflict working up to a decision before our eyes. And this dynamic effect is so overwhelming that beside it all else seems a mere means to this end. So it comes about that the effect of such a building is not merely not impaired when it is left uncompleted; its appeal and its power is actually increased. The inconclusiveness of the forms, which is characteristic of every dynamic style, gives emphasis to one's impression of endless, restless movement for which any stationary equilibrium is merely provisional.[50]

'The Parliament of Fowls'

Chaucer's third dream-poem was *The Parliament of Fowls*, which probably dates from 1382. In style, it is considerably more settled and composed than the two earlier dream-poems. Italian influences, which had affected only the content of the *House*, have now been absorbed stylistically too, and it is written not in the octosyllabic couplets of the two earlier poems, but in rime royal stanzas. The effect is less of rapid movement, whether gay or nervous, than in the earlier poems, and more of 'a grave sweetness and a poised serenity';[51] though colloquial touches are by no means excluded, and indeed stand out more sharply in this more dignified setting. Here more than ever Chaucer shows his awareness of the long and complex tradition of visionary writing, but it is now as much a matter of deft and pervasive allusion as of explicit reference. In structure, however, Chaucer remains very close to *The Book of the Duchess*. Indeed, one might guess that, after *The House of Fame*, where, under the impact of insoluble personal problems, he had pushed the use of dream-methods for literary creation so far as to make the poem unfinishable, he now decided to follow more exactly the causal sequence that had proved so successful in his first dream-poem. As in the *Book* there is a long introductory section, in which the narrator is still awake and reads a book about a dream, which then provides motivation for his own dream. As in the *House*, the narrator is a devotee of love but only in books, not through experience:

For al be that I knowe nat Love in dede,
Ne wot how that he quiteth folk here hyre,
Yit happeth me ful ofte in bokes rede
Of his myrakles, and his crewel yre. (8–11)

quiteth pays; *hyre* wages

But, in laying its emphasis on the narrator as would-be lover rather than poet of love, the *Parliament* is nearer to the *Book* than it is to the *House*. However, the distinction is not very clear-cut; there are one or two explicit references to the narrator as poet, and there is also a pervasive suggestion that love and poetry can be seen in the same terms, as creative experiences, which are highly desirable and yet difficult of achievement.[52] It is significant that the narrator invokes Venus not only as the cause of his dream, but also for help 'to ryme and ek t'endyte' (119) when he comes to set it down.

The narrator is introduced as reading one particular book, 'a certeyn thing to lerne' (20). What that thing is, we are never explicitly told, and at the end of the poem he resumes his search in 'othere bokes' (695); but here perhaps the poem is truly dreamlike, in that it solves the Dreamer's problems (at least for us) in the very act of reflecting them. The thing sought is surely found in the dream itself, without the Dreamer being aware of it, though if asked to define it one could only say that it is the meaning of the whole poem, which cannot properly be expressed in other terms. To put it more crudely than the poem does, what the narrator is seeking is presumably the meaning of that love which is the major subject of medieval courtly poetry, but which he sees chiefly as a cause of suffering; what he finds in the dream is a subtle placing of love in the larger context of the social order and of the relationship between the natural and the human, nature and culture. But to put it like that *is* to put it crudely, for the poem itself is deliberately enigmatic; it holds back from direct statements and conceptual formulations, and prefers to explore and order experience in the way dreams actually do, through images. Perhaps it would be better to say, through symbols, using 'symbol' in its Jungian sense as 'the expression of an intuitive perception which can as yet, neither be apprehended better, nor expressed differently'.[53]

The book the narrator of the *Parliament* is reading is the *Somnium Scipionis* itself, 'Tullyus of the drem of Scipioun' (31), of which he proceeds to give a compact summary. It is seen as a threefold vision of judgment, according to the traditional formula embodied in the *Divine Comedy*, except that earth takes the place of purgatory between heaven and hell:

Chapiteris sevene it hadde, of hevene and helle
And erthe, and soules that therinne dwelle. (32–3)

In the summary the emphasis is on heaven, that 'blysful place' which
is the reward of the good; and the word 'blysse' is repeated three times,
and the phrase 'blysful place' twice, in this brief passage. Another
repeated phrase is 'commune profit': heavenly bliss is the reward above
all of those who have pursued the welfare of the community rather than
private profit or even personal salvation. Finally the narrator, as it gets
dark, puts the book down, dissatisfied with its teaching,

For both I hadde thyng which that I nolde,
And eke I nadde that thyng that I wolde. (90–1)
nolde did not wish; *nadde* did not have

That is enigmatic indeed, but similar statements are made elsewhere in
Chaucer's poems, for example in *The Complaint unto Pity* and *The
Complaint to his Lady*, and they always refer to the situation of the
unrequited lover, who has the suffering that he does not wish but lacks
his lady's mercy, which he does desire.[54] So in one way these lines
probably refer to what we already know, the narrator's role as one who
has had no success in love. But a similar phrase is also used by Philosophy
in the *De Consolatione*, to refer to the general state of man, who seeks
mistaken means to arrive at that ultimate good which is his goal, and
therefore suffers from a perpetual anxiety, because 'the lakkide som-
what that thow woldest nat han lakkid, or elles thou haddest that thow
noldest nat han had' (III, pr. 3. 33–6). Thinking of *The House of Fame*,
we might feel inclined to see the dissatisfaction as that of the medieval
courtly poet, conscious of lacking the 'love-tidings' he needs if he is to
produce the expected kind of poetry, and finding in the *Somnium
Scipionis* a philosophical doctrine which seems to be of no use to him,
because it contains nothing about love (except, significantly, in the
phrase 'that lovede commune profyt' (47)). The dream will reconcile
these contradictions, and will provide the poet with 'mater of to wryte'
(168); but in its immediate context the statement is mysterious, used to
express a state in which the mind is dissatisfied for an undefinable cause,
weary as night falls, but still seeking for a truth that will answer its
longings.

The narrator falls asleep, and dreams that Scipio Africanus stands at
his bedside, just as Scipio the younger saw him in the book he has been
reading. As in the two earlier dream-poems, there is an ambiguity
concerning the status of the dream, which implies an ambiguity in the
status of the poem itself, and by extension of imaginative fiction in

general. The only theory about the causation of dreams which is stated in this poem occurs in a stanza I have mentioned before, which sees all dreams as reflecting states of body or mind: the hunter dreams of hunting, the sick man of drinking, the lover of success in love, and so on. And the narrator seems to assume the truth of this theory at the very end of the poem, where, after his awakening, he goes on reading more books in the hope that they will so affect his mind that one day he will have a dream that will do him good:

> I hope, ywis, to rede so som day
> That I shal mete som thyng for to fare
> The bet, and thus to rede I nyl nat spare. (697–9)

(Indeed I hope [or expect] some day to read in such a way that I shall dream some thing that will bring me greater success, and thus I will not refrain from reading.)

But he has already expressed doubt –

> Can I not seyn if that the cause were
> For I hadde red of Affrican byforn,
> That made me to mete that he stod there (106–8)

– and, as we have seen, he goes on to say that it was Venus who made him dream as he did. Taken literally, this would imply that the dream was a *somnium coeleste*, inspired by the goddess of love in her planetary form; taken metaphorically, it would indicate that it was a *somnium animale*, inspired by the narrator's waking thoughts of love. Then again, a dream which introduces a venerable figure such as Scipio Africanus the elder would count, according to Macrobius, as an *oraculum*, like the younger Scipio's own dream. If this were true, then the *Parliament* would be the kind of vision that *The House of Fame* stopped short of being; on the other hand, as J. A. W. Bennett has remarked, Chaucer 'reduces to a minimum Africanus' oracular function: the latter becomes a benevolent compère rather than the embodiment of divine wisdom'.[55] Are we to see the dream which follows as offering supernatural guidance, or as a fantasy woven by the Dreamer's mind out of his waking preoccupations and his reading? Chaucer does not commit himself to any answer to this question, nor to the question which by implication follows from it: are we to see a poem like this as a mere deceptive fiction, or does it offer access, through imagination, to truth?

Like the waking section, the dream in the *Parliament* follows closely the pattern of *The Book of the Duchess*. A preliminary section describes the dream-place (forest or garden), and then comes what appears to be the real subject of the poem (meeting with Black Knight or gathering of birds). We shall find in the *Parliament* as much as in the *Book* that what may seem merely a preliminary diversion is in fact related to the main subject through the kind of linkage that belongs to dreams. Africanus leads the Dreamer to the gate of a walled park, reminiscent of the walled garden of the *Roman de la Rose*. Over it are written two inscriptions 'of ful gret difference' (125), one at each side. These derive from the single inscription over the mouth of hell in Dante's *Inferno*, which promises grief and despair to all who enter. But Chaucer's inscriptions are, characteristically, more ambiguous. One promises:

> Thorgh me men gon into that blysful place
> Of hertes hele and dedly woundes cure;
> Thorgh me men gon unto the welle of grace,
> There grene and lusty May shal evere endure.
> This is the wey to al good aventure.
> Be glad, thow redere, and thy sorwe of-caste;
> Al open am I – passe in, and sped thee faste! (127–33)
>
> *hele* health; *lusty* joyful

Then the other:

> 'Thorgh me men gon,' than spak that other side,
> 'Unto the mortal strokes of the spere
> Of which Disdayn and Daunger is the gyde,
> Ther nevere tre shal fruyt ne leves bere.
> This strem yow ledeth to the sorweful were
> There as the fish in prysoun is al drye;
> Th'eschewing is only the remedye!' (134–40)
>
> *Daunger* resistance; *were* weir

The Dreamer is paralysed by the contradiction between the two inscriptions, but Africanus tells him that they are meant to refer only to one who is 'Loves servaunt' (159), and therefore not to him. And so he 'shof' (shoved) the Dreamer in through the gate, telling him that he can only be an onlooker, not a participant, but that he will at least gain material for his poetry.

What is behind the gate is evidently a garden of love, like that in the *Roman de la Rose* and its successors, and the inscriptions are saying that love is both heaven and hell. It is the 'blysful place' promised to the good in the *Somnium Scipionis*, with imagery of health, flowing water, and greenness; it is also a place of dryness, sterility and death, which can be avoided only by never entering the garden in the first place. The dream of a heaven and a hell is explicable psychologically through the influence of the vision of judgment read about in the *Somnium Scipionis*; but now the heaven and the hell are the same place – an original variant on the traditional pattern of visions. So far as the dream is to be thought of as providing material for poetry, one might also suggest that two contrary states of the imagination are indicated by the double inscription. The imagery of dryness and sterility recalls the desert outside the temple of Venus in book I of *The House of Fame*, which I suggested was a symbol, among other things, of the failure of inspiration; the imagery of growth and flowing water, on the other hand, suggests a renewal of creativity. Love, as the subject for poetry, can provide either or both of these.

The Dreamer enters the garden, and it proves to be a typical paradise-landscape, with a meadow and a river, a temperate climate, leaves that are always green, day that lasts for ever, birds singing like angels, and harmonious music sweeter than was ever heard by God 'that makere is of al and lord' (199). It contains the whole variety of natural species, instanced by lists of trees and of animals. But it soon becomes clear that this seeming paradise, as in the *Roman de la Rose*, is really a pseudo-paradise of idealized desire. In it 'Cupide, oure lord' (212) sharpens his arrows, 'Some for to sle, and some to wounde and kerve' (217), and his bow lies ready at his feet. The Dreamer sees personifications of pleasing qualities such as Pleasure, Courtesy and Beauty, but also others less pleasing, such as Foolhardiness, Flattery and Bribery, and, most forcefully described, with a real shudder in the rhythm of the last line, Cunning:

> ...the Craft that can and hath the myght
> To don by force a wyght to don folye –
> Disfigurat was she, I nyl nat lye. (220–2)
> *can* knows how; *don by force* compel

Now he presses further into the garden, and comes upon a temple of brass, the atmosphere of which is at once exotic and sinister. It may have Patience and Peace sitting at the door, but inside the air is hot with lovers' sighs, which make the altar flames burn more fiercely, and which he sees are incited by 'the bittere goddesse Jelosye' (252). The description of this temple is based on that of the temple of Venus in Boccaccio's *Teseida*; but in the *Parliament*, unlike book I of *The House of Fame*, we are not told to whom the temple is dedicated. Chaucer tells us that the 'sovereyn place' in it is held by Priapus, and leaves us to guess that it is his temple rather than Venus's. Priapus is the god of the phallus as well as of gardens, and a recent scholar has suggested that 'Chaucer's direct reference to the story in Ovid's *Fasti* of Priapus' thwarted attempt to make love to the nymph Lotis clearly marks the temple as a place of sexual frustration'.[56] Moreover, the Dreamer tells us that

Ful besyly men gonne assaye and fonde
Upon his hed to sette, of sondry hewe,
Garlondes ful of freshe floures newe. (257-9)
(People were eagerly attempting and endeavouring to set on his head garlands
full of fresh new flowers, of various colours.)

The emphasis on *attempting* to do this is not in Boccaccio, who says merely
that there were garlands of flowers about the temple; and, though the
modern reader may think of a notorious incident in chapter 15 of *Lady
Chatterley's Lover*, the suggestion Chaucer intends is probably that the
cult of sexuality cannot be so easily prettified, however 'besyly men
gonne assaye and fonde'. In a dim corner, the Dreamer finds Venus performing a kind of striptease act, which draws an approving snigger
from him. The temple is hung with broken bows, symbolizing the lost
virginities of those who 'here tymes waste / In hyre servyse' (283-4),
and it is decorated with paintings of famous figures from myth and
legend who died for love.

From this hothouse atmosphere, the Dreamer re-emerges into the
garden 'that was so sote [sweet] and grene' (296), and walks about to
recover from his insight into obsessive sexuality. There he sees another
goddess, contrasting with Venus. This is Nature,

> ...a queene,
> That, as of lyght the somer sonne shene
> Passeth the sterre, right so over mesure
> She fayrer was than any creature. (298-301)
> *shene* bright; *over* beyond

Chaucer does not describe her in detail, but, with another of the poem's
allusions to the visionary tradition, simply says that she looked just as
Alanus described her in the *De Planctu Naturae*. Now, however, the birds
of different species, which in Alanus were pictured on her garments,
have come alive, and they are all crowded round her, awaiting her
judgment. The day, we learn, is that of St Valentine, when the birds
choose their mates; and it is likely that the *Parliament* was composed to
form part of the St Valentine's day celebrations in Richard II's court.
1382 was the year of Richard's marriage, at the age of fifteen, to Anne
of Bohemia. Nature is later described as God's deputy, 'vicaire of the
almyghty Lord' (379), but there is little emphasis on her subordination
to some higher realm of values. By contrast with the *Roman de la Rose*,
this poem lays its stress not on the limitation of Nature's realm but on
its extensiveness, though it is also concerned with the intricate relationships between the natural and the human. Nature is so surrounded with
birds, the Dreamer says, that 'unethe was there space / For me to stonde,

so ful was al the place' (314–15); and indeed, from this point on, the Dreamer drops almost completely out of sight, as if the birds had squeezed him out of the poem; and so does Africanus, his guide. This is one way in which the *Parliament* is very different from both of Chaucer's earlier dream-poems: the subject-matter of the dream itself becomes so solid and energetic that it elbows the Dreamer aside, and instead of a contrast of points of view between Dreamer and guide there is a contrast *within* what the Dreamer sees. There may be a connection between this disappearance of the Dreamer's point of view and the poem's lack of emphasis on the Dreamer as poet; here it is what is seen that is important, not the role of the person who sees it.

The first things seen are all the species of birds, described in five stanzas, each bird with its own epithet or attribute, which serves to humanize it or to align it with some aspect of human life – the noble falcon, the meek-eyed dove, the thieving crow, the gluttonous cormorant, the wise raven, and so on. These are traditional epithets, evidence of the longstanding human tendency to think of birds as constituting a society parallel to human society. We may compare this list with the earlier list of trees in the garden. Both are concerned not simply with description of the natural world, but with the interaction of the natural and the human. The epithets in the list of trees call attention to the usefulness of the different species to men: the oak for building, the box for making pipes, the fir for ships' masts, the yew for bows, and so on. The list of birds, on the other hand, presents them as independent of human beings but parallel to them. The anthropologist Claude Lévi-Strauss has suggested some reasons for this attitude towards birds, which

can be permitted to resemble men for the very reason that they are so different. They are feathered, winged, oviparous and they are also physically separated from human society by the element in which it is their privilege to move. As a result of this fact, they form a community which is independent of our own but, precisely because of this independence, appears to us like another society, homologous to that in which we live: birds love freedom; they build themselves homes in which they live a family life and nurture their young; they often engage in social relations with other members of their species; and they communicate with them by acoustic means recalling articulated language. Consequently everything objective conspires to make us think of the bird world as a metaphorical human society: is it not after all literally parallel to it on another level? There are countless examples in mythology and folklore to indicate the frequency of this mode of representation.[57]

There are also countless examples in medieval literature, among them Clanvowe's *Cuckoo and the Nightingale*, which we shall consider later, and the earlier English poem *The Owl and the Nightingale*, in which the two birds are used to articulate a whole range of binary contrasts among human attitudes.

In *The Parliament of Fowls*, under Nature's arbitration, the birds are choosing their mates. Like men in medieval society, they are divided into several broad classes: the birds of prey, those that live on worms, those that live on seeds, and water-fowl. Fittingly, in terms of the human hierarchy of the Middle Ages, Nature begins with the noblest, the birds of prey, and among these with the highest, the royal eagle. But here there is a difficulty, for there are three candidates for the hand – or wing – of the beautiful female eagle, the formel, whom Nature herself is holding on her hand. They are, naturally, three male eagles, or tercels. Each speaks in turn to stake his claim to her: the first rests his claim essentially on the total humility of his devotion, the second on the length of his service as her admirer, the third on his exclusive loyalty. The statement of these claims, in a style of appropriately courtly amplitude, occupies some time, but meanwhile the other classes of birds are anxious to express their own views. Their attitudes are often less courtly than those of the aristocratic birds, and the poem echoes with cries of 'kokkow' and 'quek quek'; indeed, our last reminder of the Dreamer's presence as an observer occurs just here, when he complains that 'thourgh myne eres the noyse wente tho' (500). Nature determines that each class of birds shall select its own spokesman to offer a solution to the dilemma. The falcon, for the birds of prey, says that there is no further possibility of discussion, and the three tercels must fight to the death, unless the formel can choose among them herself. The goose, for water-fowl, offers the simple solution that any of the tercels who is not loved by the formel should choose another female as his mate – an uncourtly view, which is treated with ridicule by the sparrowhawk and the other 'gentil foules alle' (575). The turtledove, on behalf of the seed-fowl, claims that each of the tercels must show his loyalty to the formel by loving no-one else until he dies, even if she should die first – a *reductio ad absurdum* of courtly claims for the transcendent value of personal emotion, in which we are perhaps intended to see a touch of bourgeois sentimentality. The duck agrees with the goose: there are other fish in the sea, other stars in the sky:

> 'Ye quek!' yit seyde the doke, ful wel and fayre,
> 'There been mo sterres, God wot, than a payre!' (594–5)

The last verdict is that of the cuckoo, for the lowly worm-fowl, the *vylayns* of bird-society: since the eagles cannot agree, let them remain solitary all their lives. Another *gentil* bird, the small falcon called a merlin, protests against this in most *ungentil* language, calling the cuckoo 'wormes corupcioun' (614); but at this point Nature intervenes again.

In the paralleling of different types of bird with the attitudes supposed to be appropriate to different social classes, there is a close resemblance to the way in which primitive men use the categories built into nature as means of thinking about their own lives as part of human culture. In many areas of life such habits of thought have been retained by civilized societies too, so that, as Lévi-Strauss puts it, 'The differences between animals, which man can extract from nature and transfer to culture, . . . are adopted as emblems by groups of men in order to do away with their own resemblances'.[58] In the *Parliament* the poet of a highly civilized society to some extent reverses the original process: the already existing human groupings, and the attitudes which accompany them, are transferred to the realm of the birds, a realm which remains under the dominion of Nature. There are objectively and permanently different species of birds; but they are only birds, after all. One consequence of this is that we can think about their differences of attitude, even towards so central a subject as love, with amused tolerance. The irreducible birdlikeness of the eagle in *The House of Fame* had a similar function, in preventing us from being able to take him too seriously as a figure of authority. This part of the poem, the actual parliament of the birds, is very funny, not least as a parody of the unruly parliament of Chaucer's own time. Its amusing aspects, indeed, have perhaps tended to overshadow the rest of the poem. A second consequence of the way in which the birds remain birds is that Nature, the mother of them all, can call them to order, if necessary somewhat sharply: 'Holde youre tonges there!' (521) or '"Now pes!" quod Nature, "I commaunde here!"' (617). Their different degrees of *worthinesse* are not conceived as a merely historical phenomenon, but are ratified as part of Nature's 'ryhtful ordenaunce' (390). And she is in a position to insist that their mating must be by mutual agreement, by *eleccioun* (621) rather than by the force that the earlier temple of brass seemed to imply.

Finally, towards the end of the dream, a provisional solution to the dilemma of who shall mate with the formel is achieved by moving out of the realm of birds and back into that of men and women. Nature allows the formel to make her own choice – which was what the falcon had originally urged. Nature herself, it appears, is on the side of the *gentil*, even though she 'alwey hadde an ere / To murmur of the lewednesse [coarseness] behynde' (519–20). She advises the formel, saying that were she not Nature but Reason she would counsel her to choose the first of the tercels; but the actual choice she leaves to the bird herself. The formel, however, declines to choose; she does not yet wish to serve Venus or Cupid, and she needs more time to make up her mind. This too Nature grants. She allows her until the next St Valentine's day to make her choice, and meantime the three tercels have a year to prove their devotion to her. With this problem removed for the time being, all the other birds can now choose their mates. They choose immediately, and before their departure they sing a roundel in honour of Nature, the exquisite lyric 'Now welcome, somer, with thy sonne softe' (680). The noise of the birds' 'shoutyng' when the song is finished awakens the Dreamer from his sleep, and the poem ends with him reading still more books, in the hope of one day having a dream that will do him good.

There is a striking contrast between the evident dissatisfaction of the Dreamer with his dream, which he thinks has not given him what he was seeking in his books, and the satisfying completeness which most readers find in the poem that contains the dream. The difference is that between the conscious mind, always seeking for rational solutions to life's problems on the 'bookish' level of philosophy, and the unconscious mind, which achieves mastery over problems by enacting them in the form of concrete images rather than through rational analysis. One scholar writes of all Chaucer's dream-poems that 'The great originality of these poems is in their attempt to exploit the possibilities of *dispositio* – over-all structural arrangement – in ways more complex and meaningful than anything the [rhetorical] manuals suggest in their perfunctory treatments of it.'[59] This is particularly true of *The Parliament of Fowls*: the meaning of the poem is conveyed through certain contrasts embodied rather than stated in the dream-experience, and it was surely his sensitive understanding of dreams that enabled Chaucer to go beyond the inadequate treatment of *dispositio* in the *artes poeticae*. There is, for example, the contrast between the temple of Priapus and Venus and the garden of Nature, between love conceived as enslaving obsession and love conceived as natural impulse, operating within the orderly hierarchy of Nature; then there is the further contrast, within the natural order, now seen as mirroring the human order, between different attitudes towards love. We *feel* the contrast between the enclosure of Venus and Priapus and the freedom of Nature (and we may note that the temple is set within Nature's garden: Nature is more inclusive than sexuality). This freedom, always combined with order, is enacted in the parliament, where every attitude is allowed freedom of expression. This is how the 'commune profit' of the *Somnium Scipionis* is achieved in

Nature's realm, which in one way encloses and in another way is homologous with the realm of human society. The cuckoo even uses the phrase
'comune spede' (507), which means the same as 'commune profit'. And
the freedom of speech and choice includes a freedom not to choose, or
at least to defer choosing. The poem ends unexpectedly, so far as the
suitors are concerned: this mating season for them brings not the
achievement of love but its deferment. This has the advantage of finally
transferring the freedom of discussion to the poem's audience. As some
scholars have suggested, *The Parliament of Fowls* leads up to a *demande
d'amour*, a love-question to be settled by the courtly listeners as *they* think
fit. Whom should the formel choose next St Valentine's day? It is for
us to decide. Moreover, the deferment of the choice implies a richer
civilization than merely seasonal activities might lead us to expect.
Human love, the poem implies, involves not merely the gods of sex and
their temple of illicit passions, but the possibility of resisting Nature, or
at least of gaining a certain margin of freedom within which to choose
the time and manner of one's submission. No doubt, as Jean de Meun's
La Vielle puts it, quoting Horace,

> qui voudroit une forche prandre
> por soi de Nature deffandre
> et la bouteroit hors de sai,
> revandroit ele, bien le sai (13991–4)

(if anyone wanted to take up a pitchfork to protect himself against Nature and
shove her out of himself, she would come back, I know well).

But human beings, though they may not be able to overcome Nature
completely, at least are not like birds in being so absolutely dominated
by natural impulse that they cannot resist the mating season. The
subject of the poem, as I have argued, is that central subject of anthro-
pological study, the relation between nature and culture. The dream,
then, though it does not satisfy the Dreamer, does weave the thoughts
that had been preoccupying him, both from books and from life, into
a new and more richly significant pattern. Love, heaven, hell, the
'commune profit': all these appear, transmuted, in the dream, which
offers, like myth, an imaginative mastery over the problems of human
life.

The mastery is only imaginative, of course, and that is one meaning
of the poem's dream-framework. Once the dream is over, the Dreamer
may still be troubled by problems so fundamental to human nature that
they cannot be abolished. Moreover, the poem in its texture, its 'feel',
is genuinely like a dream. It may make use of conceptual thought, but
it does so in the most tentative way, with conceptual oppositions largely

replaced by concrete contrasts, and one contrast merging dreamlike into another. Such a delicate structure could not have been created by a poet who was truly in the dreamlike state in which he represents himself. A superb intelligence is at work in *The Parliament of Fowls*, and some words written about a great poet of the twentieth century would apply equally well to this poem of Chaucer's:

The poet's magnificent intelligence is devoted to keeping as close as possible to the concrete of sensation, emotion and perception. Though this poetry is plainly metaphysical in preoccupation, it belongs as purely to the realm of sensibility, and has in it as little of the abstract and general of discursive prose, as any poetry that was ever written.[60]

The 'Prologue' to 'The Legend of Good Women'

The *Prologue* to *The Legend of Good Women* is the last of Chaucer's dream-poems, and it stands alone in his work in existing in two distinct versions, F, dating from about 1385–6 and G, a revised version which probably dates from 1394 or later. This brings us to the period of Chaucer's most mature work. The *Prologue* is certainly later than *Troilus and Criseyde*, the translation of Boethius, and the first versions of *The Knight's Tale* and *The Second Nun's Tale*, because all of these are mentioned in it; and yet Chaucer is still using and further developing the dream-poem. For him, contrary to the common assumption, the dream-poem cannot have been a mere literary artifice which appealled to him only in his early, imitative period. The *Prologue* is perhaps the most puzzling and enigmatic of Chaucer's dream-poems, although it is the shortest, and is comparatively simple in outline. It begins with a discussion by the narrator of the relative values of personal experience and of the authority of old books – a topic familiar from *The House of Fame*. He is himself a devotee of books, but in May at least he leaves them behind and goes out into the meadows to perform his devotions to his favourite flower, the daisy. This he praises at some length, and then explains that one May morning he went out in this way, listened to the birds singing in praise of spring and love, and adored the daisy all day long. Then, at night, he slept in the garden and had a dream. In it the God of Love appears to him, accompanied by a beautiful lady who in appearance is like a transfigured daisy. The God and his company of ladies themselves worship the daisy, and then the God notices the Dreamer. What, he asks, is *he* doing so near the God's own flower? It would be better for a worm to be near it than for the Dreamer to do so, because the Dreamer has written works which are heresies against the religion of love, and which persuade wise men not to believe in women's trustworthiness – namely, the *Romance of the Rose* and *Troilus and Criseyde*. (The G text inserts at this point a list of books possessed by the Dreamer from which he could have drawn stories of the faithfulness of women.) But the beautiful daisy-like lady defends the Dreamer against the angry God, arguing that his works were translations, that he had not noticed that they were heretical, that he may have been writing under the orders of some patron, and that in any case he is now repentant. The God of Love, as a just ruler, ought to be merciful, not harsh. And she mentions a whole string of works which the Dreamer has also written, 'Al be hit that he kan nat wel endite' (F 414): *The House of Fame*, *The Book of the Duchess*, *The Parliament of Fowls*, the story which later became *The Knight's Tale*, and many lyrics. She adds that he has also written works of 'other holynesse' (F 424) – belonging, that is, not to the religion of love but to Christianity – and she mentions some of these. She proposes that the Dreamer should be forgiven if he agrees to write in future about women 'trewe in lovyng' (F 438). The God magnanimously consents, and the Dreamer thanks the lady, explaining that, whatever his sources intended, his own purpose was only to blame false lovers. The lady tells him that he must henceforward spend his time writing of good women and false men, and that, even though not a lover himself, he must 'speke wel of love' (F 491). The God of Love now identifies the lady by reminding the Dreamer that he has at home a book which tells how Alcestis, who died to save her husband from death, was afterwards transformed into a daisy. That is who the lady is, and the Dreamer must write of her too. Lastly, the God returns to his home in paradise, and the Dreamer is left to proceed with his task. Only in G is his awakening mentioned. There follow nine stories of 'good women', mostly taken from Ovid. The last is unfinished, and the work as a whole is incomplete, since the *Prologue* has mentioned nineteen legends to be recounted.

In many ways the *Prologue* to *The Legend of Good Women* belongs to the category established by Chaucer's earlier dream-poems, and indeed it further develops certain possibilities inherent in that category. For example, the opening discussion of experience and the authority of books is from one point of view a generalization of issues raised in the earlier poems. Each of them had begun with a story from a book by 'these olde wyse' (F 19) – Ovid, Virgil, Cicero – and each of them had gone on to counterpoint the adventures of an inexperienced dreamer against the authority encountered in his dream. In the *Prologue*, moreover, the discussion begins with the example of 'joy in hevene and peyne in helle'

(F 2), of which we know only from books, since no man has been there and returned; and yet each of the dream-poems, including the *Prologue* itself, claims to be a record of experience of a kind of heaven; though, yet again, each of them is no more than a book. The confident affirmation with which this section of the *Prologue* concludes –

> Wel ought us thanne honouren and beleve
> These bokes, there we han noon other preve (F 27–8)
> *preve* experiential proof

– dissolves into ambiguity as one thinks about it. To take another example, we saw that in *The Parliament of Fowls* the existence of the poem was justified by the fact that the dream had been sent to the poet in order to provide him with material for poetry. In the *Prologue*, this justificatory function of the dream is taken further, and the commands received in the dream justify the existence not just of the dream-poem itself but of the sequence of other poems attached to it. This conception of the dream-prologue proved to be highly influential on subsequent writers, particularly in Scotland, and I shall return to it later.

Like *The Book of the Duchess* and *The Parliament of Fowls*, the *Prologue* appears to be associated with some courtly occasion. In it, Chaucer twice refers to the courtly cult of the flower and the leaf, a kind of game at the court of Richard II, in which the courtiers divided into two parties or mock-chivalric orders, in order to provide a framework for the discussion of questions of love.[61] Chaucer refers to this cult only to assert that the cult of the daisy which is a central theme of his poem does not imply that he supports the party of the flower against that of the leaf. His poem, when he reaches the actual legends, is going to be concerned with stories dating from long before the flower and leaf game was invented:

> Ne I not who serveth leef, ne who the flour;
> Wel browken they her service or labour;
> For this thing is al of another tonne,
> Of olde storye, er swich stryf was begonne. (F 193–6)
> *not* know not; *browken they* may they enjoy; *of... tonne* drawn from a different barrel

The cult of the daisy, too, was not an invention of Chaucer's, but has a courtly background in a number of French 'marguerite' poems, especially by Machaut and Deschamps.[62] Both cults seem to have been associated with the courtly May games, which were probably aristocratic imitations of popular seasonal festivities. The dream in the *Prologue* takes place on the night of May the first in the F-text, and 'Whan passed was almost the month of May' (G 89) in G; possibly these two dates indicate occasions on which the poem was read aloud. The birds and their celebration of the mating season are repeated from the *Parliament*, and the *Prologue* also has the birds referring to St Valentine's day. The F-text refers specifically to the queen, when the God of Love instructs the Dreamer to send his book of good women, once complete, to 'the quene, / On my byhalf, at Eltham or at Sheene' (F 496–7). The queen in question is Anne of Bohemia, and the G-text must date from after her death in 1394, because it deletes this reference to her and the palaces; indeed, Richard II, in his passionate grief, had ordered the palace at Sheen to be destroyed. The strength of these bonds linking the *Prologue* to its setting in court life is an important source of the poem's puzzling quality. One cannot help suspecting that crucial elements in its meaning may relate to some situation outside itself, to which we no longer have the key. However that may be, the conception of Chaucer as court-poet is familiar to us from his other dream-poems.

The *Prologue* employs the dream for a purpose which we can now easily recognize. It is a secularized version of an otherworld vision, in which an authoritative figure appears to the Dreamer and conveys to him commands and teaching beyond those available to him in his waking life in this world. As in the *House* and the *Parliament*, the content of the vision relates to Chaucer's role as a courtly poet of love. As in the *Parliament*, the narrator is presented from the beginning as a devoted student of 'olde bokes' (F 25) – those very 'olde bokes' from which he is eventually to draw the legends of good women. He has no personal experience of love, and in this he is much inferior to the courtiers who form his audience, whom he addresses as 'lovers that kan make of sentement' (F 69) (lovers who are able to write poetry based on their own feelings). They are the reapers of the harvest of poetry, and he comes behind gleaning 'any goodly word that ye han left' (F 77); he has to apologise to them for merely repeating what 'ye han in youre fresshe songes sayd' (F 79). Just as in the *Parliament*, then, the vision comes to him as a way of providing matter for his poetry; only now it is not, as it was in both the *Parliament* and the *House*, a reward for his devoted service, and a new inspiration to him, but a penance for what he has done wrong, and he remains uninspired, nothing but a humble translator. It is true that the vision concludes with a doctrinal assurance of a more general kind, of exactly the sort that earlier visionaries had brought back from the world beyond death. The God of Love tells him,

> But er I goo, thus muche I wol the telle:
> Ne shal no trewe lover come in helle. (F 552–3)

(There is of course an intentional ambiguity in that message, which might refer either to Christian truth or to a secular parody of it, such as is enunciated by Genius in the *Roman de la Rose.*) But the main body of the vision focuses more distinctly than any of Chaucer's earlier dream-poems on poetry itself, and it throws fascinating light on Chaucer's role as a poet.

The Dreamer is even more firmly identified with Chaucer as poet than he was in *The House of Fame.* He has written all of Chaucer's works, and the list of them, which Chaucer modestly puts in Alcestis's mouth rather than his own, acts as a form of self-advertisement. Chaucer can evidently assume, as Machaut could in writing the *Jugement dou Roy de Navarre,* that some of his earlier work is sufficiently well known to his audience, and perhaps sufficiently controversial, for a contradiction of it to be a plausible starting-point for a new poem. Yet the Dreamer evidently wrote Chaucer's work in total unawareness of what he was doing – while dreaming, as it were. He was only translating, and *Troilus and Criseyde* was as simply a translation as *The Romaunt of the Rose. Troilus* indeed offers itself as being not just the story of Troilus and Criseyde, but the story of how a naive and incompetent court-poet, a mere servant of the servants of the God of Love, performed the task of translating it. The *Prologue* goes even further than this. It argues not just that *Troilus and Criseyde* is only a translation, but that it is a translation by a writer who did not grasp the meaning of his source. The defence Alcestis suggests against the God of Love's angry accusation is not that *Troilus* is really a poem in praise of the love of women, despite Criseyde's unfortunate lapse, but that Chaucer had failed to understand that the story was directed *against* the love of women:

> Therfore he wrot the Rose, and ek Crisseyde,
> Of innocence, and nyste what he seyde. (G 344–5)
> *nyste* knew not

Later, Chaucer as Dreamer hesitantly suggests a slightly different explanation: it is true that he failed to understand what his sources meant, but he thought he was telling the story as an *exemplum* warning against falseness in love, and therefore in favour of true love:

> what so myn auctour mente,
> Algate, God woot, yt was myn entente
> To forthren trouthe in love and yt cheryce,
> And to ben war fro falsnesse and fro vice
> By swich ensample; this was my menynge. (F 470–4)
> *what so* whatever; *Algate* nevertheless; *cheryce* cherish; *ben war* beware

But Alcestis quickly tells him to hold his tongue; the God of Love has been remarkably merciful to him, and he had better not argue about the matter, or presume to have theories about his own work:

> And she answerde, 'Lat be thyn arguynge,
> For Love ne wol nat countrepleted be
> In ryght ne wrong; and lerne that at me!
> Thow hast thy grace, and hold the ryght therto.' (F 475–8)
>
> *countrepleted* argued against; *at* from

Instead let him proceed with his penitential task of writing about women who were true in love, and about men who betrayed them in the way which is so sadly typical of the earthly world in which the Dreamer leads his waking life:

> And telle of false men that hem bytraien,
> That al hir lyf ne do nat but assayen
> How many women they may doon a shame;
> For in youre world that is now holde a game. (F 486–9)
>
> *ne do nat* do nothing

This abrupt treatment of the Dreamer is also similar to what we have seen in earlier dream-poems. He is a person of no importance in his own dream, fiercely rebuked by the authoritative figure who confronts him, and unable even to think of an excuse for his misdoings until one is suggested for him by Alcestis; and then rapped over the knuckles by Alcestis herself for attempting to explain what he thought he was doing in his own poetry. The Dreamer says very little indeed: he is a comically inadequate figure, far more at home diligently reading and translating old books in his earthly life than when he is transported to the presence of the God who defines the doctrine of all true love poetry. But, somewhat as in the encounter between the Dreamer and the Black Knight in *The Book of the Duchess*, the meeting of the simple Dreamer with the princely figure in his dream sets up ironic reverberations which also affect that princely figure. We all know that Chaucer really understood what he was doing when he wrote his poems, that his task as 'translator' of *Troilus and Criseyde* was really of a quite different order from his task as translator of the *Roman de la Rose*, and that, after all, the Chaucer who cuts such a poor figure in his dream is also the Chaucer who wrote the poem in which the dream occurs, the creator of the God of Love as well as the trembling poetaster who thankfully accepts penance from him. The God, we are prepared to believe (and in this we have Alcestis's encouragement too), is a literary tyrant, a censor who insists that reality shall be presented only in a certain light; and the poet, in his simplicity, may have stumbled into a more truthful picture of things. This profound ambiguity about the status of Chaucer as court-poet is developed, as usual, out of the essential ambiguity in the status of dreams.

From one point of view, the dream in the *Prologue* is obviously a distorted reflection of the Dreamer's waking life, a *somnium animale*. In his dream he finds himself in the same meadow into which he had gone earlier to do his devotions to the daisy; indeed, in the G-text the point at which he falls asleep is moved forward in the poem, and part of F's description of the real meadow becomes in G a description of the dream-meadow. In his waking life he has been entirely preoccupied with the daisy; in his dream he sees a lady who is, as it were, a daisy personified and transfigured, and he at once recognizes the similarity:

> And she was clad in real habit grene.
> A fret of gold she hadde next her heer,
> And upon that a whit corowne she beer
> With flourouns smale, and I shal nat lye;
> For al the world, ryght as a dayesye
> Ycorouned ys with white leves lyte,
> So were the flowrouns of hire coroune white.
> For of o perle fyn, oriental,
> Hire white coroune was ymaked al;
> For which the white coroune above the grene
> Made hire lyk a daysie for to sene,
> Considered eke hir fret of gold above. (F 214–25)

real royal; *fret* ornament; *beer* wore; *fluorouns* petals; *and* (l. 217) if; *leves lyte* small petals; *o* one

The French 'marguerite' poems provide a link between the flower and the pearl, because in French *marguerite* means both 'pearl' and 'daisy'. Obviously enough, this dream-lady is a projection of the Dreamer's waking thoughts; but beyond this we do not find in the *Prologue* any of the complex psychological motivation for the dream which is part of Chaucer's other dream-poems, and above all of *The Book of the Duchess*, nor do we find much sign of adaptation of the constructive methods of dreams to provide imaginative linkings within the poem. The drama of the dream is self-sufficient; its outlines are strongly drawn, and there seems to be no network of hidden correspondences beneath them. This might suggest that the poem is better considered in its other aspect, as a vision coming from outside the Dreamer's mind, under supernatural influences, a *somnium coeleste*.

The standing of the dream as a *somnium coeleste* is indicated in a number of ways. The poem begins with a reflection on heaven and hell, and on the fact that we get all our information about those interesting places from books, written by men who have never been there. But the dream itself is presented as a vision of heaven, imagined as a paradisal landscape of the usual kind. It is a flowery meadow, evidently a kind of outskirt of paradise itself, which the God of Love and his company are visiting temporarily. 'I moot goon hom,' the God says, '– the sonne draweth west – / To paradys, with al this companye' (F 563–4).[63] The God has 'aungelyke' wings (F 236), and the whole situation is like that inside the garden at the beginning of the *Roman de la Rose*: a secular version of the religious vision of the other world, based on a pseudo-theology of sexual love. The relation between the religion of love and Christianity is never clarified; as we have seen, the God of Love is able to promise that no true lover will go to hell. The world of the dream is also the world beyond death: Alcestis, the nineteen ladies immediately attendant on the God, and the multitude of other women who were true in love, are all apparently people who have lived and died on earth, and whose stories (like that of Blanche in *The Book of the Duchess*) are to be given a more lasting life in Chaucer's poetry. The God reminds the Dreamer of the story of Alcestis, and thus, as in other dream-poems, the theme of hell is touched on in this literary heaven. Alcestis is

> She that for hire housbonde chees to dye,
> And eke to goon to helle, rather than he,
> And Ercules rescowed hire, parde,
> And broght hir out of helle agayn to blys. (F 513–16)
>
> *chees* chose

Her story is completed with an Ovidian metamorphosis: Alcestis was turned into a daisy, and this emerges as the apparent justification for Chaucer's initial devotion to the daisy. Thus the flower is a symbol of love itself, a human love which can conquer even death. That is why the God of Love refers to it as 'my flour' (F 318) and even 'my relyke, digne and delytable' (F 321). It is, we may suppose, the depth of the narrator's devotion to the daisy which opens the way to the revelation in his dream of the flower's heavenly meaning and the course of action to which it directs him – the writing in future of legends of good women. Medieval devotional writers sometimes recognize a type of dream which is halfway between a *somnium animale* and a *somnium coeleste*, a type in which previous devotion leads on to supernatural revelation. Richard Rolle, for example, mentions a kind of dream which derives from 'thoghtes before that falles to Criste or hali kyrk, revelacion comand after'.[64] Perhaps in the *Prologue* we might recognize a secular equivalent to this type of religious vision. There is, however, one difficulty in this view of the poem. It is that there is not really any book Chaucer could have possessed that would have told of the metamorphosis of Alcestis into a daisy, because this event in the myth seems to have been invented by Chaucer himself. Thus the link between the daisy and Alcestis is apparently fictional, and completely arbitrary; if we are to accept it at all, it will have to be on the assumption that the dream is really an inspired revelation.

We seem to be thrown back on the acknowledgment that the poem contains an enigma. The devotion to the daisy expressed in the waking section has a peculiar fervour, which feels almost genuinely religious:

> She is the clernesse and the verray lyght
> That in this derke world me wynt and ledeth.
> The hert in-with my sorwfull brest yow dredeth
> And loveth so sore that ye ben verrayly
> The maistresse of my wit, and nothing I.
> My word, my werk ys knyt so in youre bond
> That, as an harpe obeieth to the hond
> And maketh it soune after his fyngerynge,
> Ryght so mowe ye oute of myn herte bringe
> Swich vois, ryght as yow lyst, to laughe or pleyne.
> Be ye my gide and lady sovereyne!
> As to myn erthly god to yow I calle,
> Bothe in this werk and in my sorwes alle. (F 84–96)

wynt directs; *sore* ardently; *nothing* not at all; *it soune* its sound; *after* according to; *mowe* may; *pleyne* lament

A recent scholar has written of this passage that 'It is possible…to read the praise of the daisy both as a beguiling tribute to a modest, charming flower and as a sly and cheeky mockery of the worshipful lover and the worship of love'.[65] But my own impression is that the emotional temperature of the passage is higher than 'beguiling tribute' suggests, nor can I detect any 'sly and cheeky mockery' in it. If the passage is serious, it might be possible to explain it as alluding to the source of poetic inspiration itself. The mistress of the poet's wit is surely his muse; and if we could understand the vision of this 'white goddess' as being one of the power that makes Chaucer a poet, then it would be possible to see the *Prologue* as a culmination of the tendency that has been developing through Chaucer's dream-poems, the tendency to use the dream as a way of writing about imaginative fiction itself. The legends that follow are to bring back to life ladies who died ages ago; insofar as they succeed, it is the power of the poet's imagination that enables them to transcend death; what could be more appropriate than that this power should be embodied in his dream in the person of Alcestis, who herself overcame the power of death? But the question would still arise, why

Chaucer should have attached the vision of Alcestis to the existing tradition of 'marguerite' poems. What relation was there between his inspiration as a poet and the real or imaginary lady – perhaps called Margaret? – who is alluded to in the daisy-imagery? Behind the poem must surely lie some courtly situation which would clarify its obscurities. There have been attempts to identify the lady symbolized by the flower, none of them conclusive; and I think we shall have to resign ourselves to ignorance.

3

THE ALLITERATIVE
TRADITION

'Pearl'

Like the *Prologue* to *The Legend of Good Women*, *Pearl* is a dream-poem in which the Dreamer meets a beautiful lady, crowned with a single orient pearl; and in both poems this lady is represented as being a transfigured version of an object precious to him in his waking life – a daisy or a pearl. One is tempted to guess that Chaucer had read *Pearl* (which dates from about the same period as the *Prologue*, or perhaps a little earlier), just as the opening of *The Squire's Tale* makes one suspect that he had read *Sir Gawain and the Green Knight*, which is generally attributed to the same anonymous author as *Pearl*. In both cases, the similarities could be due to the influence of the same literary traditions on both poets, rather than to the influence of one poet on another; but it is at least possible that Chaucer had read the work of the *Pearl*-poet, who appears to have belonged to a cultural orbit similar to his own. The *Pearl*-poet's work[1] belongs to the fourteenth-century Alliterative Revival, and was probably written in the north-west Midlands, but it is no less courtly than Chaucer's, being composed perhaps for some great baronial court rather than for the king's court in London. It is also no less avant-garde than Chaucer's. It seems highly likely that the author of *Pearl*, like Chaucer, was influenced by Dante,[2] who was otherwise scarcely read in fourteenth-century England, while the central figure and the effects of light and colour in *Pearl* associate the poet with the 'enthusiasm for subtle variations of pale colors, especially white' and the interest in 'effects of transparency, translucency, and reflection' which mark fashionable French art of the late fourteenth century.[3]

Pearl begins with its narrator in a beautiful garden bitterly lamenting the loss of a pearl, which has fallen into the earth. He is described as if he were a jeweller, regretting the loss of a precious stone. He then falls asleep, and has a dream in which he meets a beautiful lady, whom he gradually recognizes as being identical with his lost pearl. In the course of the dream, *we* gradually come to recognize that the lost pearl was itself a figure of the loss of a human being: the death of a person, who is eventually though obscurely identified as the narrator's daughter, who died in infancy. At first he is delighted to see her again in his dream, and thinks that now he can join her and they can resume their life together. But they are on opposite sides of a river, and he has to grasp that she is now transformed from what she was on earth, and that he is not yet fit to join her in the heavenly world. She is a queen in heaven, and a bride of Christ himself, the Lamb of God. The Dreamer finds what she tells him difficult to take in and to believe: he cannot reconcile this high reward, granted to one he still thinks of as a child, with his notions of God's justice. But he has no choice; he can only believe what he is told; and he eventually asks to be shown the place where she now lives, the heavenly Jerusalem. He is not allowed to enter it, but he sees from across the river that it is just as St John described it in his Apocalypse. Inside it he sees the Lamb followed by a procession of maidens, including his own pearl, and at this he is so overwhelmed with emotion that he attempts to cross the river and join her. The effort wakes him from his dream, and at the end of the poem he is left in the garden in which he fell asleep, wishing that he had been patient enough to dream on and see more of God's mysteries, but now content that his pearl is serving God.

This is a poem which in several ways goes back to the primary tradition of religious visions discussed at the beginning of this book. It derives explicitly from the Apocalypse of St John, which is its main source for the description of the heavenly city:

In the Apokalypce is the fasoun preved,
As devysez hit the apostel Jhon.[4] (983–4)

(The manner of its architecture is shown in the Apocalypse, as it is described by John the Apostle.)

It may also be indebted indirectly to later works such as the *Apocalypse of St Paul* and the various visions of saints and holy men in the early centuries of Christianity. Like the writings discussed earlier, it is a vision of a certain place, and also of certain doctrines. The place is first the paradisal landscape on the near side of the river, and then the heavenly Jerusalem beyond it. The doctrines taught by the Maiden, the supernatural guide encountered in this place, are many. Some, such as that grief for the dead is misplaced, that men must submit to God's will, and that they can hope by God's grace to gain a heavenly reward, are commonplaces of Christian teaching, of which the Dreamer needs to be reminded because, though he knows them in theory, he has not realized their implications for his own life. Others are more specific contributions to fourteenth-century Christian thought: among these are the Maiden's strong emphasis on God's grace, her argument that baptized children, dying in innocence, could obtain as high a reward as the righteous who gained salvation by good works, and her use of the parable of the vineyard to prove that all the saved receive equally the reward of eternal life, though their states in heaven may differ in other respects. *Pearl*, then, is an explicitly religious work, as none of Chaucer's dream-poems is. We have seen how the tradition of religious visions was secularized in French dream-poetry, from the *Roman de la Rose* onwards, and was refocused on human rather than divine love; but *Pearl* does not simply go back behind this secularization. Its author was familiar with, and makes use of, the secular as well as the religious tradition of love-visions. It is a poem that owes almost as much to the tradition of the *Roman de la Rose* as it does to the Apocalypse of St John, and it makes use of the dramatic projection of the Dreamer and his point of view in the highly sophisticated way that had been developed in fourteenth-century secular dream-poems. It is about both earthly and heavenly love, earthly and heavenly values; it is also about the relationship between the earthly and the heavenly, which it sees as involving both continuity and discontinuity. *Pearl*, then, is related in complex ways to a complex structure of literary traditions; and, though it often has an immediate appeal to modern readers (for it is one of the greatest single works of medieval English literature), a full appreciation of it depends on our trying to recapture the bearings which the poet took, and expected his audience to take, on the traditions of dream and vision.

Once the narrator's dream is over, he identifies it as a 'veray avysyoun' (1184); but he has earlier referred to it more humbly as a 'sweven' (62) and a 'drem' (1170). It is certainly possible to understand much of it as a *somnium animale*, with psychological origins and realistic effects. Like the narrator of the *Prologue* to *The Legend of Good Women*, the *Pearl*-narrator falls asleep in a beautiful garden which is itself one version of the paradisal *locus amoenus*. It is full of brightly coloured flowers, and of spice-plants which give forth a delicious fragrance, and the air is filled with music. The season is not the usual spring, but August, harvest-time, 'Quen corne is corven wyth crokez kene' (40) (when corn is cut with sharp sickles). Though unusual, this is not unprecedented, for it is also the time of the dream in Nicole de Margival's *Panthère d'Amours*. Inside his dream, the Dreamer finds himself in a place which he does not recognize – 'I ne wyste in this worlde quere that hit wace' (65) (I did not know where in this world it was) – and which at first sight seems unfamiliar, but which we may gradually recognize as a transmuted version of the earthly garden. The Maiden in the dream refers to it as 'this gardyn gracios gaye' (260), and there too the air is full of music and odours, and there are spice-plants and fruit-trees – and also, this time, the running stream which is a constant feature of the landscape of paradise, a refreshment which was perhaps significantly missing from the earthly garden. But in the dream all this has been transformed into something less languidly autumnal, something sharper, harder, brighter, even painfully bright. There are glittering cliffs of crystal; trees with indigo-blue trunks and silver leaves; river-banks as bright as gold thread; and the very gravel underfoot and the pebbles on the river-bed are made of pearls. The hardness of this jewelled landscape is present in the very sound of the verse –

> The gravayl that on grounde con grynde
> Wern precious perlez of oryente (81–2)
> *con grynde* crunched

– and, though the precious stones on the river-beds may remind us of the crystals in the well of Narcissus in the *Roman de la Rose*, the general effect is of a climate less sweet and more alien.

It is a world which the Dreamer must explore for himself, finding his way to the river, looking longingly across to the other side –

> For if hit watz fayr ther I con fare,
> Wel loveloker watz the fyrre lond (147–8)

(For if it was beautiful where I was walking, the land beyond was lovelier still)

– and then suddenly noticing there a person who is completely still and whom he feels he recognizes:

> I segh, byyonde that myry mere,
> A crystal clyffe ful relusaunt;
> Mony ryal ray con fro hit rere.
> At the fote therof ther sete a faunt,
> A mayden of menske, ful debonere;
> Blysnande whyt watz hyr bleaunt.
> I knew hyr wel, I hade sen hyr ere. (158–64)

(I saw, beyond that pleasant water, a crystal cliff, gleaming brightly; many splendid beams of light rose from it. At its foot there sat a child, a very gracious and courteous maiden; her mantle was gleaming white. I knew her well, I had seen her before.)

In this part of the poem, everything is happening with frightful slowness, as sometimes in real dreams, paced by the heavy beating of the Dreamer's heart. It takes a whole twelve-line stanza for the Maiden to raise her head, another stanza for her to stand up, and four more for her to curtsy to the Dreamer and address him. There can be no doubt that what he sees in his dream is a reflection of the preoccupation of his waking mind.

He has been thinking miserably of the lost pearl; now, in his dream, she reappears, but changed from a mere precious stone, and equally from the small child that we eventually learn the precious stone symbolized, into a lady of daunting spiritual grandeur, though one who at this first meeting is still called a *faunt* (infant). It is, on one level, an obvious example of wish-fulfilment of the type frequently experienced by the bereaved, who dream of meeting again a dead loved one. On another level, the meeting with the child is dreamlike in being an archetypal experience, such as Jung claims to find in dreams. According to him, 'In dreams [the child] often occurs as the dreamer's son or daughter', and he writes that

the 'child' paves the way for a future change of personality. In the individuation process, it anticipates the figure that comes from the synthesis of conscious and unconscious elements in the personality. It is therefore a *uniting symbol* which unites the opposites; a mediator, bringer of healing, that is, *one who makes whole.* Because it has this meaning, the child-motif is capable of...numerous transformations...: it can be expressed by roundness, the circle or sphere...[5]

The dream-child who is also a spherical pearl offers a remarkably close parallel to this archetypal pattern.

In detail, it is by no means the case that the whole poem is realistically dreamlike, but it has many dreamlike touches. There is the way, for example, that, even though the Dreamer is separated from the heavenly city by the river, he can still see what is happening inside it. And there is the way his unquenchable longing for his pearl leads him to plunge desperately into the river to reach her, and that very effort awakens him. Similar incidents occur in secular dream-poems – in *The Book of the Duchess* it is the striking of a bell within the dream that awakens the Dreamer, and in *The Parliament of Fowls* the noise of the birds – and it is common enough for real dreams to end as a result of some commotion inside them. What really happens is no doubt that we sometimes incorporate into the fiction of a dream some external disturbance which is about to wake us up, such as the ringing of an alarmclock. Finally, once the dream is over, the narrator is left in a state of only partial satisfaction, changed in attitude and yet still feeling that his waking life is a 'doeldoungoun' (1187) (dungeon of sorrow). This feeling, that the solution propounded or enacted by a dream to the problem which gave rise to it is only partially satisfying to the dreamer, seems to be very true to real life, and is also paralleled in secular dream-poems, as in *The Parliament of Fowls*, where the Dreamer is left still searching through his books and hoping for a better dream.

It is possible, then, to see the dream in *Pearl* in terms of a naturalistic psychology, as a *somnium animale*; but to see it only in that way would be to miss much of the poem's significance. As I have said, the narrator himself calls his dream a 'veray avysyoun'. In doing so, he is probably implying that it should be categorized in a very specific way. It may well seem to us that there ought to be a clear distinction between a dream and a vision, but we have seen that in the past writers about dreams, from Macrobius onwards, considered the vision, coming from some supernatural source outside the visionary's body and mind, as one type of dream. The same terminology continued to be used by medieval writers on the spiritual life, though they were perfectly aware that there was an element of metaphor involved in this way of talking about supernaturally granted visions, because the highest 'visions' of this kind do not really take the form of things seen. St Augustine, for instance, had assumed that as a preliminary to genuine mystical experience, 'all dreams and revelations that come by imagery' would disappear; and St Bernard claimed that the soul aiming at mystical experience 'will be far from content that her Bridegroom [of the Song of Songs, i.e. Christ] should manifest Himself to her in the manner which is common to all; that is by the things which are made, or even in the manner peculiar to a few, namely, by dreams and visions'.[6] But the metaphor was nevertheless found useful, and medieval devotional writers regularly use 'sleeping' and 'dreaming' as images for describing spiritual experience, even that highest kind of spiritual experience which involves a direct contact between the soul and God, and which does not take the form of visual images. Thus Richard of St-Victor, an influential devotional writer of the twelfth century, when discussing one of the best-known Scriptural cases of vision, the dream of Nebuchadnezzar interpreted by Daniel, writes as follows:

We fall asleep before seeing a dream. As by a dream of the body [*somnium corporis*] the bodily senses are quieted, we rightly understand by a dream of the mind [*somnium mentis*] a separation [*alienatio*] by which the memory of all outward things is completely cut off. Thus to see a dream is to pass over in the mind into the secret place of divine contemplation. Hence he sleeps and sees a dream who, through ecstasy of the mind, rises into the contemplation of divine things.[7]

This is a good description of what happens in *Pearl*. What the Dreamer experiences is not a *somnium corporis* but a *somnium mentis*, which leads him into divine contemplation, in the form of his vision of the heavenly Jerusalem and the Lamb of God. When he has the dream, he is not in the body. He explains that his body remained in the earthly garden, while his spirit leapt out of it on a quest for heavenly mysteries:

Fro spot my spyryt ther sprang in space;
My body on balke ther bod; in sweven[8]
My goste is gon in Godez grace
In aventure ther mervaylez meven. (61–4)

(After a time my spirit sprang from that place; my body remained on the mound; in a dream my spirit went, in God's grace, on an adventurous quest where marvels occur.)

These are his words at the beginning of the dream. Towards the end of it, he returns to this point, and insists that he could not have been in the body when he saw the heavenly Jerusalem, because the sight would have killed him; human senses would not be able to endure such splendour:

For I dar say wyth conciens sure,
Hade bodyly burne abiden that bone,
Thagh alle clerkez hym hade in cure,
His lyf were loste anunder mone. (1089–92)

(For I venture to say, with complete conviction, that if a man in the body had endured that favour, though all scholars had had him under their care, his life in this world would have been lost.)

In these lines, with their obvious allusion to St Paul's 'whether in the body, or out of the body, I know not; God knoweth', the Dreamer is claiming that, unlike St Paul, but like St John (in Apocalypse 1:10), he knows that his experience came to him not 'in the body' but 'in the spirit'. In speaking of the danger of loss of life, he is perhaps thinking of cases like that of Galahad in the *Queste del Saint Graal*. Galahad went 'in Godes grace / In aventure ther mervaylez meven', saw in the flesh the spiritual mystery underlying the Holy Grail which was the object of his quest, and at once died. As Malory describes it, 'then he began to tremble ryght harde whan the dedly fleysh began to beholde the spirituall thynges'; and next, after a little conversation, 'he kneled downe tofore the table, and made hys prayers. And so suddeynly departed hys soule to Jesu Cryste'.[9] The *Pearl* Dreamer, then, by not being in the body, avoids a fate like Galahad's. He describes St John's experience in the Apocalypse as a 'gostly drem' (790), and his own dream can be classed as an equivalent, though less complete, experience. 'Gostly drem' is the Middle English equivalent to what St Augustine calls a *visio spirituale*, a type of vision in which spiritual forces affect the imagination as if they were sensory images;[10] and St Bernard too explains that, through the influence of angels, spiritual realities may be translated in the mind into 'images and figures of lower (that is, earthly) things'.[11]

Richard of St-Victor, in the passage quoted above, refers to the mystic's 'contemplation of divine things' as occurring through an 'ecstasy of the mind', or *excessus*. This is a technical term in medieval mystical theology, to refer to the 'carrying away' of the internal sense by God, an 'abduction' which, in accordance with the common medieval use of erotic language for religious matters, is often referred to as a *raptus* or 'ravishing'. Precisely this term is used in *Pearl* with reference to the vision of the heavenly city: 'felde I nawther reste ne travayle, / So watz I ravyste wyth glymme pure' (1087–8) (I felt neither rest nor toil, I was so ravished by that pure radiance). What occurs in this mystical *excessus* is not a loss of consciousness, but rather a heightening of consciousness on a different level; this is why the image of dream is so appropriate to describe it. When we dream, we dream that we are awake; and, as we have seen, even in secular poems such as those of Chaucer, the dream begins with an awakening into a world that seems fresher and livelier than that of waking life. It is likely enough that secular dream-poets too were influenced by the frequent statements of the paradox of 'wakeful sleep' in religious writers such as St Bernard, who refers to contemplative experience as 'a sleep of life, and even a wakefulness' (*vitalis vigilque sopor*).[12] St Bernard and other devotional writers relate this paradox to a verse in the Song of Songs, 'I sleep, and my heart waketh' (5:2) (*Ego dormio, et cor meum vigilat*). A typical example is to be found in the widely read English work by a contemporary of Chaucer and the *Pearl*-poet, Walter Hilton's *Scale of Perfection*:

This is...the wakeful sleep of the spouse, of the which Holy Writ saith thus: *Ego dormio, et cor meum vigilat.* I sleep and my heart waketh...The more I sleep from outward things, the more wakeful am I in knowing of Jhesu and of inward things. I may not wake to Jhesu but if I sleep to the world. And therefore, the grace of the Holy Ghost shutting the fleshly eyes, doth the soul sleep from worldly vanity, and opening the ghostly eyes waketh into the sight of God's majesty hid under cloud of His precious manhood.[13]

A passage such as this, which could be paralleled many times in medieval devotional writing, gives a good brief description of the nature of the Dreamer's experience in *Pearl*. While his bodily eyes are shut in sleep, he wakens spiritually, and his spiritual eyes see God's majesty, not as it is in itself (which is granted only to the greatest mystics), but 'hid under cloud' – the figure of the Lamb seen by St John in the Apocalypse. His vision includes the heavenly city, St John's New Jerusalem, and he stresses repeatedly that he saw it just as St John did. Like St John, the Dreamer sees the city in great detail, and he is able to list each of the twelve precious stones of which its foundations are made. But, for all the sensory presence of 'emerade...so grene of scale' (1005) (emerald so green of surface) and 'amatyst purpre wyth ynde blente' (1016) (amethyst purple mixed with indigo), it is a symbolic city too, as the Maiden explains to him before he sees it. He asks how he can see Jerusalem, which is in Judaea; she gives the traditional answer that there are two Jerusalems – the earthly city where Christ was crucified, and the heavenly Jerusalem which is the goal of all our lives, and which means 'syght of pes' (952) (vision of peace). This interpretation is also to be found in devotional writings. Walter Hilton, for example, explains that, spiritually, Jerusalem means contemplative experience itself:

Ghostly to our purpose, Jerusalem is as mickle for to say as sight of peace, and betokeneth contemplation in perfect love of God. For contemplation is not else but a sight of Jhesu, which is very peace.[14]

The whole world of the dream in *Pearl*, not only the heavenly city but also the fantastic crystalline and metallic landscape which the Dreamer sees first, is claimed to be a real supernatural world. It is presented with none of the ironies and ambiguities which surround the dream-world in Chaucer, but quite straightforwardly as a reality. Here for once, it seems, the dream-framework does not raise the question of the self-justification of the poem which it frames, and is not a means of making the poem reflexive. The poem reflects not its own being but an authen-ticated reality outside itself; and we may connect with this the fact that in *Pearl*, unlike Chaucer's dream-poems, the Dreamer never appears in the role of poet. He is an eye and a human soul, not one engaged in the questionable activity of creating poetic fictions. The standing of the poem as a fiction is excluded from consideration, as the Dreamer encounters a spiritual reality which is ultimately a cloud shielding the Godhead itself.

The Dreamer, however, does not fully realize this; and it is in this area, of his adequacy to respond to and understand his visionary experience, rather than in the status of the experience itself, that an important element of the questionable enters the poem. The Dreamer carries into the supernatural world of his dream the values and expectations which belong to his natural waking life on earth, and the resulting contrast between the Dreamer's materialism and the spiritual nature of the world in which he finds himself is a central motive of the whole poem. We have seen how the dramatic projection of the dreamer and his point of view had been developed in secular dream-poems in France and England, and how what was projected was normally a partially fictional version of the poet's real situation. We need not assume, in *Pearl*, that the unproblematic reality of the dream-world implies that the narrator's situation in waking life directly symbolizes that of the poet, with no element of fiction. There has been much discussion of this aspect of *Pearl*, turning on the question whether we are to assume that the poet had really lost a small daughter by death, or whether the lost pearl is the symbol of an abstraction. At one extreme stand those who would see the whole poem as 'the sincere cry of a father's heart at the grave of his infant girl'; at the other, those who would interpret the pearl as standing allegorically for innocence or some other abstract quality.[15] We do not have to choose whether or not to see the poem as genuine autobiography, because that question is not raised in the poem itself. *Pearl*, indeed, is perhaps the most completely self-enclosed of all medieval dream-poems: the most perfect in its artistry, pearl-like in its circularity of structure, so 'smothe' that its surface gives no purchase for any attempt to lever apart the real and the imagined. Unlike the *Prologue* to *The Legend of Good Women*, it is not a poem which makes us feel that we need to identify its real-life occasion in order to appreciate it fully. And within its self-enclosure, we do not have to choose between the pearl as a person and the pearl as symbol, because this poet, like Dante or even to a lesser extent like Chaucer in *The Book of the Duchess*, turning a real dead duchess into a partially symbolic 'goode, faire White', was perfectly capable of seeing a real historical person as a sign or figure of some larger value.[16] After all, something of this kind regularly happens in real dreams, were a character who 'is' someone we know may also be (to use Freud's term) 'over-determined' and charged with other meanings.

The situation of a dreamer ill at ease in his own dream is one that has become familiar to us from the secular dream-poems of Chaucer; in *Pearl* it reappears, but with a new precision of meaning, related to the 'guaranteed' value of the dream-world itself. The link between the earthly Dreamer and his heavenly dream is of course the pearl itself. In the opening section in the earthly garden, most of the language used seems to define the pearl as a jewel, which has 'trendeled [rolled] doun' (41) and been lost for ever; though even here some of the language is ambiguous, and could equally well apply to a person. 'So smal, so smothe her sydez were' (6) might be part of a description of the poet's mistress in a secular love-poem. At the same time there are clear indications that the narrator's grief is excessive:

> A devely dele in my hert denned,
> Thagh resoun sette myselven saght.
> I playned my perle that ther watz spenned
> Wyth fyrce skyllez that faste faght;
> Thagh kynde of Kryst me comfort kenned,
> My wreched wylle in wo ay wraghte. (51–6)

(A desolating grief lurked in my heart, though reason reconciled me. I lamented my pearl which was imprisoned there [in the earth] with fervent arguments, contending obstinately; though the nature of Christ showed me comfort, my wretched will ever strove in woe.)

In the dream, when the Dreamer meets the Maiden and recognizes her as someone he already knows, it becomes clear to us that at a deeper level the pearl is not a thing but a person; and we come to see what was at fault in the narrator's attitude in waking life towards the loss of his pearl. It is not just that he showed excessive, though unquestionably moving, grief at the loss of a precious stone, but that he was treating a person as if she were a thing. In the fifth section of linked stanzas, the word *jueler* (jeweller) occurs in each refrain-line, and it is applied to the Dreamer both by the Maiden and himself. His attitude towards the loss of a human being by death has been like that of a jeweller towards the loss of a precious stone: a possessive and ultimately egoistic attitude, because as a Christian he must believe in the survival of the human soul after death. Thus his grief is really for himself, not for her. This emerges clearly in the first speech he addresses to her. His opening words are about his own sufferings, and he then immediately turns, almost reproachfully, to the contrast between her happiness and his misery:

> 'O perle,' quod I, 'in perlez pyght,
> Art thou my perle that I haf playned,
> Regretted by myn one on nyghte?
> Much longeyng haf I for the layned,
> Sythen into gresse thou me aglyghte.
> Pensyf, payred, I am forpayned,
> And thou in a lyf of lykyng lyghte,
> In Paradys erde, of stryf unstrayned.
> What wyrde hatz hyder my juel vayned,
> And don me in thys del and gret daunger?
> Fro we in twynne wern towen and twayned,
> I haf ben a joylez juelere.' (241–52)

('O pearl,' I said, 'adorned with pearls, are you my pearl that I have lamented, grieved for alone at night? I have concealed much sorrow for you, since you slipped away from me into the grass. I am melancholy, worn out, greatly afflicted, and you are set down in a life of pleasure, in the land of Paradise, untroubled by strife. What fate has sent my jewel here, and put me in this grief and great distress? Since we were torn in two and parted, I have been a joyless jeweller.')

The Dreamer does not simply require new information: his whole attitude expresses a sickness which needs to be cured, just as Boethius in the *De Consolatione* needs to be cured of his discontent with the misfortune that has come upon him. And because of this, it is not enough for him to be brought into contact with the heavenly world in his vision; being the kind of person he is – a kind of person with whom we can readily identify ourselves – he persistently fails to understand what he sees and learns there. His first thought is that 'Paradys erde' is a physical place like any other, and that now that he has found his pearl he can rejoin her there for ever. (Scipio made the same mistake in the *Somnium Scipionis*.) He is sharply corrected by the Maiden, who begins by saying,

> I halde that jueler lyttel to prayse
> That levez wel that he segh wyth yye (301-2)

(I consider that jeweller little deserving of praise who well believes what he sees with his eyes).

This is disturbingly paradoxical: what else has an earthly jeweller to rely on but his sharp eyesight? But it does not imply (as it surely would in a Chaucerian dream-poem) that he is mistaken in what he things he sees in his vision. What it implies is that he should not have needed a vision to convince him that God was not lying when he promised 'your lyf to rayse, / Thagh Fortune dyd your flesch to dyye' (305-6). She goes on to remind him that man is cut off from the heavenly paradise by the consequences of Adam's sin in the earthly paradise, and that to achieve her state he must first die. Later difficulties of understanding concern the status of the Maiden in the heavenly world. She tells the Dreamer that, though she was 'ful yong and tender of age' (412) when he lost her, she is now a bride of the Lamb, who has

> Corounde me quene in blysse to brede
> In lenghe of dayez that ever schal wage (415-16)

(crowned me queen, to flourish in bliss for a length of days that shall continue for ever).

He objects that she cannot be a queen, because Mary is queen of heaven, and further because she has not done enough to deserve it. As an earthly man, he thinks of the heavenly hierarchy in earthly terms, and assumes that, for the Maiden to be a queen, Mary must have lost her heavenly crown. He naturally finds it difficult to grasp that

> The court of the kyndom of God alyve
> Hatz a property in hytself beyng:
> Alle that may therinne aryve
> Of alle the reme is quen other kyng,
> And never other yet schal depryve (445-9)

(The court of the kingdom of the living God has a property inherent in itself, that everyone permitted to arrive there is queen or king of the whole realm, without depriving anyone else).

The question of how the Maiden can deserve her high reward leads into the heart of the doctrinal aspect of the vision. In complaining that God's courtesy is too generous towards the Maiden, the Dreamer is allowed to expose himself with a comic effect strongly reminiscent of the treatment of Chaucerian dreamers. The rhythm and language of his speech express protest and indignation, yet he is naively measuring countess against queen, one earthly rank against another, thus showing that he has quite failed to grasp what the Maiden told him about the paradoxical hierarchy of heaven:

> That cortaysé is to fre of dede,
> Yyf hyt be soth that thou conez saye.
> Thou lyfed not two yer in oure thede;
> Thou cowthez never God nauther plese ne pray,
> Ne never nawther Pater ne Crede;
> And quen mad on the fyrst day!
> I may not traw, so God me spede,
> That God wolde wrythe so wrange away.
> Of countes, damysel, par ma fay,
> Wer fayr in heven to halde asstate,
> Other ellez a lady of lasse aray;
> Bot a quene! Hit is to dere a date. (481–92)

(If what you have said is true, that courtesy [of God's] is too generous in its action. You did not live two years in our world; you never knew how to please God or pray to him, and never knew paternoster or creed; and made a queen on the first day! I cannot believe, God help me, that God would so wrongly turn from the true path. It would be desirable, maiden, by my faith, for you to hold the rank of a countess in heaven, or else of a lady of lower status; but a queen! That is too high a goal.)

The Dreamer's pious expletives – 'so God me spede' and 'par ma fay' – serve to underline the naively blasphemous nature of his complaint of God's excessive generosity with what is God's alone to give. The Maiden uses the parable of the vineyard to demonstrate that God may do what he will with his own, but the Dreamer still argues that what she has said is 'unresounable' (590), because it contradicts God's justice. Once more, however, his conception of justice is earthly, and he has to learn that God's grace – a major theme of the theological thought of the fourteenth century – is sufficient to salvation, and that in any case the Maiden, as an innocent, has a juster claim to salvation than a just man, who has inevitably sinned, however many his good works.

The Dreamer is apparently satisfied on this point, but he is to expose himself still further, with a comedy mixed with pathos. He learns from the Maiden that she is a bride of the Lamb, and because his conception of marriage is earthly, he assumes that this must imply that she is the

Lamb's only bride. There are many beautiful ladies, he says, who have done much to serve God,

> And thou con alle tho dere out dryf
> And fro that maryag al other depres (777–8)

(and you have driven out all those worthy creatures, and expelled all others from that marriage).

He thinks of her as being 'stout and styf' (779), in elbowing aside all her rivals – terms belonging to the idiom of martial heroism, and manifestly quite inappropriate to the exquisite lady to whom they are addressed. Just as he had to be informed before that all in heaven are kings or queens, so now he has to learn that all innocents are brides of the Lamb. There are 144,000 of them, John's Apocalypse being the authority for this symbolic number; and once more this detail sets the Dreamer's materialistic imagination to work. Such a large number of maidens must need a huge dwelling – perhaps some 'wonez [dwellings] in castel-walle' (917), since it would be ill done if 'so cumly a pakke of joly juele' (929) had to lodge in the open. He begs to see where they live, and his answer comes with his vision of the heavenly Jerusalem. Through its transparent walls, he sees the Lamb and his brides, his own pearl among them; and this brings about the last of his errors. He cannot believe that he is really forbidden to cross the river to reach them, plunges in, and brings the whole vision to an end. Thus he brings his series of blunders to a climax which not even a Chaucerian dreamer could surpass.

Pearl focuses on a relationship between the Dreamer and the pearl-Maiden which is intensely dramatic, and which is both comic and touching, because the Dreamer's repeated misunderstandings are so obviously wrong, and yet so obviously belong to the familiar world of everyday values and assumptions which we share with him. The poet never pretends that he or his audience can attain a comfortable superiority towards the Dreamer, by sharing in a full understanding of the values of the heavenly world to which the Maiden now belongs. The effect is thus very different from that of, say, *Paradise Lost*, where Milton does sometimes seem to pretend that he and we can see the story from God's point of view. In *Pearl*, for all the sharp detail of the vision, the heavenly order remains a mystery, glitteringly beautiful, and yet resistant to human understanding and even sympathy. The poem conveys its doctrine to us by engaging our emotions as well as our intellects in a dramatic encounter; but because that doctrine concerns heavenly values, it must inevitably be asserted at the expense of the Dreamer, who belongs so firmly to our earthly world. We have seen how, in the field of doctrine, he undergoes a whole series of disturbing reversals of expectation – reversals, that is, of the expectations he has instinctively and inevitably brought with him from the earthly world which is his home. Such reversals are also to be found in the whole dramatic and symbolic framework of the dream.

We understand from the poem that the lost pearl was the Dreamer's daughter on earth. The clinching factor in this identification comes at the very end of the work, when the narrator commits his pearl to God, 'In Krystez dere blessyng and myn' (1208), a formula which was regularly used in medieval letters, and almost invariably from father to child.[17] Until this last moment, the poet has been careful not to identify the relationship too specifically, because he does not wish the relevance of his poem to be confined to fathers and daughters, or even to parents and children; he wants to extend it to take in all close human relationships. The poem is not only to be about paternal love, but about human love in its most general sense, in the light of death and in the still harsher light of eternal life. But there have been many hints in the language used throughout the poem that the pearl was a child on earth. A major reversal of expectation comes when the Dreamer finds that in the heavenly world it is the child who has authority over him, not he who has adult or parental authority over her. His dream is an *oraculum*, but one which he is unwilling to accept as such, because the authoritative figure who speaks to him in it is not, as Macrobius indicates, 'a parent, or a pious or revered man', but one whom he is accustomed to think of as needing his guidance. In the life after death she has become one of those who 'thurghoutly haven cnawyng' (859) (possess perfect knowledge), and he finds it extremely difficult to adjust himself to this situation. Again and again, as we have seen, he feels impelled to contradict what she has told him, and consequently he receives a series of rebukes from her – a situation which a medieval audience, even more than ourselves, must have felt to be deeply unnatural. When he sees her for the last time in the heavenly city, in the procession of brides of the Lamb, he still thinks of her as 'my lyttel quene' (1147). It is as if a fond father were watching his small daughter acting in a school play, and the contrast between the tender and unpretentious intimacy of his feelings and the unreachable grandeur of her new position is painfully moving.

Another reversal of expectation, in the poem's symbolic framework, relates to its central symbol of the pearl. Nearly all readers would agree that the pearl-Maiden is in some sense the same as the material pearl which the Dreamer lost in the garden;[18] and, if this is so, the pearl at least provides continuity between the widely separated spheres of heavenly and earthly, dream and waking. Because the pearl is an image of value, of preciousness, this implies an assurance that there is some continuity, after all, between heavenly and earthly values. The dreamer may be a jeweller, a man of mercantile, materialistic values, but the Maiden speaks to him of another jeweller, the merchant of the parable, who 'solde alle hys goud, bothe wolen and lynne, / To bye hym a perle watz mascellez' (731-2) (sold all his goods, both woollen and linen, to buy himself a pearl that was spotless). The pearl is the kingdom of heaven, which the Maiden already possesses, and which she urges the Dreamer too to purchase for himself. But at an early stage of the poem, any hope we might share with the Dreamer of a smooth transition between the earthly and the heavenly is shattered by one beautiful image the Maiden uses. She tells the Dreamer that, in grieving over the loss of a gem that was dear to him, he is acting madly:

> Me thynk the put in a mad porpose,
> And busyez the aboute a raysoun bref;
> For that thou lestez watz bot a rose
> That flowred and fayled as kynde hyt gef.
> Now, thurgh kynde of the kyste that hyt con close,
> To a perle of prys hit is put in pref. (267-72)

(You seem to me fixed in a mad resolve, and to be troubling yourself for an inadequate reason; for what you lost was only a rose, which flowered and faded as nature granted it. Now, through the nature of the chest which enclosed it, it has proved to be a pearl of value.)

(The *kyste* is to be understood both as the box in which a jewel is kept safe and as the coffin in which the dead child was buried.) From the point of view of the heavenly pearl, the earthly pearl was no true pearl at all, because it was no more lasting than a rose; and a rose is both the persistent emblem of a merely human love, or the idealized lust of the *Roman de la Rose*, and the traditional example of the transience of all earthly things. In this image, the whole complex tradition of religious and secular visions of love which lies behind *Pearl* is summed up; but it is summed up in such a compressed way that the Dreamer is unable to understand it, and from this point for another four hundred lines the poem ceases to speak the language of symbolism, and uses instead that of literal exposition.

The Dreamer is an inadequate vessel for the experience of his dream. The content of the dream comes in the first place, we may suppose, from his own mind, and especially from his obsessive thoughts of the lost pearl. But into it are infused larger meanings, which a modern Jungian would probably see as emerging from the collective unconscious, and which a medieval Christian would have seen as deriving from a supernatural realm of whose existence all knew but to which few had immediate access. Some of these meanings, such as that of the relationship between rose and pearl, are more fully available to the poem's audience than they are to the Dreamer at the time of his dream. The Dreamer's inadequacy to receive fully the message of his dream reaches its height, as we have seen, at the moment when by his own impulsive act he brings the dream to an end. But the effect the poet achieves by this is very different from that of incompleteness, as when *The House of Fame* simply breaks off short, because the *Pearl*-poet gives at least a hint of what the Dreamer lost by his abortive attempt to cross the river-barrier. As always, his understanding and his motivation are limited by his nature as an earthly man: it is love, a love with which we can deeply sympathize, but still a possessive and selfish love, which has impelled him to try to join his pearl in the heavenly Jerusalem. But when he wakes up, he laments his own rashness, and regrets the possibilities of deeper visionary experience that he has lost by it:

> To that Pryncez paye hade I ay bente,
> And yerned no more then watz me gyven,
> And halden me ther in trwe entent,
> As the perle me prayed, that watz so thryven,
> As helde, drawen to Goddez present,
> To mo of his mysterys I hade ben dryven. (1189–94)

(If I had always submitted to that Prince's [i.e. God's] pleasure, and desired no more than was granted me there, and restrained myself there, faithful in will, as the pearl that was so fair begged me, likely enough, drawn into the presence of God, I would have been brought to more of his mysteries.)

The Dreamer, of course, does not know what these divine mysteries might have been; but the poem, through its imagery, gives us at least a hint. The central symbol, of the pearl itself, is constantly developing in meaning and implication as the poem proceeds, and towards the end it shows signs of developing in one particular direction. The pearl is, in its most material sense, a jewel, and the Dreamer has several times referred to the pearl-Maiden too as a jewel, from the moment of his first meeting her:

> A juel to me then watz thys geste,
> And juelez wern hyr gentyl sawez (277–8)

(This newcomer was then a jewel to me, and her noble sayings were jewels).

But when the vision of the Lamb of God begins, this term is also applied to the Lamb himself, whose followers 'Al songe to love that gay juelle' (1124) (all sang in praise of that fair jewel). Other key qualities of the pearl are also found in him: he is pure white – 'quyt jolyf' (842) – and spotless – 'wythouten spottez blake' (945). Finally, when the Dreamer actually sees the Lamb for the first time, he perceives this whiteness explicitly as pearl-like: 'As praysed perlez his wedez wasse' (1112) (his raiment was like precious pearls). Surely we have here a pointer towards the potential culmination of the visionary experience, in which the pearl would be identified with the Lamb, and the Dreamer would recognize in the precious stone the ground of its own worth; or, to put it differently, would recognize in the human soul the image of the perfection of God. But a perception of that kind would belong to a level of mystical experience of which the Dreamer is incapable. Such a perception would scarcely be expressible in words or images, and from that point of view too it is appropriate that the vision should break off before arriving at a goal which poetry could hardly encompass.

The Dreamer's inadequacy does not mean that his dream has conferred benefits only on the poem's audience but not on him. In Chaucer's dream-poems there is no indication that the narrator's dream has any subsequent effect on his waking life, except insofar as it provides material for his work as a poet. Indeed, in *The Parliament of Fowls*, as we have seen, he is dissatisfied with his dream-experience, can make nothing of it (except a poem), and goes on reading books just as before in the hope of having another dream that will profit him more. But in *Pearl* the Dreamer is changed by his dream: not converted with implausible completeness to a diametrically opposite frame of mind or mode of life, but certainly changed from the desperate anguish with which he was previously facing the loss of his pearl. The pearl *is* lost to him; the dream offers no escape into fantasy from the fact of death, any more than it does in *The Book of the Duchess*; and he is still sorrowful:

> A longeyng hevy me strok in swone,
> And rewfully thenne I con to reme (1180–1)

(A heavy longing overwhelmed me, and then I began to lament sorrowfully).

But he is now nearer to being reconciled to his loss, glad that his pearl has pleased God, and regretfully aware of the limitations set to human desire. In the dream, the Maiden had described him as 'put in a mad porpose' (267); now *he* describes as mad those who strive against God's will:

> Lorde, mad hit arn that agayn the stryven,
> Other proferen the oght agayn thy paye. (1199–200)

(Lord, those who strive against you or who propose to you anything contrary to your wishes are mad.)

Now at last he can *give* his pearl to God, with a father's blessing: 'sythen

to God I hit bytaghte / In Krystez dere blessyng and myn' (1207–8) (then
I committed it to God, with Christ's precious blessing and mine). This
bettering of his state of mind is precisely what medieval devotional
writers noted as a chief sign that a spiritual experience was genuinely
inspired by God. Walter Hilton, for example, writes as follows of
contemplation:

though it be so that it astonish [bewilders] thee in the first beginning, nevertheless
afterwards it turneth and quickeneth thine heart to more desire of virtues,
increases thy love more both to God and to thine even-christian, also it maketh
thee more meek in thine own sight; by these tokens may thou know then that
it is of God.[19]

In *Pearl* the narrator's closing thoughts are not of himself (as they were
in the opening section) but of the whole body of his fellow-Christians,
as he wishes that not only his own pearl but all of them may be members
of God's household and precious pearls to him:

> He gef us to be his homly hyne
> Ande precious perlez unto his pay. (1211–12)

(May he grant us to be his household servants and precious pearls to his
pleasure.)

The 'Piers Plowman' tradition: 'Winner and Waster'

Although *Pearl* was a product of the revival of alliterative poetry which
took place in the west Midlands in the fourteenth century, it was also
a poem which absorbed many other influences, to form a unique synthesis, which demands the separate treatment I have given it. But there
are several other alliterative dream-poems, which belong more exclu-
sively to the Alliterative Revival, have enough in common to form a
distinct tradition of their own, and are therefore best considered as a
group. The most famous of them is William Langland's *Piers Plowman*,
which is indisputably one of the major works of Middle English literature. The others, all anonymous, include *Winner and Waster*, *The Parliament of the Three Ages*, *Mum and the Sothsegger*, and *Death and Life*. Quite
apart from the common debt of all these poems to an ancient tradition
of alliterative writing, found in poetic style, in particular turns of phrase,
and perhaps in a general earnestness of moral outlook, there appears
to have been some influence of one poem on another, and they all make
strikingly similar use of the dream-framework itself. By far the most
influential of them was *Piers Plowman*, whose popularity is attested by
the survival of over fifty manuscripts, and this will be my main subject.
Of the others, *Winner and Waster* has been argued to be earlier than *Piers*

Plowman, and it is therefore of special interest, as indicating the nature of the tradition of alliterative dream-poetry which may have been available to Langland when he began work on the first version of *Piers Plowman.* It is possible, though less likely, that *The Parliament of the Three Ages* is also earlier than Langland's poem, and even that it is by the same poet,[20] and I therefore consider these two poems alongside each other.

Winner and Waster, if Gollancz is correct in dating it at 1352–3, is one of the earliest poems of the Alliterative Revival, and is consequently earlier than any of the English dream-poems I have so far considered. It begins with a prologue: first a few lines about the founding of Britain by the mythical Brutus – a conventional framing device for an alliterative poem – and then the poet begins to talk about his own time. He sees it as a degenerate age, in which a western man like himself dare not send his son to the corrupt south, and in which great lords give their favour to beardless jesters instead of true 'makers' (21),[21] men who themselves compose (perhaps orally) the poems they recite. Already, then, the dream-poem is associated with a concern for the status of poets and poetry; and indeed this poet briefly shows a highly sophisticated capacity for playing with the fictional illusion, as he asserts that a mere child 'That never wroghte thurgh witt thies wordes togedire' (25) will be more admired than 'the man that made it hymselven' (28). He is imagining a future recitation of his own poem, and is writing lines which will force the audience to question whether the reciting 'I' is the same as the creative 'I'. Inside the dream there is one similar movement of the 'I' between illusion and reality, when the fictional dream-king (who is yet the real Edward III) calls for wine, and the Dreamer deftly shifts roles to become the reciter for a moment:

> Me thoughte I sowpped so sadly it sowede bothe myn eghne.
> And he that wilnes of this werke to wete any forthire,
> Full freschely and faste, for here a fitt endes. (215–17)

(It seemed to me that I drank so deep that it bleared both my eyes. And let him who desires to know any more of this work quickly refill his cup, for here a fitt [section] ends.)

The poet, whose eyes are already, within the fiction, closed in sleep, blears his eyes with drink, so that there has to be an interval in the dream, in which the reciter and his audience can also refresh themselves. But there are no other signs in the poem of this consciousness of the dream as fiction, and the Dreamer is elsewhere no more than an observer of the events of his dream.

The dream begins early in the first fitt. The poet is wandering alone in the west country, through a landscape with paradisal touches: a flowery sunlit meadow, full of singing birds, next to a flowing stream. As night falls, he sleeps and has a dream in which 'Me thoghte I was in the werlde, I ne wiste in whate ende' (47) (it seemed to me that I was in the world, I did not know in what quarter). That line is of great importance, as can be seen by comparing it with the similar line at the beginning of the dream in *Pearl*: 'I ne wyste in this worlde quere that hit wace'. In *Pearl* the implication is that the dream is set in some other world than this, whereas in *Winner and Waster* it is set in this world. It is generally true of the tradition to which *Piers Plowman* belongs that dreams offer an insight into life in this world rather than information about the other world, and that the paradisal landscape is one in which the dreamer falls asleep rather than one in which he finds himself in his dream. The *Winner and Waster* Dreamer sees two armies drawn up to fight. He also sees a pavilion inscribed with a translation of the motto of the order of the Garter, 'Hethyng have the hathell that any harme thynkes' (68), and, as he peers inside it, he sees a noble king prepared for hawking. The king appears to be Edward III, the actual ruler at the time of writing, and he sends a knight as messenger to the two armies, to order their leaders to come before him and make peace. That the scene belongs to the poet's own life and time is confirmed by what we learn of the two armies. Their leaders are called Winner and Waster, and they represent the two great principles which the poet sees as underlying the economic activity of his world – winning and wasting, gathering in money and goods and spending them. The leaders come before the king to explain their quarrel; they conduct a vigorous disputation or flyting, and thus a war of words takes the place of the physical battle they were about to start. Eventually the king adjudicates between them by sending each of them to an appropriate place: Winner is to reside with the cardinals at Rome, and among those grasping men he will be able to lie in silk sheets; Waster is to go to Cheapside, the contemporary centre of extravagance and consumption. Winner in particularly is to hold himself ready to return when the king resumes his wars in France. It is clear enough that the world of the dream is precisely the real world, seen with the eye of a satiric moralist. The end of the poem is missing, but there was probably little more to come; and the main body of it establishes the nature of the dream with unmistakable clarity.

There is no question either of complex psychological motivation or of supernatural revelation: the dream simply gives an insight into contemporary life on the economic level. The insight purports to be neither personal nor inspired, but simply objective; through most of the poem we are unaware of the Dreamer's presence, and we simply listen to what is said by Winner, Waster, and the king. The poet, who is so proud of his skill as a 'maker', pretends only to be reporting what he has in fact made; and what he reports is correspondingly unproblematic. There is a conflict between Winner and Waster, but it is not one which engages the Dreamer personally. The conflict is seen from above, from the point of view of a king whose authority is unquestioned, as an economic pattern, a dynamic tension between two tendencies, which underlies the world we experience when we are awake. It must be added that the criteria the poem assumes are moral and even religious; this is not the 'scientific' economics of later centuries. Each of the disputants invokes God's support against the other: thus Winner threatens Waster with God's wrath – 'That es firste the faylynge of fode, and than the fyre aftir' (291) – while Waster assures Winner that, because his feasting feeds the poor, 'It es plesynge to the Prynce that paradyse wroghte' (296). Perhaps the poem comes closest to using dream as the medium of prophecy in Winner's apocalyptic denunciations – 'The more colde es to come, als me a clerke tolde' (293) – and in his contrast between the extravagant dress of lords and the poverty of the Holy Family, with no possessions 'Safe a barne in hir barme, and a broken heltre / That Joseph held in hys hande' (418–19) (except a baby in her [Mary's] bosom, and a broken halter that Joseph held in his hand). But the poet is careful to hold the balance between the two sides, and does not appear to be committed to the view that God supports one rather than the other.

The pattern disclosed by the dream has nothing abstract about it; and this is another way in which the poem differs from the textbook on economics which would be its modern equivalent. The successive speeches of Winner and Waster load the pattern with concrete detail, so that we get a series of glimpses of social reality, sometimes summarized, sometimes exemplified in little scenes which tend towards grotesque comedy. I give two examples, both from speeches by Winner. The first describes how Waster visits the tavern – a splendidly vigorous and noisy scene, brought to a close with a tellingly understated moral:

> And thou wolle to the taverne, byfore the toune-hede,
> Iche beryne redy withe a bolle to blerren thyn eghne,
> Hete the whatte thou have schalte, and whatt thyn hert lykes,
> Wyfe, wedowe, or wenche, that wonnes there aboute.
> Then es there bott 'Fille in!' and 'Feche forthe!', Florence to schewe,
> 'Wee-hee!' and 'Worthe up!' – wordes ynewe,
> Bot when this wele es awaye, the wyne moste be payede fore. (277–83)

(And you will go to the tavern, outside the upper end of the town [i.e. in the disreputable suburbs], where everyone is ready with a bowl of drink to blear your eyes, to promise you whatever you want and what pleases your heart, wife, widow, or wench, who lives nearby. Then there is nothing but 'Fill it up!' and 'Bring it out!', to make Florrie [the barmaid] appear, 'Wee-hee!' and 'Whoa there!' – plenty of words, but when the pleasure is over, the wine must be paid for.)

Any reader of the confession of Gluttony in *Piers Plowman* (B v) will find that tavern-scene familiar; and it must surely have been from *Winner and Waster*, or from some non-extant poem in the same tradition, that Langland developed his more elaborate treatment of excess.[22] In both cases there is an intimate relation between the moral abstraction and the everyday life in which it manifests itself; and this is one of the points of my second example. Here Winner contemptuously describes how Waster's estate is ruined by his extravagance:

> Alle that I wynn thurgh witt he wastes thurgh pryde;
> I gedir, I glene, and he lattys goo sone;
> I pryke and I pryne, and he the purse opynes.
> Why hase this cayteffe no care how men corne sellen?
> His londes liggen alle ley, his lomes aren solde,
> Downn bene his dowfehowses, drye bene his poles;
> The devyll wounder the wele he weldys at home,
> Bot hungere and heghe horses and howndes full kene! (230–7)

(All that I gain through shrewdness, he wastes through pride; I gather in, I glean up, and he quickly lets go; I secure things and pin them down, and he opens the purse. Why has this wretch no concern about the price of corn? His lands all lie fallow, his tools have been sold, his dove-cotes have fallen down, his pools have dried up; a hell of a lot of property he possesses at home – nothing but hunger and high horses and keen hounds!)

In the last line of that quotation, the abstraction hunger exists on exactly the same level as the concrete objects, horses and hounds; it is identical with them in every way, sharing the same syntactical role and even the same alliteration. This is a typical example, on the level of poetic language, of the whole view of life expressed by *Winner and Waster*, which sees moral abstractions as having exactly the same kind of reality as concrete objects. The word 'hunger' does not have to undergo formal personification in order to achieve equality with horses and hounds: there is no character called Hunger in the allegory of *Winner and Waster* (though there is in *Piers Plowman*). In both poems, the worlds of moral abstraction and social concretion interpenetrate at every point, a process found at its most telling in the montage-effect when Winner sees Waster's table, covered with glittering dishes, as a jewelled cross, the symbol of all that, for him, Waster's extravagance opposes:

> To see the borde over-brade with blasande disches,
> Als it were a rayled rode with rynges and stones. (342–3)

Finally, it must be added that, although *Winner and Waster* allows its two great tendencies to enact a violent conflict of words, it does not propound any solution of a kind that would bring the conflict to an end. The situation is firmly within the king's grasp: he is the supreme authority in the poem, and the poet implies that such problems can be brought under control by political means. But not even the king can abolish winning and wasting, or grant either a decisive victory, because the poet accepts them both as permanent tendencies in human nature. All the king can or need do is to assign them to their proper places, and make use of them himself as seems expedient. The poem's religious implications are not finally brought to bear on its political and economic meaning.

'*The Parliament of the Three Ages*'

The same cannot be said of *The Parliament of the Three Ages*, which reads in some ways like an attempt to take further a development begun in *Winner and Waster*. Here the paradisal setting is again that of the Dreamer's waking life;

> In the monethe of Maye when mirthes bene fele,
> And the sesone of somere when softe bene the wedres, (1–2)[23]

and it includes the usual flowery meadow, with singing birds, alongside a stream. And, once more, the world of the dream is that of real life, even though it is 'whate I seghe in my saule' (103) and gives a power to see a conflict of personified abstractions underlying the details of everyday reality. There are now three abstractions instead of two, Youthe, Medill Elde (Middle Age) and Elde (Old Age), but initially the conflict is between the first two only (lines 169–264). Youthe is strongly reminiscent of Waster and Medill Elde of Winner. Youthe is a huntsman, a lover and a warrior, riding 'ane heghe horse' (111) and dressed in green lavishly decorated with embroidery, gold and precious stones. Medill Elde is more soberly attired in russet and grey, and

> One his golde and his gude gretly he mousede,
> His renttes and his reches rekened he full ofte –
> Of mukkyng, or marlelyng, and mendynge of howses...(140–2)
> (He mused deeply on his money and his property, he often reckoned up his rents and his riches – muck-spreading and marling and repairing houses.)

Youthe consciously prefers the expensive pleasures of the senses, and especially hawking, to Medill Elde's anxiety about possessions, and

Medill Elde's objection to him is just like Winner's to Waster, and is phrased with a similar concreteness:

> Where es the londe and the lythe that thou arte lorde over?
> For alle thy ryalle araye renttis hase thou none,
> Ne for thi pompe and thi pride, penyes bot fewe;
> For alle thi golde and thi gude gloes on thi clothes;
> And thou hafe caughte thi kaple, thou cares for no fothire. (185–9)

(Where are the land and the people that you are lord of? For all your noble attire you have no rents, and for all your pomp and pride only a few pence; for your money and your property glitter on your clothes; once you have caught your horse, you do not worry about its fodder.)

But in two ways the *Parliament* goes beyond *Winner and Waster*. One is in the large and decisive part played by the third disputant, Elde; the other is in the inclusion of a lengthy prologue concerning the Dreamer's waking life. In neither respect can it be said that the poet achieves an unqualified success, but what he was attempting to do is of great interest.

Elde's intervention has the professed purpose of putting an end to the strife between Youthe and Medill Elde. He explains that he was once like Youthe, a handsome, well dressed lover; then he was like Medill Elde, dedicated to land and wealth; but at last he was overtaken by age, who reduced him to ugliness and feebleness, 'And now es dethe at my dore that I drede moste' (292). All men have to pass through death, and he proceeds to illustrate this truth by telling the stories of the Nine Worthies (three famous pagans, three famous Jews, and three famous Christians): all achieved great deeds in their lives, but all were overcome by death. 'Of siche doughety doers looke what es worthen' (461) (see what has become of such valiant men of action). Then, more briefly, he summarizes the stories of famous wise men and famous lovers, to point the same moral: *Ubi sunt?* where are they now? The conclusion is that all earthly things are vanity, whether they are the desires of youth or of middle age, and that men can only rely on amendment and confession. With this Elde departs, saying 'Dethe dynges one my dore, I dare no lengare byde' (654), and the Dreamer wakes. Thus Elde introduces a value-system which transcends that accepted by both Youthe and Medill Elde, for all the violence of their disagreement. For them, as for Winner and Waster, and indeed for the king who is set over them, the great question at issue concerns the right use of earthly goods; but Elde's argument is that all earthly goods are transient – 'the wele of this werlde worthes to noghte' (637) – and that man must turn his thoughts elsewhere. This is a familiar variety of the very powerful strain of *contemptus mundi* in medieval Christian thought, and the *exempla* of the Nine Worthies and the great wise men and lovers are familiar illustrations of it. But this section of the poem is so long as to unbalance the work completely. Medill Elde is allowed only 14 lines, Youthe only 74, but Elde has 389. Moreover, there is pitifully little imaginative pressure in Elde's treatment of the Worthies: the poet shows small interest in the stories he is telling, and he even manages to confuse Joshua with Moses. In this part of the poem there is a formalism, and a shoddy formalism at that, that seems to derive from an absence of that strong personal involvement in the critique of worldly values which is manifestly present in *Piers Plowman*.

There is also a lack of balance in the poet's treatment of the waking prologue, though here at least he does not seem to have lost interest in what he was doing. In the prologue the narrator of the poem is presented not (as in *Winner and Waster*) as a *maker* but as a huntsman, engaged in a solitary poaching expedition. He sees a great hart, and carefully stalks it, though his task is made more difficult because he is troubled by gnats and because the hart has a younger deer as a watchman. He succeeds, however, in shooting the hart, sends his dog after it, and finds it dead. He cuts it up in the approved fashion of the time, and carefully hides the meat in a hole, covered with fern, so that no forester should find it. After this he feels tired and sits down, and it is then that he falls asleep and has his dream. At the end of the poem, he is awakened by a bugle blowing, finds that it is now evening, and makes his way back from the woods to the town. There can be no doubt about the vividness of the prologue, with its air of stealthy suspense and its keen response to the world of the senses; here indeed the poet has found a theme which engages his interest. Where doubt arises is in relation to the relevance of the prologue to the dream. It might be, of course, that no special relevance was intended: perhaps the prologue was intended to capture the interest of an audience that loved hunting, as a means of persuading them to attend to the moralizing of the dream; or perhaps, like the prologues of fourteenth-century French poems such as the *Dis des Quatre Sieges* or the *Jugement dou Roy de Navarre*, it had no more specific purpose than to provide a contrast with the dream. On the other hand, it seems possible to make out certain psychological links between the prologue and the dream, of a kind we found to exist more definitely in Chaucer's dream-poems.[24]

The dream-content may be influenced by the Dreamer's waking preoccupations, even though he himself appears in it only as an onlooker and overhearer. In the prologue, the fertile natural scene is overshadowed by anxiety and then by death. The narrator – a perfect example of *homo economicus*, pursuing his own profit without regard to society – engages in a poaching expedition, deals out violent death, so that 'The breris and the brakans were blody byronnen' (62), and then carefully stores up his spoils where no-one else could take them from him; and it seems natural enough that he should dream of an encounter between Youthe, who is a huntsman, Medill Elde, who is obsessed with storing up goods, and Elde, who is the harbinger of death. It might be argued that, as in Chaucer's dream-poems, the interest of such links is not only psychological but thematic: the poet has perhaps made some attempt to use the creative methods of the dreaming mind to weave the diverse material of his poem into patterns of recurrence and development. Thus one recent commentator has argued that 'In the picture of the camouflaged huntsman, waiting patiently until the hart stoops to his food before hitting him with a deadly arrow from his crossbow, the poet has given us a powerful allegory of Elde's "warning to be ware".'[25] It might be added that the narrator appears again in a brief epilogue, from which it seems that he has learned from his dream. The sun has set, bringing the bright day to an end, as death brings an end to life; and the huntsman now abandons his winnings and walks back to human society. In the poem's closing lines, he applies Elde's message to himself not as a solitary individual, but (in a way similar to the final stanza of *Pearl*) as one of the community of Christians:

> There dere Drightyne this daye dele us of thi blisse,
> And Marie, that is mylde qwene, amende us of synn. Amen. Amen.
>
> (664–5)

But in the end, it is difficult to convince oneself completely that the poet has made constructive use of dream-methods. He shows none of Chaucer's interest in dreams as such, nor even of the *Pearl*-poet's concern to define precisely the nature of his dream; and the strong sense of the Dreamer's personality which we gain from the prologue does not appear in the dream itself. There is also the fact that so much of what should have been the crucial part of the dream seems merely perfunctory. Inherent in the scheme of *The Parliament of the Three Ages* is the possibility of a complex and interesting dream-poem in the 'modern' manner of its time; but the poet did not in fact bring that possibility to fruition.

'Piers Plowman': the A-text

Piers Plowman exists in three distinct versions, referred to by modern scholars as A, B and C, and probably written between about 1369 and the middle 1380s – just the period when Chaucer was writing his series of dream-poems, and when the *Pearl*-poet too was at work. It is now generally accepted that the three versions were written in succession by the same poet, William Langland, who was probably a clerk in lower orders, born in the west Midland area, the chief home of alliterative poetry, but living in London. In the B and C versions *Piers Plowman* is a poem of some seven thousand lines, and it is often deeply obscure and difficult of interpretation. In the last twenty years alone it has been the subject of a dozen books and hundreds of articles, and there can obviously be no chance of arriving at a definitive interpretation of it in a few pages here. But I believe that much light is thrown on it if it is seen specifically as a dream-poem. In what follows, I begin by discussing the A-text, a procedure I adopt for two reasons. One is that it is the only text of which there exists at the time of writing a reliable modern edition based on a consideration of all known manuscripts. George Kane's edition probably brings us substantially closer to Langland's actual words than any other edition does, and the stylistic effect is certainly sharper and more telling, less blurred by scribal misunderstandings and would-be improvements, than in any other edition of any of the texts. My other reason for beginning with A is that I have come to believe that the poet's abandonment of the A-text at an inconclusive point, and his later revision of what he had written and resumption from that point, are essential keys to the understanding of the poem. This aspect of *Piers Plowman* was perceptively discussed earlier in this century by R. W. Chambers, by whose work I have been much influenced;[26] but Chambers was writing in response to a controversy about the poem's authorship, and was aiming primarily to establish that all three texts were by the same poet. That controversy is now effectively settled,[27] but this does not mean that Chambers's approach has become obsolete. He was concerned with the writer's presentation of himself as writer of the poem *in* the poem; and in my view that is a crucial part of its existence as a dream-poem.

The A-text in particular originates (though it certainly does not end) in the tradition to which *Winner and Waster* and *The Parliament of the Three Ages* belong. Like them, it begins as a vision of this world, seen by a Dreamer who falls asleep in a paradisal landscape. In *Piers Plowman*, this landscape is reduced to a mere sketch: there is none of the lavish detail of the prologue to the *Parliament*, with its primroses, periwinkles, and penny-royal, its cuckoos, wood-pigeons and thrushes, but only the bare outline of 'a May morwenynge on Malverne hilles,' when

> I was wery forwandrit and wente me to reste
> Under a brood bank be a bourne side,
> And as I lay and lenide and lokide on the watris
> I slomeride into a slepyng, it swiyed so merye. (A Pro. 5, 7–10)[28]
>
> *swiyed so merye* flowed so pleasantly

This bareness is characteristic of *Piers Plowman* generally; it is unusual among the poems of the Alliterative Revival in avoiding verbal decoration and poetic diction, and it seems certain that it was aimed at a public different from the aristocratic audiences for whom most alliterative poems were probably written.

Once asleep, the narrator immediately dreams, and in his dream he finds himself 'in a wildernesse, wiste I nevere where' (A Pro. 12). That the wilderness represents this world is made clear by the C-text's addition that he saw 'Al the welthe *of this worlde* and the woo bothe' (C 1.10). This does not imply that supernatural values are excluded; on the contrary, as the Dreamer looks about him, he sees that the 'fair feld ful of folk' (A Pro. 17) where human action is played out is set between a high tower on a hill and a massive keep in a valley; and he soon learns that the tower belongs to Treuthe (or God) and the keep to Wrong (or the devil). The world between them is that of political and economic reality; that is, of moral confusion, an agitated bustle of apparently meaningless activity, like an ant-heap, in which, significantly, winning and wasting are prominent:

> Summe putte hem to plough, pleiyede ful selde,
> In settyng and sowyng swonke ful harde;
> Wonne that thise wastours with glotonye destroiyeth.
> And summe putte hem to pride, aparailide hem thereaftir,
> In cuntenaunce of clothing comen disgisid. (A Pro. 20–4)
>
> *selde* seldom; *swonke* worked; *aparailide hem thereaftir* dressed accordingly; *cuntenaunce* outward show

The scene is more obviously symbolic than in *Winner and Waster*, and perhaps the sense of confusion is stronger: here there are not two clearly opposed armies (the Dreamer will not be able to see the field in that way until the poem's closing section), but a busy and noisy mass of people all going about their own activities, good or bad. On the other hand, the Dreamer of *Piers Plowman*, unlike his counterparts in *Winner and Waster* and *The Parliament of the Three Ages*, has an authoritative guide, in the form of Lady Holychurch, a beautiful yet terrifying being

– 'I was aferd of hire face theigh heo fair were' (A 1. 10) – who corresponds to Boethius's Philosophy or the Maiden in *Pearl*. Her first words,
alluding ironically to the fact that this is dream, are 'Sone, slepist thou?'
(A 1. 5), and she proceeds to explain the scene the Dreamer sees, and
to answer his question 'How I may saven my soule' (A 1. 82) by telling
him of the supreme value of *treuthe* (integrity or honesty, but also a name
of God). Surely, with such guidance, the Dreamer will be able to find
his way through the wilderness, and will emerge from his dream enligh-
tened and satisfied?

I think it likely that when Langland began to compose the A version
of *Piers Plowman* he intended a poem which would not differ too greatly
in kind from *Winner and Waster*, and that what we have in the poem's
three versions is, among other things, the record of how he came to see
that he would have to go further, and create a radically new kind of
dream-poem. For the moment, the hope is still for a political solution
to the economic and moral disorder of society. When the Dreamer asks
Holychurch how he shall recognize 'the false' (A 11. 4), she refers him
to a woman 'wondirliche clothide' (A 11. 8), who is called Mede (reward,
bribery), and who is going to be married next day to Fals. At this point
Holychurch leaves, and the Dreamer tells us what he saw further. It is
the allegorical representation of a problem in economics, and one that
belonged to the real world of Langland's time. In a society which has
traditionally seen the social contract as involving an exchange of goods
and services, what is to be thought of payment in money? Is it merely
bribery, or is the cash nexus a proper bond between men? Mede is
dangerous: Holychurch herself sees her as a rival, for

> In ths Popis paleis heo is prevy as myselve;
> And so shulde heo not be, for Wrong was hire sire;
> Out of Wrong heo wex to wrotherhele manye. (A 11. 18–21)
> *prevy* familiar; *wrotherhele* the ill-fortune (of)

If her marriage to Fals is completed, corruption will spread throughout
society: the lands conferred on her by the marriage settlement include
most of the seven deadly sins. She, Fals, and his cronies ride off to
London to obtain a licence for the marriage, but news of their journey
reaches Conscience, and he informs the king, who orders the arrest of
the company, showing himself aware that 'holy chirche for hem worth
[will be] harmid for evere' (A 11. 166) if they are left at large. It appears
that, as in *Winner and Waster*, a political solution will be possible. But
Fals and his followers run away, leaving Mede alone and trembling to
face the king's wrath. Such are her charms, that she is treated with great

kindness by clerks, justices and friars, and with courtesy by the king himself. He asks her to marry Conscience instead; Conscience refuses, and they argue about the validity of reward; Conscience says he will not kiss Mede until Reason orders him to do so, and Reason is sent for. Meanwhile, Mede's insidious power is shown in the case of Peace's bill of complaint against Wrong, which ends with Peace being bribed to beg for mercy on his deadly enemy. When Reason comes, his advice is simple:

> and it so were
> That I were king with croune to kepe a reaume,
> Shulde nevere wrong in this world that I wyte mighte
> Be unpunisshit at my power, for peril of my soule,
> Ne gete my grace thorugh giftes, so me God helpe! (A IV. 120–4)
> *and* if; *wyte* know of

All that is necessary is for the king to put an end to 'wrong'; but we have learned that Wrong is the keeper of the dungeon in the valley – a permanent principle, it seems, part of the essential structure of the world. As the king himself ruefully remarks, 'Ac it is wel hard, be myn hed, herto to bringe it' (A IV. 146). This section of the poem ends with the king, Reason and Conscience agreeing to stay together, and the court going to church – a triumph of good advice and good intentions, but with no guarantee that society can really be reformed on this basis.

Here the Dreamer wakes; and one way in which *Piers Plowman* differs from other dream-poems is that it consists of a series of dreams, with brief waking intervals between them, the effect of which is both to fragment the dream-world and, at times, to remind us of the waking world running alongside it and interacting with it. This interval is brief: the Dreamer confirms our sense that nothing has been finally settled by wishing that he had 'yslepe saddere [more soundly] and yseyn more' (A v. 4). The new dream has the same setting as the old: 'the feld ful of folke that I before tolde' (A v. 10). Conscience (replaced by Reason in B and C) preaches a sermon in which he asserts that recent tempests and pestilences were God's punishments for sin, and gives advice. This includes

> He bad Wastour go werche what he best couthe,
> And wynne that he wastide with sum maner craft. (A v. 24–5)

There is still the expectation that a king will impose political solutions to society's problems: for example, members of religious orders are warned that unless they keep to their rule, 'the king and his counseil' (A v. 38) will take away their possessions. The sermon is so effective that it leads to confessions by figures symbolizing the seven deadly sins. Langland, however, does not conceive of the sins as emblematic figures, in rigid postures and with fixed attributes, in the way they are presented by Spenser in *The Faerie Queene* I. iv. For him, they are representative individuals, sinners rather than sins, with their own names and characters and life-histories, confessing at various lengths, and in ways which do not artificially separate one sin from another (lechery is associated with gluttony, envy with anger, and so on). The consequence is that repentance is a real possibility for them, as it is not for Spenser's sins. If Spenser's sins ceased to sin they would cease to exist, but for Langland's sinners the possibility of a change of heart is always open, though we may not feel sure that all of them are going to seize it. This is one illustration of a general truth about *Piers Plowman*: that its allegorical characters have a fluidity which is more genuinely dreamlike than anything to be found in other poems. The poem's underlying stream of ideas and impulses is continuous, but it takes now one form, now another. The sins are now sinners; earlier they were lands settled on Mede; later they will be stains on the cloak of Hawkyn, the representative of the active life, and later still members of an army led by Antichrist fighting against Piers and his followers. Piers himself is the supreme example of this protean tendency, as he takes the various forms of ploughman, overseer, Christ's human nature, and Pope. As a result, the overall effect of reading *Piers Plowman* is more like the experience of dreaming than that of reading any other poem discussed in this book. We saw a movement towards such fluidity in *Winner and Waster*, where hunger became a personification for a single line and then relapsed into being an abstract noun; but Langland pushes this tendency much further, and sometimes indeed pushes it to the point at which his readers become baffled and dispirited. The world of his dreams becomes truly a wilderness at times, a world in which everything is slippery and problematic, nothing is what it seems, and rational analysis is defeated.

This certainly appears true of what follows from the confessions. The folk on the field are granted absolution by Repentance, and they set out on a pilgrimage to Treuthe. But no-one knows the way there. First they meet a man dressed as a palmer, decked out in all the symbols of pilgrimage; but Treuthe – or truth – is the last thing he knows about. At this point Piers Plowman enters the poem for the first time. He is simply a ploughman, a common labourer, but he claims to know Treuthe well, to be one of his workmen, and to find him 'the presteste [promptest] payere that pore men knowen' (A VI. 38). He proceeds to tell the way to Treuthe's tower: it takes the form of an allegorization of the ten commandments, and he promises the people that, after contrition and amendment, Grace will unlock the gate that was shut by Adam and Eve, and 'Thou shalt se Treuthe himself wel sitte in thin herte' (A VI. 93). Already, with this teaching, *Piers Plowman* is beginning to reach out beyond the scope of *Winner and Waster* into the realm of the spiritual: the ultimate goal of the pilgrimage is that inner paradise of contemplation which the Dreamer of *Pearl* glimpses across the river. But Piers assumes that for the time being this journey must be delayed: he will guide the people to Treuthe, but only after he has ploughed his half-acre. The ploughing of the half-acre is a further allegory of the attempt to set up a just society, now seen not as an end in itself but as a means to salvation. At times it appears that the ploughing is a preliminary to the pilgrimage; at other times, when Piers speaks of being Treuthe's 'pilgrym at the plough' (A VII. 94), it seems that the ploughing itself is a pilgrimage; but in either case it is assumed that political and economic means will gain the spiritual end. Piers takes on the role of overseer in a social microcosm, and attempts to set up the ideal feudal state towards which the whole poem has been looking forward. The different social groups – knights, ladies, priests, workmen – are all to perform their appropriate functions: the normal remedy suggested by medieval writers for the ills of society. But soon difficulties begin to emerge. As the day passes, some lazy workmen 'sungen at the ale, / And holpen to ere [plough] the half akir with "Hey, trolly, lolly!"' (A VII. 107–8), and some pretend to be cripples so that they can eat without working. Piers denounces them as 'wastours' (A VII. 122, 124), at which they arise into full personification and threaten him:

> Thanne gan Wastour arise, and wolde have yfoughte;
> To Peris the ploughman he profride his glove. (A VII. 139–40)

Winning and wasting are beginning to be seen in a different perspective from that of *Winner and Waster* itself. There, the viewpoint was that of the poet's aristocratic patrons, and a waster was a lavish spender; but Langland's viewpoint is lower down the social scale, where the need to work if one is to eat is more apparent, and wasters are those who refuse to join in the community's work, but expect to live on the product of their fellows' labour.

Piers first calls on the knight to perform his social function by protecting him and society from 'wastours that waite wynneres to shende [destroy]' (A VII. 148). But Waster is not frightened by the knight, and so Piers summons Hunger to 'Awreke [avenge] me on wastours...that this world shendith' (A VII. 158). Hunger is all too willing to attack the wasters, and indeed would kill them but for Piers's charity. In consequence, everyone sets to work again, and Piers begs Hunger to depart.

But on the half-acre, as in the fourteenth-century England of which it is a microcosm, famine is not so easily dismissed. Hunger gives Piers some general advice, amounting to a gospel of work which is one of the poem's most deeply felt truths:

> Kynde Wyt wolde that iche wight wroughte,
> Other with teching, other telling, or travaillyng of hondis,
> Actif lif other contemplatif; Crist wolde it alse. (A VII. 231–3)

(Natural intelligence demands that every man should work, at teaching, or ploughing, or manual labour, active or contemplative life; Christ wishes this also.)

The people's work brings a good harvest, and they eventually manage to send Hunger to sleep 'with good ale and glotonye' (A VII. 285). But now once more Waster refuses to work, and the whole disastrous cycle of famine, labour, prosperity, gluttony, famine, begins over again. In the closing lines of this episode the problems of the half-acre merge into those of contemporary England, as the Dreamer prophesies famine to the men of his waking world, and once more employs the old contrast between winning and wasting:

> I warne yow werkmen, wynneth while ye mowe,
> For Hungir hiderward hastith hym faste.
> He shal awake thorugh water, wastours to chaste. (A VII. 302–4)
> *awake thorugh water* be aroused by floods; *chaste* punish

The familiar reference to winning and wasting does not conceal the fact that *Piers Plowman* has now diverged from the pattern of *Winner and Waster*. Society's economic problems cannot after all be solved by political means, even when an ideal workman takes the place of the king; this is the conclusion to which the second dream leads. But it has not so far called in question Piers's own position, as Treuthe's loyal servant; even if society as a whole cannot be saved by his efforts, surely he and all the good men whom he represents can be certain of their individual salvation. Even this is made doubtful by the final part of the second dream. Treuthe hears of what has happened on the half-acre, and sends a pardon to Piers and all who help in his work, including kings, bishops, honest merchants, labourers, and even those who are genuinely unfit to work. At this a priest steps forward and offers to explain the pardon to Piers, for its actual contents have not yet been read. As Piers unfolds it, we are reminded of the Dreamer's presence in his own dream:

> And I behynde hem bothe beheld al the bulle.
> In two lynes it lay, and nought o lettre more,
> And was writen right thus in witnesse of Treuthe:
> *Et qui bona egerunt ibunt in vitam eternam;*
> *Qui vero mala in ignem eternum.* (A VIII. 92–6)

As the priest points out, the Latin means simply that those who do well will go to eternal life, while those who do evil will go to eternal fire, and he concludes that it is not really a pardon at all. It seems that Piers's earlier confidence in his relationship with Treuthe was misplaced. He had seen Treuthe as a prompt payer; like the lord of the vineyard in the parable, 'He withhalt non hyne his hire that he ne hath it at eve' (A VI. 39) (He does not keep back his wages from any workman, so that he lacks them at evening). But, as the *Pearl* Dreamer had to learn, the parable is enigmatic; and while it may be true that the ploughman, the type of the poor labourer on whose work society depends for its sustenance, is closest to God, the pardon seems to indicate that the relations between God and man cannot be fully seen as a matter of 'mesurable hire', because there can be no measure linking God's fullness with fallen man's emptiness. In anger Piers tears the pardon, an act that marks a crisis in which he abjures his earlier concerns and the attitudes and expectations of the half-acre scene:

> I shal cesse of my sowyng...and swynke not so harde,
> Ne aboute my belyve so besy be namore;
> Of preyours and of penaunce my plough shal ben hereaftir,
> And beloure that I belough er, theigh liflode me faile. (A VIII. 104-7)
>
> *swynke* labour; *belyve* living; *beloure...faile* scowl at what I formerly laughed at, even though my livelihood should be lacking

Like the birds, he will rely on God to provide his food. The priest sarcastically suggests that Piers is 'lettrid a litel' (A VIII. 119), and that if he were a priest he might take the Psalmist's 'Because I have not known learning' (Psalms 70:15) as his text. Piers in replying quotes Proverbs 22:10 - 'Cast out the scoffer and contention shall go with him' - and at this point the Dreamer is awakened by the noise of the argument. Langland has contrived a splendidly enigmatic close to the dream, giving us much food for thought as to whether or not the pardon *is* a pardon, and as to the nature of the new way of life that Piers has resolved to adopt. And indeed Langland himself, as narrator, proceeds to ponder with almost Chaucerian uncertainty on the reliability of dreams as a guide to truth. In a poem which began by depicting a world as solid and certain as that of *Winner and Waster*, everything has become problematic. A new start has to be made, and it seems as though Langland himself may have been baffled and uncertain how to proceed.

What has happened in the poem so far - the *Visio*, as this part of it is usually called - is not only that the dream-world has disintegrated into an uncertainty that is frighteningly like some real dreams; it is also that the Dreamer's own role has been called in question, in a way it never is in *Winner and Waster* or *The Parliament of the Three Ages*, but which has striking similarities with the treatment of the Dreamer in Chaucer. Though the Dreamer plays little part in his own dreams in the *Visio*, being no more than an observer or at most a questioner, there is no pretence that he is not a poet. In A 1, Holychurch commands him to teach others her doctrine that *treuthe* is the best treasure: 'Lerith it thus lewide [ignorant] men, for lettrid it knowith' (A 1.125). Langland's public may well have included the unlearned in reality; it must surely have included at least the literate laity who appear to have been readers of the devotional prose of the time. The likeliest theory about Langland's way of life is that he wandered about saying prayers for various families who supported him for his spiritual services,[29] and it may be that he also entertained and instructed them with alliterative verse. This would explain why Holychurch goes on to urge him to sing of love to his patrons:

> love is the levest thing that oure Lord askith,
> And ek the plante of pes; preche it in thin harpe
> Ther thou art mery at mete, yif men bidde the yedde. (A 1. 136–8)[30]
>
> *levest* dearest; *yedde* sing

Whether or not this was really his way of life, Langland regularly represents himself in his poem as a kind of wandering minstrel; and he shows a peculiar sensitivity on the subject of minstrels. At the very opening of his first dream, he sees minstrels among the folk of all trades on the field (A Pro. 33). The first of his many digressions is devoted to distinguishing between those minstrels who 'gete gold with here gle, giltles, I trowe' and those who 'Fonden hem fantasies and foolis hem make' (invent absurdities and make themselves fools) and are 'Judas children' (A Pro. 34–6). The distinction is recognizably related to that in the prologue of *Winner and Waster* between genuine 'makers of myrthes' and uncreative childish minstrels, but in Langland the thought has become more intimate, more an expression of uneasy conscience than of easy *saeva indignatio*. Already *Piers Plowman*, like other dream-poems, is showing a tendency to become reflexive, in this case by expressing the poet's doubts about his own vocation. What is a poet, after all, but a creator of fictions, like Liar who flees from the king's threats along with Fals's other followers, and finds himself 'nowhere welcome for his many talis' (A II. 179)? And surely Langland may have felt himself to be included in Piers's warning to the knight on the half-acre:

> talis thou hate,
> But it be of wysdom or of wyt, thi werkmen to chaste;
> Holde with none harlotis, ne here nought here talis,

And nameliche at mete suche men eschewe,
For hit arn the develis disours, I do the to undirstonde. (A VII. 45–9)

chaste correct; *harlotis* rascals; *nameliche* especially; *disours* storytellers; *do* give

Hunger's gospel of work seems to leave no place for a mere poet;[31] moreover, we get an uneasy sense from time to time that, as Dreamer, Langland is not merely an observer of an objectively existing social reality, but is himself implicated in the subject-matter of his visions. There are points at which his very consciousness of his role as observer and reporter prevents that role from being taken for granted. This happens, for example, in his comment on the inclusion of merchants in the pardon Treuthe sends to Piers:

Thanne were marchauntis merye; many wepe for joye,
And yaf Wille for his writyng wollene clothis;
For he copiede thus here clause, thei couden hym gret mede.
(A VIII.43–5)

yaf gave; *here clause* the clause referring to them; *couden* gave

Perhaps this is a hint to Langland's real patrons to reward him for his writings; but at the same time it implies that if he deserves reward it must really be for something more than copying down words for which he is not responsible. At other times Langland acknowledges more directly that the meaning of what he writes includes himself: at the beginning of the confession of the deadly sins, he tells us,

Thanne ran Repentaunce and reherside his teme,
And made Wil to wepe watir with his eiyen. (A v. 43–4)[32]

reherside repeated; *teme* text

The poet too is a sinner; and this is ultimately the reason why his satirical vision disintegrates, because he has to admit that he cannot claim a position of special privilege or immunity in relation to the world he depicts in his poem. This admission is something towards which Langland works only slowly and painfully, and it leads him to write eventually a quite different kind of poem from that which he originally intended.

One possibility would have been for Langland to end his poem with the tearing of the pardon and his own following doubts about the validity of such dreams. But, even when writing the A-text, he was too seriously absorbed in his subject to be content with such a Chaucerian withdrawal, and he attempted to continue the poem along new lines. Piers's pardon has promised salvation only to those who 'do well', and so it appears to the Dreamer that 'dowel' must now be the object of his quest. He works this out at the end of A VIII, and then, still in a waking state, sets off to seek Dowel, whom he thinks of as an allegorical person who is to be found in some specific place or among some social class. First he meets two friars, Franciscan masters of divinity, and they assure him that Dowel is permanently among their number. But the Dreamer disputes this with a scholastic *contra*, on the grounds that all men sin at times, and therefore Dowel cannot be always with the friars. One of the friars answers with a parable designed to show that Dowel is what prevents men from committing deadly sin, even though they cannot avoid venial sins. The Dreamer is not satisfied, and says he will 'go lerne betere' (A IX. 49). He wanders into a paradisal landscape like that in which the poem began, and once more falls asleep. He dreams, and in his dream is addressed by a man like himself who addresses him by name, and explains that he is Thought and has been following the Dreamer for seven years. This encounter indicates that the poem's new direction is to be introspective and personal, and that the dream-setting is hence-forward to be envisaged as the Dreamer's mind rather than, as pre-viously, the outer world. When he encounters Thought, the Dreamer is introspecting and also retrospecting. 'Thought', as we have seen, is the term used by Chaucer in *The House of Fame* to mean 'memory', the faculty that has inscribed in his brain the events of his dream; and Langland's 'Thought', which has been following him for seven years (a number we need not take literally), is presumably one of the faculties involved in the creation of his poem so far.

The Dreamer asks Thought where Dowel dwells, and Thought replies by extending Dowel into the triad of Dowel, Dobet and Dobest (which dominates the rest of the poem), and by giving definitions of each. The Dreamer is still not satisfied, but he walks about disputing with Thought 'day aftir other' until 'er we ywar were' they meet Wit (A IX. 108–9). He too is asked about Dowel, Dobet and Dobest, and he explains that they live 'nought a day hennes' (A X. 1) in an allegorized castle of romance, as the guardians of the lady Anima, the human soul, against her would-be ravisher, the devil. Wit digresses on the subject of mar-riage, explaining that only marriages based on equality of rank and loving consent produce Dowel. At this point, with an effect almost of satire, Wit's own wife, Dame Study, angrily intervenes to blame him for laying his wisdom before flatterers and fools. Nowadays, she complains, wisdom is not valued, and she wanders onto the perpetual subject of minstrels, saying that those who tell of holy things are despised, and 'harlotrie' (A XI. 31) is preferred by their noble patrons. This might seem to favour Langland, but she goes on to refer to the blasphemous conversation of clerics: they may have God in their mouths, but poor men have him in their hearts. This passage probably expresses Langland's disapproval of the separation of reason from faith in fourteenth-century thought, and its general tendency towards logic-chopping scholasticism. But surely the Dreamer himself, with his readiness to cry *contra*, is at least an amateur scholastic? And sure enough, having quoted St Paul's 'Be not more wise than it behoveth to be wise' (Romans 12:3) against those intellectuals who encourage unbelief by asking questions about God's purposes, Study turns on the Dreamer himself, classing him among these frivolous questioners:

> And now comith a conyon and wolde cacche of my wittes
> What is Dowel fro Dobet; now def mote he worthe,
> Sithen he wilneth to wyte which thei ben alle. (A xi. 87–9)
> *conyon* fool; *worthe* become; *Sithen* since; *wilneth* desires

He will never reach Dobet and Dobest until he *lives* the life of Dowel.

The poem's new course appears to be leading only to disabling contradictions. The Dreamer is in search of knowledge, but knowledge of something that cannot be known unless it is also lived – and how can living be turned into poetry? Wit is embarrassed by his wife's outburst, and signs to the Dreamer to placate her. He does so, with comic exaggeration, and Study is easily appeased, and directs him by another allegorical route to her cousin Clergy (learning) and his wife Scripture. Before he leaves, she admits that she is puzzled by Theology,

> For the more I muse theron the mistlokere it semith,
> And the deppere I devynide the derkere me thoughte. (A xi. 138–9)
> *mistlokere* mistier

This is precisely the Dreamer's condition; and in this interior allegory Study must represent his own studies. She would give up theology, were it not that it sets such a high value on love. The Dreamer finds Clergy, and Scripture gives him yet another set of definitions of Dowel, Dobet and Dobest, identifying them as good workmen, religious and bishops respectively. She goes on to say that nowadays the religious orders have become worldly, and the rich cannot expect to enter heaven. Once more, the Dreamer cannot resist putting in a *contra*. He quotes St Peter as saying that he who believes and is baptized will be saved; against which Scripture says that this text applies only to the conversion of pagans: Christians must also love God and their neighbours. In despair, the Dreamer exclaims that, for all his walking about, he is no nearer to knowing in his heart what Dowel is; because, whatever works he may perform, the fate of his soul is predestined:

I was markid withoute mercy, and myn name entrid
In the legende of lif longe er I were,
Or ellis unwriten for wykkid, as witnessith the gospel. (A XI. 261–3)
er I were before I existed

Those wise men Solomon and Aristotle are held by the Church to be damned, while the thief who appealed to Christ on Calvary was saved before the apostles or patriarchs or prophets. Not even learning can ensure salvation, and indeed it may be a danger (this was Study's argument earlier); it is simple ploughmen and shepherds who have the best chance of being saved.

Thus the Dreamer is brought to a halt by that central issue of the fourteenth century, predestination and freewill, and by the growing conviction that the quest for knowledge which is the impetus of the whole poem is of no value so far as the salvation of the soul is concerned. He is beset and hindered by doubts, which take the form of objections to what he is told by his allegorical instructors; and to them those very objections are signs that he is not serious in his quest. Clergy says that he has done his duty in teaching him Dowel,

But I se now as I seye, as me soth thinkyth,
The were lef to lerne but loth for to stodie;
Thou woldest konne that I can, and carpen hit after,
Presumptuowsly, paraventure, apose so manye
That myghthe turne me to tene and Theologie bothe.
Yif I wiste witterly thou woldest don therafter,
Al that thou askest asoylen I wolde. (A XII. 5–11)

The were lef you would be glad; *konne* know; *carpen* chatter; *apose* dispute with; *tene* annoyance; *witterly* certainly; *don therafter* act accordingly; *asoylen* explain

We have now reached the final passus of the A-text, which is found in only three of the seventeen A manuscripts, and is complete in only one of these. Its authenticity is not certain, though I think that all but the last few lines are by Langland, and that it represents his final, abortive attempt to take the A version further. Scripture urges Clergy to give the Dreamer no further help, because he did not really come to 'lerne to Dowel' (A XII. 32); and Clergy's response is to creep into a hut and shut the door after him, telling the Dreamer that he can do well or wickedly for all he cares. Scripture has told the Dreamer that he can learn nothing unless he is absolved by 'the kynde cardinal wit' (A XII. 15), and she now gives him directions for yet another allegorical journey to find 'Kynde Wit' (perhaps best translated as natural or inward understanding). He lives with Life, and the Dreamer is to be accompanied there by *Omnia-probate* (prove all things) who will lead him to *Quod-bonum-est-tenete* (hold fast that which is good).[33] The Dreamer sets out, but this last journey is destined never to be finished. He explains that before he reached *Quod-bonum-est-tenete*, while he was travelling through youth towards the prime of life, he met Hunger, and then 'a knave with a confessoures face' (A xII. 77) who is Fever, Death's messenger to Life. The Dreamer offers to accompany him, but is told instead to 'lyve as this lyf is ordeyned for the'; if he acts according to Dowel, he will be 'laughth into lighth with loking of an eye' (taken up into the light in the twinkling of an eye) (A xII. 90, 96). Here the A-text ends, with a few lines added not by Langland but by a certain John But who says that after Will had written this and other works concerning Piers Plowman he died. These lines must have been added to an A manuscript after Langland had written the B- and C-texts, and they are valuable evidence that the same man was author of all three versions.

The last four passus of the A-text, as I have said, are set in the world of the mind; and it seems reasonable to take them as an allegorical account of intellectual and moral difficulties which prevented Langland from being able to find a way of completing his poem once he had been forced to abandon the original, *Winner and Waster*-like conception. We need not believe in an exact correspondence between the allegory and Langland's biography: as in *The Book of the Duchess*, the allegorical dream can be assumed to generalize the specific facts of the individual life. These last passus, with their series of abortive journeys and new starts with no finishes, their objections and rebukes and doubts, must surely be meant to be understood as the record of a period in the poet's earlier life. In them, the dream, which began as a form of allegorical vision, objective and analytic, becomes a personal nightmare; the literary *visio* disintegrates under the pressure of painful personal experience into an all-too-realistic *insomnium*. Something of the same kind happened, as we saw, in Chaucer's *House of Fame*, and Chaucer simply abandoned the poem and passed on. For Langland that was not possible; it is as though for him the vision of Piers Plowman was so important that it could only absorb his own life. Almost inadvertently, perhaps, he had transformed the dream-poem from an objective into a reflexive form, one which would mirror his whole spiritual history, and in doing so would inevitably have near its centre the struggle to get itself written. He could proceed only by going back, rewriting his poem from the beginning, incorporating in it his subsequent experience, and making its next topic precisely the difficulties he had in continuing it at all.

'Piers Plowman': the B-revision

Some years later, then, Langland appears to have returned to the writing of *Piers Plowman*. What he did first was to revise the part he had already written, adding a number of fairly long passages, and amplifying, modifying and rearranging parts of the poem throughout; but there is no space here to consider this rewriting of the existing text. When he gets to the end, Langland completely drops the short final passus, A XII, but uses a hint from it to begin a new passus, B XI (the arrangement and numbering of passus are different in the two texts). In A XII Scripture bent scornful brows on the Dreamer and told Clergy to give him no more help. B XI begins with Scripture scorning the Dreamer, and quoting to him some words of St Bernard: *multi multa sciunt, et seipsos nesciunt* (there are many who know much, but they do not know themselves). The Dreamer weeps at this, falls asleep, and dreams again. He is, however, already asleep: this is a special kind of inner dream, in which he will come closer to knowing himself. What he sees is a vision of his own past life: possibly (as Chambers believed) of his life since he abandoned the A-text, or perhaps (if recent scholarship is right in suggesting that there are only a few years between A and B) the whole of his adult life up to the present. Fortune seizes him, takes him into the 'londe of Longynge' (B XI. 7), and makes him look in a mirror called Middle-earth, where she says he will see what he desires, and even perhaps attain it. This is a Faustian episode, in which the Dreamer is persuaded that his desire for knowledge may be slaked by earthly pleasures. Fortune's followers, Lust-of-the-flesh, Lust-of-the-eyes and Pride-of-perfect-life (the three temptations, that is, of the world, the flesh and the devil) comfort him. Despite the warnings of Elde and of Plato, the Dreamer follows the promptings of Rechelesnesse and gives himself up to the three temptations for forty-five years. We may be meant to take that as an indication of Langland's age when he wrote this passage. Lust-of-the-eyes means more to him than Dowel or Dobet, and she tells him that he need not worry about the future; the friars will get a pardon for him and pray for him, if he has enough money. But at last, he tells us, 'I foryat youthe, and yarn [ran] into elde' (B XI. 59), and then Fortune turned against him, he became poor, and the friars would not help him. If *The Parliament of the Three Ages* was written earlier than *Piers Plowman*, Langland may have borrowed from it the idea of introducing old age as a crucial factor in changing one's view of the world. But if he did, he made it more personal; now it is the poet-Dreamer who is growing old; and indeed we have been prepared for the poem to absorb his life-history by the passage in A XII in which he told us that he met Hunger and Fever while he was travelling through youth towards his prime. I must emphasize again that we need not believe that such passages are literally autobiographical, and that Langland really lived as a libertine and then repented as he felt the effects of age. We do not know what his real life was like: the important thing is that such passages give the *impression* of drawing a real life into the poem – a life which may be the typical life of the human will as described by Gower –

> The weie he secheth hiere and there,
> Him recheth noght upon what syde[34]
>
> *Him recheth* he cares

rather than the individual life of Will Langland. The dream has become a means of breaking the tyranny of chronological narrative, and making past and present, whether real or fictional, equally present, as they are to the consciousness itself, in reverie and in dream.

The Dreamer embarks on a diatribe against the friars who have let him down, but is interrupted by a cool stare from a new personification, Lewte (loyalty, justice, truth to others and to oneself), who asks why he is frowning. 'Yif I durste...amonges men this meteles avowe!' (B XI. 86) (If only I durst disclose these dreams among men!), the Dreamer exclaims; and so, once more, his activity as poet is in question. Lewte assures him that he is justified in his satirical writing, so long as he is not the first to attack any abuse:

> Thinge that al the worlde wote, wherfore shuldestow spare
> To reden it in retoryke, to arate dedly synne? (B XI. 97–8)
>
> *wote* knows; *reden* discuss; *arate* rebuke

Thus the continuation of the poem is justified, but only in its treatment of public subject-matter: the Dreamer has not yet overcome his inner difficulties, and cannot do so except by bringing them too into the poem. Scripture intervenes to support Lewte, but she proceeds to preach a sermon on the text 'Many are called, but few are chosen', which sets the Dreamer trembling and disputing with himself 'Whether I were chosen or nought chosen' (B XI. 112). This, of course, was just the problem which so troubled him at the end of the A-text, since it seemed to call in question the value of good works, the 'do well' which was the object of his quest. Now a new thought has occurred to him, which makes further progress possible, and the thought appears in his dream as a person: Trajan, the pagan who was saved simply by his works – 'love, and...lyvyng in treuthe' (B XI. 146) – despite the fact that he lacked baptism. It is not clear at what point after this Trajan stops speaking and the Dreamer starts, but this scarcely matters if we recognize that Trajan is a thought of the Dreamer's, in a dream which is little different from the stream of consciousness. The two hundred lines that follow are far from coherent, as they circle round the topics of salvation and predestination, and above all of the value of poverty, since

> For owre joye and owre hele Jesu Cryst of hevene
> In a pore mannes apparaille pursueth us evere. (B xi. 179–80)
>
> *hele* salvation

Such lines foreshadow the later development of the poor ploughman Piers into the armour of human nature taken on by Christ. Amidst its incoherence, B xi has many such beautiful and suggestive lines as that, like fish swimming in the poet's troubled mind.

Next Kynde (Nature) comes to the Dreamer, and from the mountain of Middle-earth shows him a vision of the whole world, as if he were once more seeing the field full of folk of the poem's opening, but now from a high vantage point, where man's life can be seen as part of the whole of created nature:

> I seighe the sonne and the see and the sonde after,
> And where that bryddes and bestes by here makes thei yeden,
> Wylde wormes in wodes and wonderful foules,
> With flekked fetheres and of fele coloures.
> Man and his make I myghte bothe byholde;
> Poverte and plente, bothe pees and werre,
> Blisse and bale bothe I seigh at ones,
> And how men token mede and mercy refused. (B xi. 318–25)
>
> *makes* mates; *wormes* snakes; *fele* many; *bale* misery

The juxtaposition of men and birds under the eye of Kynde may remind us of *The Parliament of Fowls*, but this feels like a moment of higher inspiration, a genuinely prophetic vision. It does not last, however. The Dreamer observes that all creatures are ruled by Reason (that is, by instincts which fit them into the order of nature), except for man. And he rebukes Reason himself for thus neglecting mankind. But Reason answers sharply, saying that it is no concern of the Dreamer's, and that if God can suffer it he can surely suffer it too. Before he blames anything living, let him see whether he himself deserves praise! This seems to undercut Lewte's encouragement of the Dreamer to expose the sins of others in his poetry, and it once more brings the Dreamer himself into the centre of the poem. At the end of Reason's answer, the Dreamer blushes and feels ashamed, and at once awakens from his inner dream, wishing that he could have learned more. As he opens his eyes, an unnamed person looks into them, and asks him what Dowel is: and his answer is, 'To se muche and suffre more, certes,...is Dowel!' (B xi. 402). The unnamed person goes on to tell him that if he had 'suffered' more (that is, been more patient) in his dream, he would have learned more, but now he has been abandoned because of his 'entermetyng' (B xi. 406) (interference). The situation is very like that at the end of the dream in *Pearl*; the Dreamer has brought his dream to an end by his own impatience, and now wishes that he could have learned more. But Langland's Dreamer has another chance. The unnamed person points out that he has been overcome by Pride-of-perfect-life, even though Fortune's two other followers, Lust-of-the-flesh and Lust-of-the-eyes, have left him as he grows older. He is like a drunkard, impervious to any rebuke from Reason; but even the drunkard may still be aroused from his ditch by Need and Shame. At this the Dreamer says, 'Ye seggen soth' (B xi. 425), and himself rises and follows his new instructor.

At the beginning of the next passus, the instructor introduces himself as Ymagynatyf, who has followed the Dreamer for forty-five years, and has made him think of his end in middle age, before it was too late. Ymagynatyf is a personification of the *vis imaginativa*, the mind's image-making faculty, and especially its power to call up images of things that are not present, whether these are future (as when the Dreamer imagines his coming age and death) or more commonly past. Such images are often at their most vivid in dreams, whether prophetic or retrospective, and it is as though the Dreamer is facing the power that makes him a dreamer (and a poet).[35] He has often been admonished by suffering and disasters to amend himself, and yet, says Ymagynatyf,

> thow medlest the with makynges, and myghtest go sey thi sauter,
> And bidde for hem that yiveth the bred; for there ar bokes ynowe
> To telle men what Dowel is, Dobet, and Dobest bothe,
> And prechoures to preve what it is of many a peyre freres. (B xii. 16–19)
> *bidde* pray

This is the sharpest questioning yet of the Dreamer's activity as a poet ('making'), and the strongest expression of his bad conscience; but it is precisely by the realization of his inner doubt that he will be able to continue his poem. His answer to Ymagynatyf has two parts: first, that his 'meddling with makings' is no more than a recreation, and as such may be harmless or even beneficial; and second, that, if only someone could tell him what Dowel, Dobet and Dobest are, he would devote himself to prayer. (After all – though he does not make this point himself – he has already had a thoroughly unsatisfactory answer from one 'pair of friars'.) Ymagynatyf tells him that Dowel, Dobet and

Dobest are faith, hope and charity, and goes on to praise charity as against wealth and 'kynde witte'. And yet, he continues, neither 'kynde witte' nor 'clergye' are to be despised: Christ himself showed learning, for example when he wrote on the ground on the occasion when the Pharisees brought before him the woman taken in adultery, saying, 'He that is without sin among you, let him first cast a stone at her' (John 8:6–8). Once more we are brought back to the case of the Dreamer, accusing others when he may be more sinful than they are. Thus *clergye* and *kynde witte* may be 'as miroures to amenden owre defautes' (B XII. 97), and the Dreamer should not dispute with the learned. The ignorant need the learned to lead them to heaven, and books are written by men but inspired by the Holy Spirit – a possible defence of Langland's own book. The birth of Christ was first made known to shepherds and men of learning (the Magi), and indeed 'To pastours and to poetes' (B XII. 149). The 'poetes' may be either the Magi or the shepherds themselves, who sang in praise of God, but in either case Ymagynatyf is supplying a further hint that poetry such as Langland's may be inspired.

He goes on to explain that he has said all this to the Dreamer because he noticed how he 'contraryedest Clergye with crabbed wordes' (B XII. 157) and said that the ignorant were more easily saved than the learned. This was in B x: it is clear that Ymagynatyf's major function is to look back over the past, and that the Dreamer is now learning something from this looking back. Ymagynatyf explains that *clerkes* are best at avoiding sin because they best know what it is. He reminds the Dreamer of how he adduced the case of the good thief on Calvary who gained salvation (also back in B x) to show that learning cannot ensure salvation; now he assures him that, though the thief was saved, he is in the lowest and least secure place in heaven. Yet no *clerke* knows why it was that thief rather than the other who asked Christ's help; and once more Ymagynatyf looks back, this time to B XI, to explain that he says this with reference to the Dreamer, who 'sekest after the "whyes", / And aresonedest [argued with] Resoun, a rebukyng, as it were' (B XII. 217–18). Only Kynde himself knows *why* things are arranged as they are; *clerkes* do not even know whether Aristotle was saved. Here the Dreamer intervenes to claim that, according to Christian *clerkes*, no man can be saved unless he believes in Christ – an argument which Ymagynatyf denies with a *contra*, and yet a further backward glance, this time to the case of Trajan, who was saved solely on account of his *treuthe*. At this point Ymagynatyf vanishes, and the passus ends. Passus B XIII begins by showing us the Dreamer waking up and then wandering about like a mendicant for many years, thinking back over the events of the last two passus, from Fortune's betrayal of him down to Ymagynatyf's last argument and his sudden disappearance. After the final act of retrospection, he sleeps again, and begins on a new dream which leaves the past behind.

I have given so much attention to these confusing opening passus of the B continuation because they seem to me crucial to an understanding of the whole poem. In them, Langland manages to find a way of continuing a work he had previously abandoned. This is partly a matter of his having seen a way through the problem of predestination: at the end of the A-text, he could see no value in human works (that is, in *doing* well), because neither they nor learning could ensure salvation; but in B XII he sees the significance of the case of Trajan, the pagan who was saved *by* God's grace, but *on account of* his own *treuthe* of thought and deed. Thus the Dreamer is assured that the quest for Dowel is worth pursuing. But what has happened in B XI–XII is not only the solution of a philosophical problem; it is also that the Dreamer has come to see himself more clearly, thus carrying out the programme implied by Scripture's *multi multa sciunt, et seipsos nesciunt*. Plunging into the depths of his own mind, where thoughts and impulses swirl unguided by logic, he comes to see that he must change himself before he can change the world; and, as poet, he comes to see that the difficulty of writing his poem must itself be part of the poem's subject.

From here the poem's course runs more smoothly, and I treat it more briefly. In the next dream comes the feast with the Doctor of Divinity, at which the change in the Dreamer's outlook is indicated by the fact that he now has Patience sitting next to him – just that quality that Reason had told him he needed, and that he had himself identified as the essence of Dowel at the end of B XI. But he is still not fully restrained by Patience, and cannot resist intervening at last to question the Doctor angrily. Next he meets Hawkyn, the representative of the active life, whose cloak is soiled with all the sins, and who is a minstrel – a kind of parody version of the Dreamer-poet himself, now seen with disillusioned clarity. What he needs above all is patience in his poverty, and Patience feeds him on allegorical food: *fiat voluntas tua* (Thy will be done). In his next vision, the Dreamer meets Anima, who includes in himself the names of many of the personified faculties he has met previously: Thought, Memory, Reason, Wit, Conscience and Love. The Dreamer makes a feeble joke about his possessing all these names, and Anima turns on him with surprising anger:

> 'now I se thi wille!
> Thow woldest knowe and kunne the cause of alle her names,

And of myne, if thow myghtest, me thinketh by thi speche!'
'Ye, syre,' I seyde, 'by so no man were greved,
Alle the sciences under sonne and alle the sotyle craftes
I wolde I knewe and couth kyndely in myne herte!'
'Thanne artow inparfit,' quod he, 'and one of Prydes knyghtes;
For such a luste and lykynge Lucifer fel fram hevene.' (B xv. 44–51)
her their; by so so long as

The desire for knowledge is itself sinful; the Dreamer will only achieve understanding when he understands and acts on that.

In the next passus the Dreamer asks what charity means, and in reply Anima begins to describe an allegorical tree of charity which grows in the garden of man's heart. Piers Plowman, he says, is in charge of it; and at the mere mention of Piers's name, the Dreamer swoons, and dreams that Piers is himself showing him the tree. The Dreamer is still full of consuming intellectual curiosity – he admits that he has 'thoughtes a threve' (B XVI. 55) (a heap of thoughts) about the props which support the tree, and which signify the Trinity. But now at last, under Piers's influence, the Dreamer manages to contain his curiosity:

And egrelich he loked on me, and therfore I spared
To asken hym any more therof, and badde hym ful fayre
To discreve the fruit that so faire hangeth. (B XVI. 64–6)
egrelich sharply; discreve describe

At the Dreamer's request, Piers knocks down apples from the tree, but the apples are human souls, and as they fall the devil seizes them. Piers hits out at the devil with one of the three props (called *Filius*, the Son), and at that moment the angel appears to Mary and announces the forthcoming birth of her son, who will joust against the devil for possession of the apples. This is the most surrealistic section of the whole poem, the least open to rational analysis, the most purely dreamlike in its combination of inconsequence with rich significance. We cannot say *where* this bizarre sequence of events is taking place: not in this world or the next – nowhere at all except in the mind of a dreamer. The apples on the tree must suggest the forbidden fruit; the 'pure tene' (B XVI. 86) which Piers shows in hitting out at the devil must recall the 'pure tene' with which he tore the pardon; there are other suggestive details. But, by not intervening with his usual questions and contradictions, the Dreamer has at last got carried on to a higher level of vision, where he can *see* the entry of the transcendent into history.

The life of Christ on earth takes its course; the Dreamer meets Faith, Hope and Charity in the forms of Abraham, Moses, and the Samaritan; and then, at the poem's emotional climax, he has his great vision of

Christ's crucifixion and the Harrowing of Hell. He wakes from this to the ringing of bells on Easter morning, and it seems that at last vision and reality are united:[36] the real world is no nightmare, but is one with the *visio spirituale*. On this real Easter day he goes joyfully to Mass with his wife and daughter. The poem might end there, and it would make a triumphant conclusion; but it is a sign of strength that it does not end there. Once more the direction changes, attention is turned to the depressing historical reality of Christianity, and the Dreamer is returned to the world of his own day, where a barn called Unity has been established by Piers – that is, Christ has left behind him the Church under the guidance of St Peter and his successors in the papacy. But the barn is being attacked by the deadly sins from without and by hypocrisy from within, and at the same time the Dreamer is being attacked by Elde – a fulfilment of the earlier threats of the inevitable end of human life. Elde makes him bald, deaf, toothless, gouty and impotent: this poem, which has absorbed the whole of its poet's life, must inevitably come to its end as he comes to his. If the poem's end, in the present, suggests the 'Last Days' of the world, it also depicts the last days of the Dreamer's life. Langland had half-seen this at the end of the A-text; now he sees it fully and clearly. Defeat seems imminent for those huddled in the barn, especially when the friar Flatterer worms his way among them; but the poem ends with the promise of a further quest, when Conscience vows to go in search of Piers Plowman, 'as wyde as al the worlde lasteth' (B xx. 379). That phrase implies both 'to the ends of the earth' and 'till the end of the world' – both spatial and temporal extension – and it reminds us that we are back in the dream-world with which the poem began: this world, the world of Langland's own time. Something has been gained: what seemed in the opening vision a mere aimless bustle on the field full of folk now shows up clearly as a battle between two armies, such as was threatened in *Winner and Waster*; but in it evil looks like defeating good.

The end is inconclusive: it points outside the poem to a further quest. One might guess that, just as in the middle of the poem Langland discovered that the way to overcome the difficulties he had in continuing it was to make them part of the poem, so he now discovered that the way to overcome the impossibility of finishing it was to make it end with no ending. It is a highly effective moment, with the glimpse it gives us of perspective beyond perspective; it is also the necessary end to the kind of work *Piers Plowman* has turned out to be. Langland is concerned with a transcendent reality, with the divine as well as the human; but, with that honesty that is so powerfully expressed in his work, he takes his stand within the human, in this world, not the next. He refuses to pretend to be able to stand firmly outside the confusing spectacle of human history, even in dreams, and to see the divinely ordained pattern complete, as God might see it. *Piers Plowman* might have followed the example of the great cycles of mystery plays that were being put together in its time; it might have claimed to show the complete cycle of human time, from Creation to Doomsday. But it does not; it sticks obstinately to what can be seen from the human standpoint, unilluminated by any other vision than what is mediated through history, or glimpsed only briefly in moments of special inspiration.

The fragmentariness of the poem, and its vagueness, are appropriate expressions of the human apprehension of transcendent realities. Despite the use the poem makes of scholastic methods (and we have seen that the Dreamer is himself a kind of barrack-room scholastic philosopher), its main effort is directed against the making of fine intellectual distinctions, and towards the building up of large ideas and images, which often have the vagueness of dreams, and are scarcely definable in theological terms, but which will have power over men's hearts and hence over their deeds. When the Dreamer has his vision of Christ riding to his crucifixion, what he sees is 'One semblable to the Samaritan and somedel to Piers the Plowman' (B XVIII. 10) – someone similar to the Samaritan and somewhat similar to Piers the Ploughman – and there the vagueness of the dream serves an important religious purpose. The process of condensation has taken place which we noticed in other dream-poems: several persons have been combined into one. But it would not suit Langland's purpose to try to make the apprehension enacted by this line theologically watertight, by attempting to establish precise intellectual relationships among Christ, the Samaritan, and Piers. His aim is rather to let one person merge into another, to accumulate meaning and emotion round certain magnetic centres, of which Piers himself is the chief.

The closest parallels to such insights are to be found not in theological writings, but in the devotional works which were so widely read in Langland's time, and which we have already considered in connection with *Pearl*.[37] The kind of parallel I have in mind is found in a statement such as this from Julian of Norwich's *Revelations of Divine Love*:

All mankind that shall be saved by the sweet Incarnation and blissful Passion of Christ, all is the Manhood of Christ: for He is the head and we be His members . . . For the longing and desire of all Mankind that shall be saved appeared in Jesus: for Jesus is All that shall be saved, and All that shall be saved is Jesus.[38]

Such a statement goes beyond the precision of theology into the suggestive and moving language of poetry and, in its identification of Jesus
with all mankind that shall be saved, it offers a striking parallel to the
merging of Piers as good workmen into Piers as the Humanity of Christ.
Meditation on Christ's human sufferings in the Passion was the most
popular form of devotion throughout the Middle Ages, and it is the
highest form achieved by the Dreamer in *Piers Plowman*, in the vision
of the crucifixion and Harrowing of Hell in B xviii. Other visions in
Langland's poem are reminiscent of medieval devotional experiences,
for example those which Richard Rolle describes in his autobiographical
Incendium Amoris. Rolle explains that once 'I was sitting in a certain
chapel, and whilst I was finding great delight in the softness of prayer
or meditation', he felt for the first time that spiritual rapture which he
describes as sensible heat or as music:

And while I sat in the same chapel, and at night before supper sang psalms as
best I could, I heard above me, as it were, the tinkling sound of psalmodists or
singers. And when in prayer with my whole desire I was intent on celestial things,
of a sudden I felt within me (I know not how) a melodious harmony, and I
received from heaven the most delectable symphony, which remained with me
in mind. For my thought was continually changed into melodious song...[39]

Rolle's baroque imagery of fire and song had no appeal for Langland,
but the last but one of his visions similarly comes when he is in church,
and in it he sees Piers as the Humanity of Christ:

> In myddes of the masse, tho men yede to offrynge,
> I fel eftsones aslepe, and sodeynly me mette
> That Pieres the Plowman was paynted al blody,
> And come in with a crosse bifor the comune peple,
> And righte lyke in alle lymes to owre lorde Jesu. (B xix. 4–8)[40]

Such moments of supreme vision come only briefly and rarely. They
generally focus on the mysterious figure of the Ploughman, and as the
poem proceeds his appearances become more intermittent and unpredictable, and yet he becomes increasingly the object of the Dreamer's
urgent longings. For example, after that most dreamlike vision of all,
in which Piers hits out at the devil beneath the tree of charity, the
Dreamer wakes, and then eagerly searches for Piers:

> And I awaked therewith and wyped myne eyghen,
> And after Piers the Plowman pryed and stared.
> Estwarde and westwarde I awayted after faste,
> And yede forth as an ydiote in contre to aspye
> After Pieres the Plowman; many a place I soughte! (B xvi. 167–71)
> *awayted* searched

The C-text adds another strange appearance and sudden disapperance of Piers: he begins speaking without its ever having been mentioned that he is present, and then, after only eleven lines, he vanishes again so secretly that no-one knows what has become of him:

> And whanne he hadde worded thus, wiste no man after
> Where Peers Plouhman bycam, so priveliche he wente. (C XVI. 149–50)

These brief appearances of an object felt to be so important are certainly dreamlike, but they are also part of the reason why the dream was found to be such a suitable image for mystical experience. The presence of God to the soul in mystical states is impermanent and unpredictable, like the things seen in a dream. St Bernard writes that

> sleeping in contemplation, [one] dreams of God; yet, as it were, in a glass and darkly, and not as yet face to face. Nevertheless, though he knows God rather by inference and surmise than by distinct view, and though he beholds him only hurriedly as he passes by, as it were by the flash of a tiny spark, yet that momentary vision arouses in him a burning love.[41]

In English, Walter Hilton similarly writes of the 'changeability of absence and presence of Jhesu that a soul feeleth', and quoting John 3:8 ('The Spirit breatheth where he will and thou hearest his voice; but thou knowest not whence he cometh and whither he goeth'), he adds, 'He cometh privily sometimes when thou art least aware of Him...But then He goeth ere thou wit it'[42] And Langland's Dreamer himself, quoting like St Bernard from I Corinthians 13:12 ('We see now through a glass in a dark manner; but then face to face'), tells Anima:

> Clerkis kenne me that Cryst is in alle places;
> Ac I seygh hym nevere sothly but as myself in a miroure,
>   *Ita in enigmate, tunc facie ad faciem.* (B XV. 156–7)
> **kenne** teach

Dream is the mirror in which the soul sees itself, and in itself sees the image of God.

Langland's Followers: 'Mum and the Sothsegger'

Piers Plowman was widely read, and its considerable influence on later writers is not surprising. Some of the works most indebted to it were not dream-poems; such for example was *Pierce the Ploughman's Crede*, which is essentially an anti-mendicant satire. Its narrator shares the experience of Langland's Will, in wandering about seeking for enlightenment from supposed authorities but always being disappointed; but he does not share the agonising uncertainty arising from the problematic, for his 'authorities' are clearly spurious, until he meets Piers, who is now simply a shrewd and honest workman who tells the truth about the friars. Closer to being a dream-poem is *Mum and the Sothsegger*. This survives in two fragments, the first of which, formerly known as *Richard the Redeless* and attributed to Langland himself, was written in 1399–1400, and offers advice to Richard II on kingly behaviour and the causes of his downfall. This is not in dream form, though one passage, apologising for a digression, implies that the writer is still thinking of himself, like Langland, as 'seeing' the content of his poem: he will leave one topic, 'For mater that my mynde is meved in now,... I wolle schewe as I sawe, till I se better' (R III. 2, 5).[43] Another passage also recalls *Piers Plowman*, and at the same time introduces what is to be the major theme of the second fragment. The narrator interrupts his own criticism of Richard by expressing a doubt as to the propriety of displeasing his liege lord:

> But it longith to no liegemen his lord to anoye
> Nother in werk ne in word, but if his witt faile (R II. 67–8)

(But it is not for any vassal to trouble his lord in either deed or word, unless the lord loses his sanity).

But his doubt is answered by Reason, and he proceeds – 'Now for to telle trouthe thus than me thynketh...' (R II. 77). 'To telle trouthe' is precisely the subject of the second fragment, and the poet no doubt had in mind the wish expressed by Langland's Dreamer to disclose to men his dream concerning the covetousness of the friars, and Lewte's assurance that 'It is *licitum* for lewed men to segge the sothe' (B XI. 92).[44]

The second fragment was probably written later, between 1403 and 1406. It argues that the officer the new king, Henry IV, most needs in his household is a 'sothe-sigger' (M 38) (truth-teller), for, though truth is hated and punished, it will eventually outlive falsehood. The poet praises Henry, but fears that evil counsellors may – and at this point 'Mum' (Silence) enters the poem, and cuts him off, saying that, since he knows that truth-tellers are hated, he is a fool to take risks. This incident clearly puts the poet himself on the side of *sothe-sigger*. Mum goes on to advise him to 'Cumpaignye with no *contra* yn no kynnes wise' (M 256); and we are reminded of the inability of Langland's Dreamer to resist saying *contra!* to those who advise him. The poet parts from Mum, and sets off on a quest for the answer to the question whether silence or truth-telling is the best. This is no doubt derived from the quest for Treuthe in *Piers Plowman*, and indeed in *Mum and the Sothsegger* the quest imperceptibly becomes one for the *sothe-sigger* himself. But there has been a reduction in scope: Treuthe for Langland was a name of God, but the later poem is concerned only with *telling* the truth about this world; and there is now no real problem, as there was in *Piers Plowman*, about the justification of the poet's own role, because it is taken for granted that his satires *are* the truth. Only the expediency of truth-telling is now in question.

But, as *Mum and the Sothsegger* proceeds, it is unexpectedly lifted to a higher level, more fully comparable with *Piers Plowman*; and this happens in a dream. The poet wanders about, finding Mum dominant everywhere, and becoming angry and bewildered. At last he comes upon a *sothe-sigger* salving his wounds, and this makes him acknowledge that it is Mum who has the pleasanter life on earth. This depressing insight drives him almost to madness, and, as he lies thinking of his fruitless wanderings, he sleeps and has a dream. The dream is obviously moti-vated by his psychological state; yet at the same time it comes to him as a revelation, which cannot be fully accounted for by his waking state of mind. He defends it in advance by taking his stance with the Scriptural dream-interpreter Daniel as against Cato's scepticism; and once it is over he expands this Scriptural defence of dreams against those who 'savery but lite' (relish but little) of them (M 1309). In the dream he finds himself in a wilderness, climbs a hill, and, looking about him, sees a panoramic view of a countryside, proliferating with natural life, and yet made richer still by human cultivation – reaped cornfields, sheep and cattle, hounds pursuing the hares. Then he moves down into the country setting, amid a 'hevenely' (M 935) chattering of birds – a vestige of the paradisal origins of this scene, which seems indeed a modern Eden before the Fall. He is refreshed by the sweet scents of fruit and flowers, and 'of my travail, treuly, toke I no kepe [care], / For al was vanesshid me fro thorough the fresshe sightes' (M 942–3). His former weariness is transformed into energy, as

> I lepte forth lightly along by the heigges
> And movid forth myrily to maistrie the hilles. (M 881–2)
> *maistrie* overcome

We are convincingly shown to be at a turning-point in the Dreamer's experience, and one which comes to him as an inspiration from outside his conscious mind. The further content of the dream confirms this. He meets a white-clad man, who is ancient, and yet

> Proporcioned at alle poyntes and pithy in his tyme,
> And by his stature right stronge, and stalworth on his dayes. (M 964–5)
> *pithy... tyme* vigorous for his time of life, *stalworth... dayes* sturdy for his age

He is the owner of the dream-garden, and also a bee-keeper, and he explains to the Dreamer how the various estates of bee-society carry out their duties harmoniously under their king, and how he helps them to kill those wasters, the drones. It is evident that the dream is an *oraculum*, in which the bee-keeper is the 'pious or revered man' who conveys valuable truths to the Dreamer. And, by one of those twists in meaning which we have come to expect of dream-poems, the Dreamer hints that the account of bee-keeping has an allegorical significance, but is able to use the fact that it is in a dream as an excuse for professing not to understand it himself:

> For hit hath muche menyng, whoso muse couthe,
> But hit is to mistike for me, by Marie of hevene. (M 1088–9)
>
> *muse* ponder; *mistike* mystical/misty

The poet who stands behind the Dreamer is thus enabled both to indicate the implications for the human commonwealth of the killing of the drones – then perhaps England would be a garden as paradisal as that over which the bee-keeper rules – and to absolve himself of responsibility for these implications.

The account of the bees thus tells a truth about society, only in a concealed form; and this raises once more the question of silence or truth-telling which has dominated the Dreamer's waking life. The Dreamer asks the bee-keeper who should have the mastery, 'Mum or the sothe-sigger' (M 1102), saying that if he agrees with everyone else that Mum should be master, then he will abandon his quest. But the bee-keeper praises him for 'thy seching...And thy travail for thy trouthe' (M 1111–12), and assures him that if he follows the *sothe-sigger* he will eventually receive God's reward. The Dreamer thanks him for resolving his doubt; but he still does not know where to find the *sothe-sigger*. The old man's answer takes us back to Langland, to Piers's promise that 'Thow shalt se Treuthe himself wel sitte in thin herte' (A vi. 93):

> Yn manis herte his housing is, as hooly writte techet,
> And mynde is his mansion that made alle th'estres.
> There feoffed hym his Fadre freely forto dwelle,
> And put hym in possession in paradise terrestre
> Yn Adam oure auncetre and al his issue after. (M 1224–8)
>
> *his...estres* the dwelling of Him who made all its rooms; *feoffed hym* put him in possession

Let the Dreamer go there quickly: he will find the truth-teller's house always open, and can easily 'have concours to Criste and come yn agaynes' (M 1245), because 'trouthe and the Trinite been two nygh frendes' (M 1248). It is fully appropriate that it should be in a dream that this poet comes nearest to Langland's identification of truth with God, whose image is imprinted in the human soul. But still, for the later poet, truth is only close to God, not identified with him. The bee-keeper now says he must depart, and he tells the Dreamer to write down what he has learned when he wakes up:

> Sith thou felys the fressh, lete no feynt herte
> Abate thy blessid bisynes of thy boke-making. (M 1280–1)
> *the* thyself

There is no trace here of Langland's doubts about the value of his 'meddling with makings': the dream justifies the poet's claim to be a truth-teller, and it is able to do so precisely because for him truth, even at its highest, means no more than telling the truth about society, and he can therefore be confident of achieving it.

The remainder of the second fragment, after this section in which the dream-setting really corresponds to a heightened inspiration in the poet, is a disappointment. The poet, having awakened, takes confidence from the old man's words, and announces that he will open up his bag of books, 'Of vice and of vertue fulle to the margyn' (M 1346), in order to counsel the king. What follows consists of summaries of the contents of these imaginary books – that is, of a whole collection of miscellaneous satires, against ecclesiastical corruption, rumour-mongering, litigiousness, the greed of great lords, and so on. These, it is claimed, form a 'newe salve' (M 1339) for the wounds of the land, which the *sothe-sigger* has long been seeking, and which Mum and his followers had carried off. But ultimately the dream has been used as an excuse for the collapse of literary form into a mere catalogue. In this section of the poem (which has come down to us in an incomplete form) there is no personal quest, as there was in *Piers Plowman* and in the earlier part of the fragment, because the poet's mind has been set at rest by his dream. There is therefore nothing to link together the various satires, and no reason within itself why the list should ever conclude.

'Death and Life'

Only one work by a follower of Langland is fully a dream-poem. This is *Death and Life*, the date of which is uncertain, because it survives only in a seventeenth-century manuscript, but which perhaps comes from the early fifteenth century. It clearly derives from the fourteenth-century tradition of alliterative dream-poems, but it also looks further back among visionary writings, to Alanus's *De Planctu Naturae*. It reads like a work at the end of a tradition, in the sense that it offers no possibilities for further development, but its author shows himself a real poet in his

combination, modification and development of earlier motifs. It opens
with a brief prologue, which assumes the position adopted at the end
of *The Parliament of the Three Ages* and *Piers Plowman*, and in innumerable other medieval poems, that death conquers all things:

> For boldnesse of body, nor blythenesse of hart,
> Coninge of clearkes, ne cost upon earth,
> But all wasteth away, and worthes to nought,
> When Death driveth att the doere, with his darts keene. (7–10)[45]
>
> *cost* quality; *worthes to* turns into

But beyond death's triumph lies the possibility of salvation through the
'royall red blood' of Christ (4). The dream confirms and amplifies this
accepted truth. It is given no psychological context, and the Dreamer
himself plays no part in it except as an excited observer and enquirer;
and neither his role as poet or dreamer nor the status of the dream itself
is ever called in question. If one had to categorize it, it would no doubt
be as a *somnium coeleste*; but the question is never raised. The poem's
essential action takes place not in the personal consciousness of the
Dreamer, but between the two allegorical figures seen in the dream.

Exactly as in *Winner and Waster*, *The Parliament of the Three Ages*, and
Piers Plowman, the waking poet wanders through a paradisal landscape,
falls asleep in it, and in his dream finds himself in this world, not some
other. He is on a mountain – a frequent symbol of spiritual elevation
– from which he can see spread out all 'The world full of welth, winlye
[joyful] to behold' (45). The poet may be remembering a line from
the opening of *Piers Plowman*, where the Dreamer sees 'Al the welthe
of this worlde and the woo bothe' (C I. 10); but if so, the absence of *woo*
from his vision is significant. For Langland, the woe of the world, as its
pairing with wealth suggests, notably includes poverty, and a fundamental problem of life, though not its ultimate problem, is the provision
of material necessities: it is our need for bread that gives meaning to
the saying that man does not live by bread alone. This dimension of
earthly experience is missing from *Death and Life*. The world that the
Dreamer sees is summarized as follows:

> Both of woods and wasts, and walled townes,
> Comelye castles and cleare, with carven towers,
> Parkes and pallaces, and pastures full many, (42–4)

and similarly the people he sees in it make up

> a seemelye sight
> Of comely kings full keene, and knights full noble;
> Princes in the presse, proudlye attyred;

Dukes that were doughtye, and many deere erles;
Sweeres and swaynes, that swarmed full thicke. (50–4)
presse throng; *deere* noble; *sweeres* squires

The preponderance of nobility and gentry over *swaynes* is noticeable. This is an aristocratic world, perhaps created by a poet writing, as Langland was not, for an aristocratic audience. Hence it is a far simpler world than that of Langland's poem, but the simplification serves the poet's purpose by emphasizing the power of death even over such fortunate creatures.

Beyond this noble company, the Dreamer sees Dame Life coming towards him. She is gorgeously dressed, kings and princes kneel to her, and her attendants are courtly personifications, such as Sir Comfort, Sir Love, and Sir Curtesye. But she is associated not only with the aristocratic order but also, more forcibly, with the natural order. She comes with light out of the east; she is dominant (we learn later) about midday; and it is not only nobles who bow to her, but trees, plants and flowers, as she, in effect, causes spring to come:

the boughes eche one
They lowted to that Ladye and layd forth their branches;
Blossomes and burgens breathed full sweete;
Flowers flourished in the frith, where shee forth stepedd;
And the grasse that was gray greened belive. (69–73)
lowted bowed; *burgens* buds; *frith* wood

Her clothing is green, but her breasts are naked, because she is the universal mother. It has been pointed out that Life derives from Alanus's Natura,[46] and just as Natura's chariot is divinely guided, so we are told of Life that 'the crowne on her head was carven in heaven' (95). Sir Comfort identifies the lady for the Dreamer, and tells him that 'Shee hath fostered and fed thee sith thou was first borne' (127).

Time is passing; at two o'clock a great horn-blast is heard from the north, and Life's ugly counterpart Death appears, described in grotesque detail, so hideous that the Dreamer says that he would have died at the sight of her if Sir Comfort had not assisted him. She grinds to powder the grass that has renewed its colour at Life's approach, the leaves fall, and she is followed by appropriate personifications such as Pryde, Envye, Morninge, 'Sorrow and Sicknesse and Sikinge [Sighing] in Hart' (187). She shoots her arrows at the 'heard' who have welcomed Life, as if she were a hunter and they were deer, and instantly kills them; we may recall the association of hunting with death in *The Parliament of the Three Ages*. At this, Life cries for help to 'the hye King of heaven' (212), and he responds 'hendlye' (213) (courteously) by sending

'Countenance' (Continence?) to tell Death to stop. Death reluctantly obeys; and thus, somewhat as in *Winner and Waster*, what was to have been a battle turns into a disputation between two personified principles. The fundamental idea of a battle between Life and Death is found in the liturgy, but the immediate source is almost certainly *Piers Plowman* B XVIII, where Death threatens to 'fordo and adown brynge / Al that lyveth or loketh in londe or in watere' (29–30), and Life promises to defend human souls from the devil and to 'forbete and adown brynge bale and deth for evere' (35). Further reminiscences of this part of *Piers Plowman* occur later in *Death and Life*. Life begins the disputation by asking why Death, following 'neither reason nor right' (238), destroys what God has created:

> How keepes thou his comandements, thou kaytiffe retch?
> Wheras banely hee them blessed, and biddeth them thrive,
> Waxe forth in the word and worth unto manye? (264–8)
>
> *banely* willingly; *word* world; *worth. . . manye* multiply

Death's answer is that she *is* acting according to 'reason and right' (260):

> I wold have kept the commandement of the hye king of heaven,
> But the bearne itt brake that thou bred up first (264–5)
>
> *bearne* man

– Adam and Eve ate the forbidden fruit, and Death rightfully punished them and all their descendents, and would willingly attack Life herself.

Life answers that Death's threats are vain, for 'I am grounded in God, and grow for ever more' (289) – which seems to imply that her scope is wider than that of Alanus's Natura – and, continuing the poem's aristocratic assumptions, she asks why Death 'uncurteouslye' (297) breaks up happy families, who deserve no punishment. Death replies that she is needed to prevent mankind from pride and sin. She has defeated all men; and she gives a catalogue reminiscent of the lists of those overcome by death in *The Parliament of the Three Ages*, including Jews, a pagan (Alexander), and Christians, and finally Jesus:

> Have not I justed gentlye with Jesu of heaven?
> He was frayd of my face in freshest of time,
> Yett I knocked him on the crosse and carved throughe his hart. (345–7)
>
> *freshest of time* prime of life

The crucifixion as a knightly tournament is probably borrowed from *Piers Plowman* (though the theme is found elsewhere), and, as in Langland's poem, the piercing of Jesus's heart by Longeus is seen as the culmination of the jousting. But the *Death and Life* poet goes further than Langland in representing all of Christ's torments as carried out by

Death herself. However, even in claiming to have defeated Jesus, Death doffs her crown and kneels; and so does Life. Life summons her company to listen, and then turns to Death and points out that she did not really defeat Jesus, but, 'When the glory of his godhead glented [shone] in thy face' (384), her falchion dropped from her hand and she retreated to hell to defend it against him. The defence of hell against the approach of Christ is again borrowed from *Piers Plowman*. Jesus raised up Life, and, 'all wounded as hee was' (402), cast light into hell's darkness, broke open its gates and bound Lucifer. He released the patriarchs, and promised Life that 'never danger of death shold me deere [harm] after' (426). Life assures her 'deare children' (438) that Death shall not harm them if they love Jesus, are baptized, and believe in the creed:

> Death was damnde that day, daring full still;
> Shee hath no might ne no maine to meddle with yonder ost
> Against Everlasting Liffe, that Ladye so true. (441–3)
> *daring* hiding

Thus the meaning of Life is explicitly extended from that of Alanus's Natura to take in life everlasting.

The vision marks a development in understanding, which comes to the Dreamer from outside himself, and which by now has exhausted him. Life blesses her company with the sign of the cross, raises up the dead, and goes over the hills followed by them:

> I wold have followed on that faire, but no further I might;
> What with wandred and with woe, I waked belive. (450–1)
> *faire* journey; *wandred* misery

Thus the dream images the Resurrection, but the Dreamer, like so many medieval dreamers, has not the spiritual capacity to enter the realm of eternal values in this life. He wakes, and the poem ends with a brief prayer. If we allow for the fact that its text has been much modernized and distorted in the course of transmission, *Death and Life* is a remarkable witness to the continuing vitality of the tradition of alliterative dream-poems in the later medieval period. The Dreamer's part has lost its earlier importance, but the vision he sees is dense, complexly organized and penetrating. In our final chapter we shall see how, in metrical verse too, the dream-poem remained a living literary form long after the fourteenth century.

4
THE CHAUCERIAN TRADITION

It is well known that Chaucer's work was a powerful and pervasive influence on the English and Scottish poets of the fifteenth century; and this is as true of dream-poems as it is of other literary kinds. But in the dream-poem, as in Chaucerianism generally, there is an important distinction to be drawn between those writers who understood what Chaucer was doing in his work and those who did not. The former responded to the creative principles of Chaucer's dream-poems, imitated those, and sometimes took them further in directions implied but not completed by Chaucer's work; the latter – a far more numerous class – imitated only the external forms of his poems, without responding to their inner spirit. Here I must be selective; and in any case there would be little profit in discussing most of the unintelligent or mediocre Chaucerian imitations. It is the intelligent ones that provide the best poems, and also, incidentally, help us best to understand what Chaucer was doing in his dream-poetry. To read Chaucer through the eyes of an intelligent late-medieval poet, who studied him not in an academic spirit but as a master who could point out new creative possibilities, can be an illuminating experience. But it will be right to look briefly at unintelligent imitation of Chaucer, partly because it was so sadly common, and partly to throw into relief the rare achievement of those poets who penetrated more deeply into Chaucer's dream-poems.

Lydgate: 'The Temple of Glass'

I begin, therefore, with one poem by Chaucer's most devoted and prolific English imitator, John Lydgate. It is *The Temple of Glass*, which has the particular interest of being a very early example of Chaucerianism, dating from the first years of the fifteenth century, just after Chaucer's death. In this poem the narrator falls asleep on a moonlit December night, and has a dream. In the first part of the dream, he finds himself near a temple of glass. Inside it he sees images of suffering lovers, and a beautiful lady praying before a statue of Venus. The lady explains to the goddess that she is bound to one man, but really loves another; the goddess answers that her unhappiness will end, and promises to ensure that the person she loves will love her in return. In the second part of the dream, the Dreamer leaves the temple and finds a melancholy man praying to Venus in an oratory, and telling her that he has long loved a lady, who apparently knows nothing of his love. Venus tells him that he must declare his love to the lady, and promises to help him. In the third part, with devastating predictability, the Dreamer goes back into the temple, and sees the man address the lady. She accepts his service, and Venus binds their hearts together with a golden chain, and gives them good counsel. The union is celebrated by the Muses, Orpheus and Amphion, and the noise of their music awakens the Dreamer, who dedicates his book to his lady. That is a skeleton summary of a poem of 1,403 lines, but it does not leave out much of the poem's action, because there is not much action in it.

The Temple of Glass is full of Chaucerian reminiscences, both explicit and implicit. Among the explicit ones are references to Alcestis, Griselda, Palamon and Arcite 'as Chaucer tellith us' (110),[1] and the characters of *The Squire's Tale*, all in the description of the decorations of the temple. There are also references by Venus to Griselda (again) and Dorigen, as *exempla* of how happiness is all the more pleasing if it follows misery. These explicit references are mostly to *The Canterbury Tales*; more interesting for our purposes are the implicit allusions, which are mainly to Chaucer's dream-poems. For example, the opening on a December night recalls that of *The House of Fame*. Next we are told that the narrator was suffering from melancholy, and was at first unable to sleep, which recalls the melancholy and insomnia of *The Book of the Duchess*. The initial vision of the temple of glass recalls the temple of Venus at the beginning of the dream in *The House of Fame*, and Lydgate's temple is standing on 'a craggy roche, / Like ise ifrore' (19–20), which reminds us of how Fame's castle was standing on 'a roche of yse' (1130). When Lydgate comes to describe his temple of Venus, there are also reminiscences of the temple of Venus and Priapus in *The Parliament of Fowls*, with its array of suffering lovers. The melancholy lover whom Lydgate's Dreamer sees in the oratory irresistibly recalls the Black Knight in *The Book of the Duchess*, though there are also touches of Troilus when he laments that his previous freedom has given way to bondage to love. When the Dreamer wakes, he regrets losing the sight of the lady in his dream, and vows that for her sake he will compose 'A litil tretise...In prais of women' (1380–1), and this reminds us of the purported origin of *The Legend of Good Women* in a dream. The regret at the loss of his vision of the lady when the dream is over perhaps suggests not Chaucer but *Pearl*. Lydgate, like the *Pearl*-poet, describes his dream as an *avisioun* (1374), and at the beginning of the *Temple* there is described a landscape of painful brilliance like the dream-landscape in *Pearl*:

> And as I did approche,
> Again the sonne that shone, me thought, so clere
> As eny cristal, and ever nere and nere
> As I gan neigh this grisli dredful place,
> I wex astonyed: the light so in my face
> Bigan to smyte, so persing ever in one
> On evere part, where that I gan gone,
> That I ne myght nothing, as I would,
> Abouten me considre and bihold. (20–28)

ever in one continuously

There can be no doubt whatever that Lydgate was well read in Chaucer; it is less likely that he knew *Pearl*, though he was probably familiar with some of its sources and analogues in visionary writing. But, in any case, all these recollections of fourteenth-century poetry relate only to externals. Lydgate is attracted by pictureque details, such as the December night with the 'pale light' of the moon darkened by 'a mysty cloude' (4, 9), or the rock of ice first glittering in the sun and then made more tolerable by a passing cloud 'With wind ichaced' (31). But he is interested in such things simply for their own sake, as a magpie is attracted by anything shiny, and it is hard to believe that the local details are governed by any larger scheme of significance. In *The Parliament of Fowls* we found that Chaucer was employing in a poem the very manner of 'thinking' that is found in dreams – thinking through sequences of concrete images – but I do not believe that the picturesque details of *The Temple of Glass* have any such purpose. In *The House of Fame*, the fact that Fame's castle was on a hill of ice had a symbolic significance – the way to fame is slippery and insecure, and one cannot be sure that a name inscribed there will not melt away – but in the *Temple* the rock of ice seems to be there simply because Lydgate had liked it in Chaucer and wanted to add to the glittery effect of his own poem.

Another way in which Lydgate shows a failure to grasp what is really happening in fourteenth-century dream-poems is in his treatment of the narrator. Lydgate was a monk at Bury St Edmund's, and though a number of his poems, including possibly this one, were commissioned by the court or by aristocratic patrons, he appears never to have written, as Chaucer did, for a courtly audience with whom he was in intimate contact. It was thus never necessary for him to project himself into his own poems, as a naive dreamer who is also an inexperienced lover and an incompetent poet; and it appears to me that Lydgate was completely insensitive to this aspect of Chaucer's poetry. He begins *The Temple of Glass*, as we have seen, by presenting himself as melancholy and unable to sleep, but there is no indication that the narrator's psychology influences the content of his dream. Lydgate was not interested in the way dreams may reflect the state of mind and point of view of their dreamers, and he therefore provides neither the psychological interest of the *somnium animale* nor the structural reflections and distortions to which this gives rise in Chaucer. Norton-Smith argues that a recurrent theme of the poem is the doctrine of contraries: we only know what something (such as love, or the sun) is really like by experiencing its opposite (frustration, or a cloud).[2] This has some truth, but there is no reason to associate the theme with the Dreamer. Within the dream he plays no part: he does not participate in an encounter with some authoritative figure, as in all of Chaucer's dream-poems, nor are we even made aware of his helplessness in relation to his dream-experience (he is not seized by an eagle or thrust forcibly through a gate). He is merely an observer, before whom the dream unfolds itself as a kind of pageant. It may well be that one part of the poem does express Lydgate's own views – that is, where the 'mani a thousand of lovers' (144) lamenting in Venus's temple are said to include those who were entered into religious orders in their youth, and who must now hide their true feelings. This was Lydgate's own situation, and, whether or not he personally had any feelings to hide, he must at least have known more about this situation from personal experience than he did about most of those with which he deals in his work. It is not, I think, mere sentimentality that makes one detect more feeling and better poetry in this passage than in most other parts of the *Temple*:

> And right anon I herd othir crie
> With sobbing teris and with ful pitous soune,
> Tofore the goddes, bi lamentacioun,
> That conseiles in hir tender youthe
> And in childhode (as it is ofte couthe)
> Yrendred were into religioun
> Or thei hade yeris of discresioun,
> That al her lif cannot but complein,
> In wide copis perfeccion to feine:
> Ful covertli to curen al hir smert
> And shew the contrarie outward of her hert. (196–206)
>
> *goddes* goddess; *conseiles* unadvised; *couthe* known; *Or* before; *curen* cover; *smert* pain

But that passage has little to do with the rest of the poem.

In view of all this, it might well be asked why Lydgate put the events of his poem into a dream at all. The most obvious reason is that it was because Chaucer had done so; but it must be added that a dream was the obvious 'excuse' for a poet to describe some scene which would be impossible in waking life. If the temple and what happens in it had to be described as being seen by someone, then it is difficult to imagine who that someone could have been other than a dreamer. But, of course, there was no compelling need for them to be described as part of what someone saw; this method was taken over inertly by Lydgate because it had not occurred to him that, in a poem of this kind, instead of writing 'I saw a temple of glass', one could simply write 'There was a temple of glass'. He assumed that non-historical landscapes, events and speeches needed to be authenticated by being introduced through a personal observer; but, on the other hand, he had given no thought to the status of that observer, either in relation to what he observed or in relation to the audience for whom he was describing it. Even Chaucer sometimes slips into the assumption that, when a symbolic setting is being described, there must be someone present to see it. For example, *The Knight's Tale* as a whole is a third-person narrative, which is not supposed to be based on its teller's personal experience; but, when he gets to the elaborate description of the temple of Mars, the Knight automatically finds himself saying, 'Ther saugh *I* first the derke ymaginyng / Of Felonye...' (*Canterbury Tales* I [A]. 1995–6). In Chaucer, this is a rare lapse; a similar inadvertency forms the whole substance of Lydgate's poem.

Lydgate has the further excuse, however, that the story he has to tell, such as it is, is apparently intended as an allegory, which requires some form of interpretation. If dreams are usually thought to have hidden meanings, there is an obvious case for presenting such a story as a dream. The chief indication that *The Temple of Glass* has some allegorical element (beyond the use of gods and temples as means of conveying ideas indirectly) comes in the poem's closing lines, where Lydgate, with characteristic imprecision, appears to be dimly hinting that the lady to whom he is dedicating the poem is the same as the lady seen in his dream. He begs her to accept the poem as it is,

> Til I have leiser unto hir heigh renoun
> Forto expoune my foreseid visioun,
> And tel in plein the significaunce. (1388–90)

The vision, then, has a *significaunce* which is not plain as it stands. The poem may possibly have been commissioned for a wedding, in which case the man and woman in the dream presumably stand for the couple to be married; though, if the lady had really been waiting long years for her first husband to die so that she could marry the man she really loved, it is difficult to believe that this would have been indicated so clearly in the poem. The problem of the dream's *significaunce* seems insoluble. Perhaps indeed Lydgate wished only to give his poem an air of importance by pretending that it alluded to some intriguing real-life situation. In this case, the dream-setting would be little more than an apology for not clarifying something that was not capable of being made clear. If so, it would be in keeping with his general treatment of the dream as providing a world in which intellectual distinctions are blurred in order to give titillating pictorial and emotional effects. The pagan goddess Venus promises the lady that eventually her sufferings will come to an end, her 'purgatorie' will cease, and she will 'forth-lyve in glorie' (375–6). It appears then that Venus must be seen as standing for a love endorsed by heaven, and indeed she has earlier been connected with 'hevenli fire of love that is eterne' (327). But what the lady is praying for, and Venus is promising, is in effect that her lawful husband will be disposed of, presumably by death, so that she can marry someone else. The poem offers a mixture of religiosity and illicit passion, which will give the desired emotional satisfaction only if we allow ourselves not so much to dream as to daydream.

Clanvowe: ' The Cuckoo and the Nightingale'

A considerable proportion of dream-poetry in the Chaucerian tradition might better be called daydream-poetry; and indeed it is not uncommon for such poems to open with a description not of sleep but of a state between sleep and waking. In one of the earliest dream-poems written under Chaucer's influence, and indeed during his lifetime, Sir John Clanvowe's *The Cuckoo and the Nightingale*,[3] we are actually told that the dream which forms the main substance of the poem came to the narrator when he was 'Not al on slepe, ne fully wakynge' (88).[4] Such an admission seems to imply the abandonment of all symbolic possibilities for sleeping and dreaming, and to reduce the dream to a mere Macrobian *phantasma*; and superficially at least *The Cuckoo and the Nightingale* may appear to be as much a case of loosely associative Chaucerian imitation as *The Temple of Glass*. It opens with a direct quotation from *The Knight's Tale*, and goes on to recount a dream of debate among the birds, obviously deriving from *The Parliament of Fowls*. Though the dream occurs in May, the Dreamer mentions St Valentine's day (the date of Chaucer's *Parliament*), and he is awakened, like Chaucer's Dreamer, by the noise of birdsong in his dream. Again, Clanvowe is probably recalling the *Prologue* to *The Legend of Good Women* when he makes the nightingale advise the Dreamer to 'Goo loke upon the fresshe flour daysye' (243) every day, to obtain relief from the pains of love. *The Cuckoo and the Nightingale* has generally been regarded as conventionally Chaucerian, in a way that would not serve to distinguish it from Lydgate's poem. A representative judgment is this: 'It follows the familiar pattern . . . There is little here that is new, and the poet excites little surprise by his handling of the theme. . . There is, however, a certain freshness in the way that the poet extols the May morning. . .'[5] In fact, however, Clanvowe's response to Chaucer is a great deal more intelligent than Lydgate's. Clanvowe plays the game of the Chaucerian dream-poem, but (partly perhaps because he was a contemporary and wrote for the same court audience) he does so with a far better understanding than most fifteenth-century poets had of the finer points of its rules.[6]

The role adopted by Clanvowe as narrator is one established by the Chaucerian dream-poem, though subtly different from that adopted by Chaucer himself. Chaucer's dream-poems assume a crucial distinction between the members of his courtly audience, who know love from experience, and the poet, whose task it is to write about love, but who knows it only from books. Clanvowe, a member of a knightly family and himself a courtier, aligns himself as narrator and dreamer with those who are experienced in love, and who can therefore speak of it 'of felyng'. On the other hand, he too is separated from the successful practice of love, by being old. (He was in his late forties when he wrote *The Cuckoo and the Nightingale*, but the role of the aged lover also belongs to a literary convention, and is found for example in Gower's *Confessio Amantis*, by which Clanvowe may have been influenced.) He explains that in May, the season of love, all true lovers are stirred by new feelings, and feelings of a mixed kind, 'Other to joy, or elles to morenynge' (24). And for himself, he continues,

> I speke this of felyng, trewely;
> For, al thogh I be olde and unlusty,
> Yet have I felt of that sekenes in May
> Bothe hote and colde, an accesse every day,
> How sore, ywis, ther wot no wight but I. (36–40)
>
> *accesse* fever

In the particular May to which the poem refers, he was 'shaken with the feveres white' (41) by love; and as he lay sleepless in bed he remembered the lovers' saying that it was better to hear the nightingale than the cuckoo. This is presumably part of the light-hearted courtly mythology, to which belong also the cult of the daisy, the opposition of flower and leaf, the custom of riding out a-maying, and so on. The nightingale is traditionally the bird of true love, while the cuckoo, with its jeering cry and its association with cuckoldry, represents a more cynical attitude. And so, early in the morning on 3 May – the day when Arcite in *The Knight's Tale* rode out to 'doon his observaunce' (*Canterbury Tales* A [1] 1500), and a date which may have had some special significance, perhaps as a day of ill luck, in the courtly calendar – the narrator walks out into a paradisal spring landscape, a flowery meadow, full of singing birds, with a river flowing past with a noise 'Acordaunt to the foules ermonye' (83). There he falls asleep, and dreams that he hears the cuckoo singing – it was evidently a token of misfortune in love to hear the cuckoo first. So he curses it, and then hears the nightingale, which he welcomes, adding that he wishes the cuckoo might be burnt.

He goes on:

> But now I wil yow tel a wonder thinge:
> As longe as I lay in that swonynge,
> Me thoght I wist al that the briddes ment,
> And what they seyde, and what was her entente,
> And of her speche I had good knowynge. (106–10)

One function of the dream, then, is to mark off the element of fantasy or fiction in this courtly poem; the birds in the dream are singing in the same meadow as in real life, but only in the dream can the narrator understand what they are saying. What the nightingale is saying, as we might expect, simply reflects the narrator's own attitudes; and she tells the cuckoo to go away because his song is so disagreeable. The cuckoo answers that his song may not be the 'nyse, queynte crie'[7] (123) of the nightingale, but at least it is 'bothe trewe and pleyn' (118). The nightingale explains that her cry of 'ocy! ocy!' means 'kill! kill!' – may all those who speak against love be shamefully slain; and, she goes on, all those who do not intend to devote their lives to love ought also to be killed. Not a very tolerant view, one may well think; and, to our surprise perhaps, the cuckoo's reaction is more civilized, and has an attractive humour:

> 'Ey!' quoth the Cukkow, 'this is a queynt lawe,
> That eyther shal I love, or elles be slawe!' (136–7)

The cuckoo goes on to argue that the life of lovers is wretched, and that he himself does not intend either to die or, while he lives, to love. At this the nightingale is deeply shocked, and she replies in a speech praising the courtly virtues of which love is the source in 'every wight that gentil ys of kynde' (150). Once more, the cuckoo's answer is less extreme, and has an authoritative sobriety and clarity of definition:

> Nyghtyngale, thou spekest wonder faire,
> But, for al that, the sothe is the contreyre;
> For loving is in yonge folk but rage,
> And in olde hit is a grete dotage. (166–9)
>
> *rage* madness

We remember that the narrator is himself an old man. The cuckoo concludes by an *argumentum ad avem*: if the nightingale herself leaves her mate for more than a moment, she will be deserted by him, and then her song will agree with the cuckoo's. The nightingale speaks of the joy love sends to those who please him; the cuckoo replies that 'Love hath no reson but his wille' (197), and that he rewards or punishes his servants quite arbitrarily, 'For he is blynde, and may not se' (202). At this the nightingale is so upset that she cannot speak another word for anger, and she calls on the God of Love himself to help avenge her on the cuckoo. It is not the God, though, who intervenes. It is the Dreamer, who shares the nightingale's views so completely that he rushes to the river, picks up a stone, throws it at the cuckoo, and chases him off.[8]

This moment at which the Dreamer intervenes in his own dream and plays god, whilst the God of Love does nothing, is amusing, and in a subtler way, perhaps, than has been generally recognized. The standard view of this poem is that it is simply a celebration of the courtly idealization of love. One recent scholar, for example, has classed *The Cuckoo and the Nightingale* along with a whole group of other 'Chaucerian' poems, remarking that 'They are love poems, and the love they celebrate is exquisite, refined and ennobling'.[9] As applied to *The Cuckoo and the Nightingale*, this would mean that the poem endorses the nightingale's view of the nature of love. The Dreamer's intervention on the nightingale's behalf might be taken to confirm that view. But this would be so only if we failed to recognize that the Dreamer is not the same as the poet. Clanvowe has responded intelligently to the characterization of the dreamer in Chaucer. The aged lover who is the poem's narrator is a violent partisan on behalf of that very God of Love of whose cruelty his own life gives evidence; and his inability to tolerate an opposite point of view, like the nightingale's similar intolerance, only proves the truth of the cuckoo's assertion that 'Love hath no reson but his wille'.

The remainder of the poem helps to make this clear. The nightingale is grateful to the Dreamer for helping her, and promises him that, though he has heard the cuckoo first this year, next year she will see that it is different – so long as she is not 'affrayed' (235). She counsels him never to believe what the cuckoo says, and he answers,

> 'Nay,' quoth I, 'ther shal no thing me bring
> Fro love; and yet he doth me mekil wo.' (239–40)

The nightingale sings a song to comfort him; and, once more, it turns out not to be a joyful celebration of love, but an execration of love's enemies: 'I shrewe hem al that be to Love untrewe!' (250). Before leaving the Dreamer, she expresses on his behalf a wish whose ambiguity he evidently fails to notice:

> And God of Love, that can ryght wel and may,
> As mekil joy sende yow this day
> As ever yet he eny lover sende! (253–5)

Finally, the nightingale flies off to the other birds to beg them to do her justice against 'that foule, fals, unkynde bridde' (270), the cuckoo. They, however, are unwilling to condemn the cuckoo in his absence, and they summon a parliament, to take place

> Before the chambre-wyndow of the Quene
> At Wodestok, upon the grene lay. (284–5)
> *lay* meadow

This deft courtly compliment, which leaves it to the audience, including perhaps the queen herself, to decide which bird is in the right, may have a concealed cutting-edge. The date fixed for this 'parliament of fowls' is not, as in Chaucer's poem, St Valentine's day, but the day after; by when, one may suppose, the married birds will be less intoxicated by love. The nightingale flies up into a hawthorn and sings a last song, so loudly that the Dreamer wakes. Even that song holds an ambiguity which is potentially damaging to the doctrine of idealized love. It consists of a single line: 'Terme of lyve, Love hath withholde me' (289). The word *withholde* might imply that the nightingale was one of Love's retainers; but it could also imply that she was kept in prison or bondage by Love, in which case 'Terme of lyve' would imply a term of imprisonment – a life-sentence.

The Cuckoo and the Nightingale is only 290 lines long, but, on its miniature scale, it indicates a sensitive reading by Clanvowe of Chaucer's dream-poems, and a lively understanding of the irony they persistently direct against the dreamer-narrator, by making the poem express only his personal, biased point of view, even while it implies the possibility of other points of view. Behind Chaucer, Clanvowe is looking back to the *Roman de la Rose*, with its opposition between love and reason, and its offering to the Dreamer of an insight into the true nature of Love's service, which he is too blind to accept or even recognize. But it is not entirely a backward-looking poem; it seems likely that the violence of the antagonism which the nightingale expresses against all who fail to worship Love in the orthodox courtly fashion may reflect the increasing bitterness of religious controversy in late fourteenth-century England. Clanvowe himself was associated with the group of 'Lollard knights', and is also known as the author of a religious tract which shows some sympathy with Lollardy.[10] It is not expressly heretical, but at least Clanvowe must have known what it was like to be a supporter (like the cuckoo) of views which were opposed and persecuted by religious orthodoxy. His Dreamer wishes to have the cuckoo burnt; and though the first burnings of Lollards for heresy were not to take place until 1401, after Clanvowe's death, the poem's poise was perhaps already somewhat difficult to maintain. For him, things may already have moved on since Chaucer, in the *Prologue* to the *Legend*, had been arraigned for heresy against the religion of love, but had suffered no worse punishment than the penance of writing tales of Love's martyrs. Clanvowe, then, was not simply imitating Chaucer; he had a real grasp of the dynamic of the Chaucerian dream-poem, and was able to apply in a new way the dramatization of the dreamer as a character at least intermittently separate from the poet. Clanvowe's Dreamer is not reluctantly snatched up or shoved into dream-experience by an authoritative guide, but intervenes most eagerly in the action of his Dream, when he stones the cuckoo; yet that very eagerness shows how little he understands of what his dream has to tell him. It was to be a long time before another English follower of Chaucer was to see so fully the implications of his master's reshaping of the dream-poem. Perhaps no other English poet before Skelton was a really intelligent reader of Chaucer's dream-poetry.

'The Kingis Quair'

In Scotland, however, the situation was different; there a number of poets were able to make a genuinely creative use of Chaucer's achievement in dream-poetry. The earliest Scottish dream-poem is *The Kingis Quair*, which has been widely attributed to King James I of Scotland, and probably dates from 1424. The attribution to James has been contested, but it is accepted by both the poem's most recent editors, and their views are followed here.[11] Like English dream-poems of the same period, it is deeply influenced by Chaucer, and also probably by Lydgate, especially his *Temple of Glass*. But it is a greatly superior poem to any of Lydgate's, and shows, even amid a certain confusion, a far deeper understanding than he ever does of what Chaucer was doing in his dream-poems. One indication of this may be mentioned now. I have argued that a crucial feature of Chaucer's dream-poems is the ambiguous nature of the dream itself, which might be either a heavenly vision of truth or a mere fantasy reflecting the dreamer's own psychological state. Just this ambiguity is stated in *The Kingis Quair*, when the dream is over and the Dreamer asks himself, 'quhare hath my spirit be?' (1222), and goes on to state the alternatives:

> Is this of my forethoght impressioun,
> Or is it from the hevin a visioun? (1224–5)
>
> *Is this...impressioun* Is this a reflection of my previous thoughts

In this poem, unlike Chaucer's, the question receives an answer. The Dreamer proceeds to beg the gods to give him some further sign if his dream truly comes from them, and at that moment a white dove flies through the window and alights on his hand, carrying in its beak a spray of gillyflowers, which have written on them in gold a messsage of hope, confirming the dream's truth. That certainty, of course, is unChaucerian; but it derives from a clear understanding of the significance of Chaucerian uncertainty.

The Kingis Quair is a substantial poem, of 1,379 lines, and it follows the Chaucerian model in embedding the dream elaborately in the Dreamer's waking life – so much so that the dream forms less than half the poem. Indeed, one might wonder whether this is a dream-poem at all, rather than, like Henryson's *Testament of Cresseid*, a narrative which includes a dream as an important episode. I suspect that James himself had not seen any need to make up his mind about this. He begins with a description of his insomnia at night, relieved by the reading of a book – Boethius, *De Consolatione* – and we naturally expect this to be the prologue to a dream. But in fact the first 133 lines of the poem are the prologue to an explanation of how he came to write a *buke* (91) telling the story of his own life; and it is that story which contains the dream, which does not begin until line 512. Thus the dream is doubly enclosed, and we become aware of it as a highly specialized area of imaginative fiction; but only at the price of a disturbing uncertainty, which continues later. The role established for the narrator in this prologue to the poem is different from Chaucer's. Like Clanvowe, this narrator is an aristocrat, and in reality probably even a king, and there can be no question therefore of his not knowing about love from experience. The story he tells purports to be that of his own love-affair. In the prologue he explains how after a sleepless night, spent reading Boethius and thinking of the rule of Fortune over his own life, he heard the bell ring for matins, and it seemed to him to say, 'Tell on, man, quhat thee befell' (77). Towards the end of the poem, too, he feels the need to justify himself for writing at such length on a merely personal subject. Subtly and yet confusingly, he makes the fantasy of the bell's message a small-scale parallel to the dubious status of the dream which is to follow, thinking to himself,

> quhat may this be?
> This is myn awin ymagynacioun,
> It is no lyf that spekis unto me,
> It is a bell – or that impressioun
> Of my thoght causith this illusioun
> That dooth me think so nycely in this wise. (78–83)
>
> *lyf* living creature; *nycely* foolishly

From the beginning, then, we are to look on the narrator as one in whom *thoght* is apt to produce *illusioun*; and at the beginning of the dream, when the gate of Venus's palace opens to him 'as quho sais, "at a thoght"' (536), he reminds us that a dream may be no more than the dreamer's thought, with the witty implication that in dreams the commonplace metaphor 'at a thought' is literally true. It will come as all the more of a surprise when we eventually learn that his dream was more than *illusioun* after all. In Chaucer, as we have seen, the dream is developed as a means of pondering on the uncertain status of imaginative fiction. In *The Kingis Quair* there is an interesting passage about the poet's need for inspiration, a 'wynd that furthward suld me throwe' (116), away from the rocks of 'prolixitee' (120); this however is not connected with the dream, but is still part of the prologue to the *buke* which contains it. The speaker of this prologue is divided between two roles, being experienced as a lover but immature as a poet. In all this there is a certain confusion: James is by no means merely imitating earlier dream-poets, but he is not sufficiently the master of the conventions of dream-poetry to re-shape them radically.

Lines 134–511 take us back into the past. This dream – and here we have a distinct innovation in comparison with Chaucer and his English followers – is to be set as fully as possible in the whole course of the dreamer's life-history, and the dream itself is to be recounted as part of past experience. Any dream-poem is written in the past tense – it says 'I dreamed', not 'I am dreaming' – but here the dream is past not just in relation to the time of writing but in relation to a series of subsequent events which serve to confirm its validity. Oddly enough, then, the

Dreamer here, establishing a present time of writing in relation to which the actual dream belongs to a somewhat remote past, whose significance in his biography is now clear, may remind one of a devotional writer such as Julian of Norwich, meditating on the meaning of a religious vision she had long ago. The narrator tells us his life-story: how in his childhood he was put to sea, captured by his enemies, and imprisoned. (This really happened to James I of Scotland, who was imprisoned by the English between the ages of eleven and twenty-nine; that is how he could have come to know the work of Chaucer and his followers earlier than any other Scottish poet.) In his prison, like Boethius, he bewailed his treatment by Fortune; he heard the nightingale singing, and wished that he might become a servant of love. Looking from his window, like Palamon in *The Knight's Tale*, he saw a beautiful girl, and fell in love with her, thus becoming her willing prisoner metaphorically as well as an unwilling prisoner in reality. He prayed to Venus to help him, begged the nightingale to go on singing, and composed a love-song to its notes (here there is no Clanvowian cuckoo). It is impossible to decide where to draw the line in this section of the poem between literary reminiscence and genuine autobiography. No doubt a real fifteenth-century prisoner might well have read Boethius and thought along Boethian lines, read *The Knight's Tale* and found Boethian thought there too, and even have fallen in love at a distance with the girl he was eventually to marry (in James's case, Joan Beaufort, whom he married immediately on his release). But at most the poem can be seen as offering a symbolic and generalizing account of the poet's real experience, in which the real sea-voyage, 'Upon the wawis weltering to and fro' (162), emerges imperceptibly from the conception of youth in general as a 'schip that sailith stereles...Amang the wawis of this warld' (101, 111). As with *Piers Plowman*, we can say no more than that it *gives the impression* of genuine autobiography, since inevitably the only evidence about the poet's inner experience is in the poem itself.

When the lady had gone, the narrator bitterly lamented his helplessness, and that same night he had his dream. In it, he is first blinded by a great light and is then carried up 'in a cloude of cristall' (525) through the various spheres of the Ptolemaic universe, until he reaches that of Venus. In Venus's sphere he finds 'mony a mylioun' (543) of those who have ended their lives in Love's service. The experience, with its reminiscences both of the Boethian flight of philosophy and of the deliverances from prison of Peter and Paul (Acts 12:7 and 16:26), has an authentically visionary feel. It has taken him to a heavenly realm which is appropriate to a religious vision, though the religion involved appears at first to be the pagan religion of sexual love. Next the Dreamer sees Cupid and Venus, and prays again to Venus to assist him in his love for the lady in the garden. She tells him to continue in his love, but warns him that he appears to be ill-matched to the lady, and that she does not have absolute power. He needs the help of other deities, and she will therefore send his spirit to Minerva, whose instructions he must obey. Minerva, the goddess of wisdom, is associated with reason and virtue; and it is becoming clear that the poem is not really (like *The Temple of Glass*) adopting a loosely defined religion of love, but is aiming at a treatment of human love as a supremely significant experience, which totally transforms the lover (see lines 314–15), but which can yet be related and subordinated to higher ethical and religious values. Before sending him to Minerva, Venus gives the Dreamer a message to pass on to men when he returns to the waking world: all the rain that has fallen recently has been her tears, falling because mankind has been negligent in following her laws. We have seen earlier cases in which Christian visionaries were similarly given information to take back from the other world to this.

The Dreamer, with Gude Hope as his guide, now departs for the palace of Minerva. Minerva tells him that his love will not prosper unless it is based on virtue and conducted with wisdom. If it is 'groundit ferm and stable / In Goddis law' (960–1), she will help him; and she does not object to desire, 'So thou it ground and set in Cristin wise' (989). Through Minerva, the author of the *Quair* makes it clear that he is not following Lydgate in using a dream-setting as an excuse for avoiding clear thought about the relationship between human love and Christian truth; on the contrary – and this will be true of the Scots poets generally – the effect of the dream is to promote clarity of thought. On these conditions, Minerva agrees to help the Dreamer, by asking the help of Fortune, who has the rule over 'all ye creaturis / Quhich under us beneth have your dwellyng' (1009–10). She discusses the various theories which relate Fortune to freewill and necessity, in order to instruct the Dreamer, who is 'wayke and feble' of 'wit or lore' (1040–1). Unlike the Chaucerian Dreamer, he needs no instruction about love, but even a king may need instruction in philosophical matters, and the Boethian doctrine here picks up the earlier references to Boethius and Fortune, both in the prologue to the *buke* (now we see why the narrator had the *De Consolatione* to hand when he was unable to sleep) and in the prologue to the poem.

Still accompanied by Gude Hope, the Dreamer now descends from the heavens to the earth, the realm over which Fortune rules, and he finds himself in a paradise-landscape of a traditional kind, which owes a particularly strong debt to *The Parliament of Fowls*. The description is beautiful in itself, but it seems to be the one part of the *Quair* which is taken over inertly from the dream-poem tradition. There has to be a paradise-landscape somewhere, because all dream-poems have paradises in them; and there has to be a catalogue of the various species of animals, each with its defining attributes, because there was a catalogue of birds in the similar section of *The Parliament of Fowls* – regardless of the fact that in the *Parliament* the catalogue found its justification as part of the poem's thought about the relation between the natural order and human culture, while in *The Kingis Quair* it is not Nature but Fortune that presides over the landscape. The Dreamer sees Fortune, the third goddess of his vision, with her wheel, and a pit beneath it 'depe as ony helle' (1129) – another of those vestiges of the early vision of judgment which we found in Chaucerian dream-poems. Men are clambering all over the wheel, climbing up and being thrown down. He begs Fortune for her aid, and she remarks that he looks so pale and wretched that he certainly seems to need it. She herself helps him on to the wheel, warning him to make the most of his success. As she says farewell to him, she plucks him by the ear so sharply that he awakes from his dream. Even kings, when they become dreamers, are subject to such indignities.

As we have already seen, the gillyflowers confirm the dream's message, and the narrator explains that thenceforward Fortune was indeed kind to him, and the gods gave him his heart's desire – presumably, the lady with whom he has fallen in love. The pattern of the *De Consolatione* has been reversed; in this case Fortune has been kind. The poem ends with a further Gothic 'flurry of curves and spikes': a speech of thanks to the gods, the nightingale, the gillyflower, and so on; an envoy commending his poem to 'the reder' (1354) (we have left behind the intimate link of poet and listeners at the Ricardian court); thanks to 'Him that hiest in the hevin sitt' (1369), who has caused our lives to be written in the stars; and a dedication of his poems to those of 'my maisteris dere, / Gowere and Chaucere' (1373–4). *The Kingis Quair* forms a most interesting example of what could be made of the dream-poem by an intelligent and sensitive fifteenth-century reader of Chaucer and his followers, for whom the oral situation in which Chaucer himself wrote had disappeared. If *The Kingis Quair* had been read by other fifteenth-century poets in Scotland, or in England, it might well have proved a fruitful influence – for example, in setting the dream so fully in the context of a life in which it represented a crucial event. But in fact there is no evidence that the poem was read at all widely in the fifteenth century.

It survives only in one late fifteenth-century manuscript, though admittedly that belonged to the Henry Sinclair who suggested to Gavin Douglas that he should translate the *Aeneid*. Dream-poetry in Scotland seems to have made a completely fresh start, going back once more to the Chaucerian model half a century later than *The Kingis Quair*.

Scottish dream-prologues

A major Chaucerian influence on the Scottish dream-poems of the later fifteenth century is the *Prologue* to *The Legend of Good Women*, and there are a number of examples of dream-poems which act as prologues to some other narrative, serving to explain and justify its existence. The simplest of these is the prologue to *Lancelot of the Laik*, a romance translated anonymously and incompletely from the French. It opens with a conventional but charming spring morning description, in which one detail at least alerts us to expect connections with the *Prologue* to the *Legend*: a mention of 'the quen alphest' (57)[12] – a scribal error, doubtless, for 'Alcest', identified, as by Chaucer, with the daisy. The narrator is tormented by the pains of a love of which the beloved lady knows nothing, and in this state

> I became into one ex[t]asy,
> Ore slep, or how I [n]ot; bot so befell
> My wo haith done my livis gost expell,
> And in sich wise weil long I can endwr,
> So me betid o wondir aventur. (76–80)
>
> *not* (for MS *wot*) know not

The uncertainty whether his state was a sleep or a religious ecstasy or something else is characteristically Chaucerian, and it is further developed at the end of the dream, when the narrator asks himself,

> Quhat may this meyne? quhat may this signify?
> Is it of troutht, or of illusioune? (160–1)
>
> *troutht* truth

In the ninety lines of the dream, a green bird comes to him, and tells him that the God of Love is angry with him because he is doing nothing to disclose his love to his lady. He answers that he dares not approach her directly, and the bird tells him that in that case he must do so indirectly, by sending her a poem 'Of love, ore armys, or of sum othir thing' (147). The translation of the romance of Lancelot is the result of this dream. The poet introduces it with great modesty, and indeed the dream-prologue is no more than one element in the modesty-convention: his only excuse for writing the poem is that he does so under the

God of Love's orders. His role, then, is different from Chaucer's: he is essentially not a poet but a lover, and the poem purports to exist only as a move in the game of love. This means that the uncertainty about the nature of the dream-experience is not used, as it is by Chaucer, to reflect on the validity of the poetic fiction itself; indeed, it has no real function, and is no more than an imitation of Chaucerian practice. Chaucer's conception of the dream-poem has for this poet distintegrated into separate formulas, though each of these is thoroughly engaging in itself.

A second example of the dream-prologue shows a fuller understanding of its possibilities, and a new development to match a new situation. Henryson's *Tale of the Lion and the Mouse*, one of his collection of *Moral Fables* (beast-fables in the Aesopian tradition, each with its moral application), has a prologue in which Aesop himself appears to the poet in a dream. It is perhaps not by chance that this, the only one of the *Fables* to have a dream-prologue, holds the central position, being the seventh of a collection of thirteen.[13] Moreover, it has an epilogue as well as a prologue, so that the dream provides a framework for the whole fable, which is supposed to be recounted to Henryson by Aesop. On a beautiful June morning (for in Scotland, where spring comes late, it was necessary to shift the conventional springtime landscape from May to June) Henryson falls asleep under a hawthorn, and he dreams that he is approached by an impressive, white-bearded man, finely dressed in the antique fashion. That the dream is an *oraculum*, like Scipio's vision of his grandfather, is confirmed when Henryson addresses the man as 'father' (1366) and 'maister venerabill' (1384).[14] When he learns that this is Aesop himself, he begs him to tell him 'ane prettie fabill, / Concludand with ane gude moralitie' (1386–7). At first Aesop demurs, on the ground that if men will not listen to preaching, there is no point in telling them 'ane fenyeit taill' (1389), a mere fiction; but when Henryson presses him, he agrees. The fable itself follows, and then in the epilogue Henryson eagerly asks Aesop, 'Maister, is thair ane moralitie / In this fabill? (1570–1). Aesop explains what the moral interpretation of the story is, and concludes with a more general moral, which would apply equally well to all the fables, wishing that justice should reign in Scotland and treason be exiled. Then he vanishes and Henryson wakes up.

On the face of it, the purpose of this dream-framework for the central fable is to provide authority and authenticity for the whole work: not just for the story of the lion and the mouse, but for all the other stories (which are similar in kind) and notably also for their moral interpretations – the dream purports to establish that those too are authentically Aesopian. But it must not be supposed that the deference to the old poet's authority excludes any implication, such as we have found in some of Chaucer's dream-poems, that the dream also represents the poet's inspiration. 'Henryson' appears in the dream precisely as a poet – a fifteenth-century Scottish poet. In a situation where it is assumed that the highest goal of vernacular poetry is not to be original but to follow classical authority, imitation and inspiration will be one and the same thing, and the Scottish poet will never be more truly inspired than when he acts as a mouthpiece for his ancient predecessor. Moreover, just as in Chaucer, the dream is used to explore some problematic element in the nature of the poetic enterprise itself. What can justify the existence of these highly entertaining animal stories, which are after all no more than frivolous fictions, 'fenyeit' in the sense that they are not and could not be true? Their only possible justification is that they have a moral significance; and accordingly each *fabula* is accompanied by a *moralitas*. But if, as Aesop is made to say, Henryson lives in a dark age, when 'The eir is deif, the hart is hard as stane' (1393) and men pay no attention to holy preaching, surely fables are unlikely to do them any good? Against this uncertainty of purpose, Henryson can set only the vague hope that he may 'leir [learn] and beir away' (1402) from such stories something that may be profitable in the future. These are the doubts that the dream articulates, without pretending to lay them fully to rest.

My third example of a Scottish dream-prologue was greatly influenced by Henryson's modification of the form. This is Gavin Douglas's prologue to book XIII of his translation of the *Aeneid*. (He composed a prologue for each book, and that to book VIII is also in the form of a dream, which satirises the state of Scottish society.) Here once more the dream is an *oraculum*, in which the authoritative figure who instructs the dreamer is the poet whose work he is translating; and once more, too, the dream is used not only to justify the existence of the translation but to express obliquely a doubt about the enterprise of writing. But in Douglas's case the tone is more clearly comic, and the dream is a kind of mock-*oraculum*, or poet's nightmare. Douglas has completed his translation of the twelve books of the *Aeneid* written by Virgil. In this prologue he wanders out on a June evening, and there is a superbly evocative description of the gradual sinking to rest of all creatures. Douglas himself falls asleep under a laurel tree, only to have his rest disturbed by a dream in which he is brusquely addressed by an old man, crowned with laurel, the emblem of poetic fame, and claiming the laurel tree as his own, but dressed in threadbare clothes (unlike Henryson's Aesop). He claims that Douglas has done him an injury, and it emerges that he is Mapheus Vegius, a fifteenth-century poet who added to Virgil's twelve a thirteenth book in which Aeneas is carried up to heaven. Why has Douglas failed to include this in his translation? Douglas defends himself by saying that if he translated any more he would be open to the accusation of neglecting 'full mony grave mater' (112)[15] (for Douglas was not only a poet but a statesman and priest, who shortly became a bishop), and that in any case a thirteenth book is no more necessary to the *Aeneid* than a fifth wheel to a cart. Mapheus Vegius points out that he, unlike Virgil, was a Christian poet, and he insists that Douglas *must* translate him, enforcing his insistence by hitting him twenty times on the back with his club. Douglas hastily promises to do what he asks, and then he wakes up.

The dream has lasted all through the short northern summer night; the dawn of the next day is described in another passage of exquisite beauty, birds and men come back to life, and Douglas proceeds to carry out his promise, though he says that after that he will attend only to 'grave materis' (188) – and this was indeed Douglas's last poetic composition, completed in 1513, though he lived another nine years. The comedy of this dream-prologue derives from the Chaucerian dream-poem, in that it applies both to the bewildered poet-dreamer and to his self-important authority. The 'inspiration' for the translation of book XIII is seen as a matter of inner compulsion of the most literal kind; but, just as in Henryson's dream-prologue, the dream expresses doubts about the poet's own role. How can a future bishop justify himself for giving so much of his life to poetry, and to secular, pagan poetry at that? That is the personal dilemma which is re-enacted, as our problems of role and identity so often are, in a dream. Once more, I do not wish to imply that the dream must be a form of sincere self-expression; perhaps Douglas was writing only what he thought would best suit his public image, but he wished at least to give the impression of expressing a personal dilemma. When we come to consider Douglas's earlier work, *The Palice of Honour*, we shall see that there too he explores, much more elaborately, his own role as poet and its relation to earthly fame and heavenly honour. Mapheus Vegius's arrogant claim to the laurel is the expression of a central theme in Douglas's work.

Dunbar

The dream-framework was a favourite device of Dunbar's, and he used it for a variety of different purposes; indeed, from his work alone it could be demonstrated that the dream-poem has no single right use. One poem, for example, is a vision of Christ's passion (Mackenzie 80),[16] which is granted to the poet when he suddenly falls into a trance while praying in an oratory – a 'dream' closely parallel to Langland's vision of Piers Plowman in B xix, and related like it to the visionary experiences of devotional writers such as Rolle and Julian of Norwich. The first part of the vision gives a detailed sensory picture of the Passion itself; the second uses personifications such as Compassion, Remembrance and Grace to describe the poet's own response to his vision, which is brought to an end when he is awakened by the trembling of the earth of Matthew 27:51. Another poem (Mackenzie 4) consists of a comic analogue of those dreams that, according to the *Liber de Modo Bene Vivendi*, 'occur through the illusions of unclean spirits'.[17] In it St Francis appears, to urge the poet to become a friar; Dunbar resists his urging, and the supposed saint turns into a devil and 'vaneist away with stynk and fyrie smowk' (48). One commentator has asserted that in this poem Dunbar 'is writing about a real dream which he actually had', that he 'is in fact receiving his religious vocation in a dream-vision from one of the great saints in person: to a devout Catholic there could be no other interpretation,' and that his rejection of the call expresses a deep inner conflict.[18] This view of the poem is merely fanciful, and disregards the broad range of types of dream with which a medieval poet is likely to have been acquainted. This *visio* is obviously spurious, and the poem's chief purpose is to satirise the pretensions of the friars, in support of the common medieval view that 'Freres and feendes been but lyte asonder' (*Canterbury Tales* iii [D] 1674).

A number of Dunbar's other dream-poems are satirical in intention. Two of them are directed against John Damian, Abbot of Tongland, an alchemist who attempted to fly with wings made of birds' feathers and was patronized by James IV of Scotland. The first hilariously describes how all the species of birds attacked him in his attempted flight (Mackenzie 38), and the satire is the sharper if one recognizes that Dunbar sees it as a travesty of Philosophy's promise to Boethius to 'fycchen fetheris in thi thought' (for 'philosophy' had also come to mean alchemy). In the second (Mackenzie 39), the poet has a vision of Fortune, who informs him that Damian will meet a she-dragon in the heavens and will beget Antichrist. Here the implication of the dream-framework seems to be double: that the abbot's associations are devilish, and that his attempt at flight belongs rather to apocalyptic fantasies than to waking life. Other dream-satires are less personal in their scope. One, in which a single vision incorporates two poems, 'The Dance of the Sevin Deidly Synnis' and 'The Sowtar and Tailyouris War' (The Battle of the Shoemaker and the Tailor) (Mackenzie 57 and 58), offers a comic vision of hell, showing first the personified sins and then the shoemaker and the tailor urged on by the devil to a grotesque tournament. It is a parody, of course, of genuine religious visions of the other world, and its last line declares its status as mere fantasy: 'Now trow this gif ye list!' The comic vision of the other world is completed in a third poem which purports to make amends to the shoemakers and tailors for the joke at their expense. Here an angel appears to the poet in a dream, to promise that, though these tradesmen may be knaves on earth, they will be saints in heaven (Mackenzie 59). Another grotesque dream-satire, but more sombre in tone, is 'The Devillis Inquest' (Mackenzie 42), in which the poet sees people of various callings dedicating themselves by their blasphemies to the devil, who stands close by and encourages them. Here the function of the dream is to provide a genuine insight into an unseen reality: in waking life we hear the blasphemies but do not see the devil who profits by them. Lastly, in a poem called simply 'The Dream' (Mackenzie 60), a vision comes to the poet 'halff sleiping' (1), in which he is visited by various personifications. Distres, Hivines and Langour depress his spirits, while others discuss the fact that the king has not rewarded him with ecclesiastical preferment for his work as a poet. It ends with Patience encouraging the Dreamer to rely on the king's generosity, but at this point a gun is shot off, and the noise wakes him. In this case the function of the dream-setting is, I believe, somewhat complex. Dream, as we have seen in other cases, is an appropriate setting for debate among personifications (particularly those which stand, as these do, for the various psychological impulses which are really reflected in dreams); in this sense the poem represents a plausible *somnium animale*. This dream, however, discloses a truth – that Dunbar has received no reward – but the plea, and the incidental satire against the pluralism of other courtiers, are softened by the fact that it is 'only a dream'. And finally the assurance of the king's generosity, followed as it is by a rude noise which brings the vision to an end, is exposed as the most insubstantially dreamlike thing of all.

Even in Dunbar's shorter poems, then, the dream can be used for complex purposes. But the poem of which on which I wish especially to focus is a longer work, *The Thrissil and the Rois* (Mackenzie 55), which, in my view, has been greatly underestimated by modern commentators. Mr Speirs sees it and *The Goldyn Targe* (Mackenzie 56) as poems from which 'life has largely escaped', while Dr Scott describes it as 'regressive and morbid..., forced, contrived, unreal, unconvincing, spurious'.[19] It is a formal occasional poem, written in 1503 to celebrate the marriage of King James IV to the English princess Margaret Tudor, and what takes place inside the dream relates symbolically to this historical event. In the dream (to summarize briefly) Dame Nature summons all the creatures to do homage to her. Among them comes the lion, from the royal arms of Scotland, whom Nature crowns as king of the beasts. Then she crowns the eagle as king of the birds. Lastly she crowns the thistle as king of the plants, gives him good advice about ruling the other plants, and advises him to love no other flower but the rose. The thistle, emblem of Scotland, stands for James IV, and the advice to love none but the rose implies that he should abandon his mistresses when he gets married. Then Nature crowns the rose – a Tudor rose, red and white in colour, set above the lily (the emblem of France), and standing, of course, for the English princess. All the birds sing a song of welcome and praise of her, and with their noise the Dreamer wakes. The concept of the gathering of the creatures under the rule of Nature, and the ending with birdsong which awakens the Dreamer, both derive from Chaucer's *Parliament of Fowls*, but Dunbar's poem is considerably shorter than Chaucer's, and much simpler in structure.

Although the events of the dream, such as they are, stand for historical events, the dream-world in which they are set is not a version of this world, as in the tradition of *Winner and Waster*, but a paradisal other world. It is imagined along traditional lines: it is a May morning, the Dreamer is taken into a 'lusty gairding gent' (44) (pleasant and noble garden), full of green leaves and sweet-smelling flowers, the air rings with the song of birds, and the language used implies the usual analogy with the heavenly world – this time it is the sun which 'In orient bricht as angell did appeir' (51). In the opening section of this book I described how this traditional dream-landscape originated in the Mediterranean area, and then spread over the whole of Europe as a literary convention without any very close relationship to the realities of the climate in any locality. In the south of England, though springtime weather is notoriously treacherous, the convention remained just plausible enough to survive intact. The breaking-point seems to have come when it was carried still further north to Scotland. Not even a Scot could believe that a Scottish spring would be paradisal, even as late as May, and we have seen how in Henryson's and Douglas's dream-prologues the month was silently changed to June. Dunbar went further, by taking up the contrast between literary convention and climatic reality and making it part of his poem's meaning. The opening section of *The Thrissil and the Rois*, before the dream begins, takes place in May. The poet lies sleeping in bed one morning, when it seems to him (and here his dream begins) that Aurora, the goddess of the dawn, looks in through his bedroom window, with a lark on her hand which sings aloud,

> Awalk, luvaris, out of your slomering,
> Se how the lusty morrow dois up spring. (13–14)
> *awalk* awake; *morrow* morning

Then May appears to him, a personification of the season, standing by his bed, dressed in flowers and glittering with sunbeams, and she too tells him to rise up and write something in her honour: the lark has aroused lovers 'with confort and delyt' (25), so why has not Dunbar risen to compose songs for them? (As in Chaucer, it is assumed that the Dreamer, a court-poet, must be a love-poet.) But at this the Dreamer rebels, and in effect tells this literary personification, May, that she is a mere fiction, and that the real Scottish May is a season of bitter winds, cold air, and silent birds:

> 'Quhairto,' quod I, 'sall I uprys at morrow,
> For in this May few birdis herd I sing?
> Thai haif moir caus to weip and plane thair sorrow.
> Thy air it is nocht holsum nor benyng;
> Lord Eolus dois in thy sessone ring;
> So busteous ar the blastis of his horne,
> Amang thy bewis to walk I haif forborne.'[20] (29–35)
> *sessone* season; *bewis* boughs

In reply to this rebellious speech, May simply smiles soberly, reminds the Dreamer that he has promised to write something in honour of the rose, and invites him to enter the world of his dream, that garden

> Illumynit our with orient skyis brycht,
> Annamyllit richely with new asur lycht. (41–2)
> *our* over

He does so, and the main content of the dream follows.

What Dunbar has done is to admit that the idealized world of his dream is only a fiction, an artifice, as is suggested, by the very words *illumynit* (like a manuscript illumination) and *annamyllit* (like a design painted on precious metal). And the sense of a contrast between the real world and the dream-world is continued when Dame Nature appears in the dream and orders Neptune, the sea-god, to prevent storms at sea,

Aeolus, the god of the winds, to make no cold blasts, and Juno to keep the heavens dry:

> Dame Nature gaif an inhibitioun thair
> To fers Neptunus, and Eolus the bawld,
> Nocht to perturb the wattir nor the air,
> And that no schouris, nor [no] blastis cawld,
> Effray suld flouris nor fowlis on the fold;
> Scho bad eik Juno, goddes of the sky,
> That scho the hevin suld keip amene and dry. (64–70)
>
> *inhibitioun* prohibition; *fold* earth; *amene* pleasant

The obvious implication of these precautions is that paradisal weather is not the norm in real life; it belongs to an art based on the exercise of the will in opposition to the natural course of events.

Dunbar, then, pointedly uses the dream-framework as a way of separating the world of art, or poetic fiction, from the world of reality. But this does not mean, as is sometimes assumed, that he is content to write an escapist and merely decorative kind of poetry, to be a 'dreamer of dreams' in the post-Romantic sense. There is of course a paradox involved in Dunbar's contrast between the dream-world of art and the waking world of nature: it is that Nature herself, the personified concept, can be seen only in the dream-world of art. Just so, in *Winner and Waster*, winning and wasting can be identified as the principles underlying everyday life only in a dream. Dream enables one to see more deeply into reality than one can in waking life; it is a form of intuition which, far from escaping from reality, lays bare its deeper structure. In the more specific terms of this particular poem, the art of poetry merges into that of heraldry – both modes of artifice which convey meaning not by imitating the surface appearance of everyday reality, but by stepping back from it, selecting certain objects, and transforming them into the symbols of ideas. The vision of the gathering of the creatures before Nature is a vision of that ordered hierarchy which in medieval times could be seen as underlying the world men directly experienced. And it does not involve pretending that the harsher aspects of experience can be dismissed or disregarded. For example, animals sometimes prey on each other, and Nature cannot be made to order them not to do so; but she can tell the eagle, as king of the birds (and hence James in his role as the enforcer of laws), to ensure that birds of prey should seize only the prey proper to them:

> And lat no fowll of ravyne do efferay,
> Nor devoir birdis bot his awin pray. (125–6)
>
> *do efferay* cause terror

And this philosophical vision of hierarchical order merges through heraldry into a political vision of concord between the warring neighbours, England and Scotland. The lion, as well as king of the beasts, is an emblem of Scotland, and is described partly in heraldic terms, standing on a 'field' of gold:

> Reid of his cullour, as is the ruby glance;
> On feild of gold he stude full mychtely,
> With flour delycis sirculit lustely. (96-8)

It is Nature who lifts him up into the heraldically appropriate rampant posture. By means such as this, political concord is shown as rooted in natural order; but the connection between the two can be seen only through an art which distinguishes itself from nature in order to conceive of nature more clearly. For Dunbar, the image of that art of intellectual vision is the dream; and he is able to re-use the traditional elements of dream-poetry – the paradisal landscape and the comically obstinate dreamer – for a purpose which is at once traditional and new.

A glance at Dunbar's other major courtly dream-allegory, *The Goldyn Targe*, will show that its treatment of landscape and weather helps to support what has just been said about *The Thrissil and the Rois*. In *The Goldyn Targe* the dream-world at first is once more a world of conscious artifice, which is also a paradise – it is actually called 'that paradise complete' (72) – beyond the power of the 'ornate stilis' (68) of Homer or Cicero to describe. But this time the subject of the dream is an allegorical love-affair, and, as it proceeds, the paradisal vision collapses, as if in a speeded-up version of the *Roman de la Rose*. The Dreamer is delivered by Danger into the power of Hevynesse, and the paradisal landscape is dissolved by that same god of winds who was the chief representative of the real Scottish climate in *The Thrissil and the Rois*:

> Be this the lord of wyndis, wyth wodenes,
> God Eolus, his bugill blew, I gesse,
> That with the blast the levis all to-schuke;
> And sudaynly, in the space of a luke,
> All was hyne went, thare was bot wildernes,
> Thare was no more bot birdis, bank and bruke. (229-34)
>
> *wodenes* madness; *hyne went* gone hence

In the next stanza, the ship which originally brought the personifications through whom the love-affair is recounted sails rapidly away again, firing its guns, and the noise awakens the Dreamer.[21] In this poem, though, dream weather and real weather have changed places, and when he wakes from this dream which has become a nightmare he finds himself in a real paradisal landscape. The love-affair was nothing but a hideous fantasy; the reality is a landscape of rhetorical artifice, in which Dunbar is the humble disciple of the three great English poets, Chaucer, Gower and Lydgate. Like the 'Chaucer' of the dream-poems, he retreats gladly from the pain of love to the comforting artifice of literature; and yet, comparing his work with that of his great predecessors, he feels that 'Rude is thy weid, disteynit, bare and rent' (278) – an obvious parallel to the final state of the landscape in the dream, after Aeolus has been at work. In Dunbar's hands the dream-poem has become a hall of mirrors, in which reality and artifice reflect each other in perpetually recurring paradox.

Skelton: 'The Bowge of Court'

This and the two dream-poems which follow it, one by Douglas and another by Skelton, come from the very end of the medieval period, and are included not only for their own merits, but in order to show how the tradition of dream-poetry, far from being ossified, was capable of being adapted to convey vigorously the characteristic concerns and attitudes of the arriving Renaissance. *The Bowge of Court* is John Skelton's earliest surviving major work, dating from 1498, yet it already brings a number of innovations to dream-poetry. The spot where the narrator falls asleep is identified more specifically than ever before as a real place, Powers Key at Harwich (34–5);[22] as Dreamer, the narrator acquires the identity of a personification, Drede (fear, anxiety); and the setting of the dream is on board a ship – though admittedly it is an allegorical vessel, the *Bowge of Court* (court rations). In the brief waking section at the beginning, Skelton introduces himself as a would-be poet, who wishes he could emulate the great allegorical writers of the past. They clothed truths in 'coverte termes' (10), but he has no such power 'to illumyne' (20); and so his perplexity wearies him and he falls asleep. It is autumn, at a time when the moon, 'full of mutabylyte' (3), rules over men and smiles scornfully 'At our foly and our unstedfastnesse' (6). This prepares us for a dream which can be seen as a *somnium coeleste*, albeit of the lowest kind (since the moon's is the lowest of the heavenly spheres), and which will deal with mutability and human folly and unsteadfastness. Moreover, autumn is in general a time of frequent dreams, which tend to be meaningless *insomnia* or nightmares, according to John of Salisbury.[23] Are we to expect a dream about folly or a foolish dream? The familiar ambiguity in the status of dreams is already hinted at in the opening lines. But the dream's leading image is clearly provided by the Dreamer's waking experience; he falls asleep on the quayside of an important port, and so it is natural enough that he should dream about the arrival and departure of a ship.

In a further prologue within the dream (36–126), before the ship sets sail and the poem's action commences, the symbolic significance of its contents is made clear, partly by the Dreamer's own experiences and partly by an authoritative but anonymous voice. The traditional love-allegory has undergone a sharp modification. There is, it is true, a great lady, Dame Saunce-Pere (Without Equal), whose chief gentlewoman is Daunger, and who sits

> In a trone wiche fer clerer dyde shyne
> Than Phebus in his spere celestyne,
> Whoos beaute, honoure, goodly porte,
> I have to lytyll connynge to reporte. (60–3)

But Saunce-Pere is present not as the object of the Dreamer's love, but as the owner of the 'shyppe, goodly of sayle' (36) which has just arrived at the port. She is engaged in trade, a chancy occupation – hence the inscription on her throne, 'Garder le fortune que est mauelz et bone' (67). (Take care of fortune, which is both bad and good) – and the Dreamer finds her by following merchants who are flocking to see her 'royall chaffre [merchandise]' (54). The allegory of love, then, has become an allegory of trade. But the trade in turn is that of courtly life under the absolute monarchy of the Tudors. The merchandise is favour, which all eagerly seek, including the Dreamer, who tells Daunger he has come 'to bye some of youre ware' (79). He has 'but smale substaunce' (94), but another gentlewoman, Desyre, lends him the 'precyous jewell, ...Bone aventure [good luck]' (97–8) to help him make his way to favour. However, she warns him that it is essential to make a friend of the steerswoman of the ship, that 'Fortune' who is named on Saunce-Pere's throne. The Dreamer along with the other merchants rushes to seek Fortune's friendship, and she, of course, 'promysed to us all she wolde be kynde' (124). Thus we are given to understand in this explanatory prologue that life on the ship is an emblem of court life; and indeed the mutability of the moon and Fortune was nowhere more sharply felt than at the early Tudor court (to which Skelton belonged). But life at court is no more than a special case of life in the world, over which Fortune had been shown as ruling capriciously in visionary writings from Boethius onwards; and life in the world was traditionally imaged as a vessel tossed by a stormy sea, as in *The Kingis Quair*. There can be no doubt that this dream is set, like those in the tradition of *Winner and Waster*, not in a heavenly other world but on earth.

Like many dreamers before him, Skelton is at a loss in the strange realm of his dream. We have already been told that among the merchants at the port 'coude I none aquentaunce fynde' (45), and he continues to be alone and friendless on the crowded ship. On it he meets 'Full subtyll persones in nombre foure and thre' (133) – a number which may suggest some analogy with the seven deadly sins. The first is Favell, the flatterer, who assures him that he is in high favour with Fortune, and that while Favell is on his side, 'Ye maye not fall' (170); and yet his assurances are already undermined by the hint that 'here be dyverse to you that be unkynde' (161). The Dreamer cannot quite rely on his 'doubtfull doublenes' (178), and his uncertainty is increased when he overhears a conversation in which the second subtle person, Suspycyon, asks whether they were speaking of him, and he and Favell agree to abandon Drede. Suspycyon warns him against Favell, and tells him that 'here is none that dare well other truste' (202). His third acquaintance is Hervy Hafter (Dodger), an inquisitive gossip, who once more congratulates him on having Fortune's favour, and once more undermines his assurance with 'I praye to God that it maye never dy' (271). Now the Dreamer overhears a second conversation about himself, between Hervy and Disdayne, in which Disdayne shows his envy that this mere newcomer has achieved such favour that 'It is lyke he wyll stonde in our lyghte' (305), and they agree to pick a quarrel with him. Disdayne does so, asking him threateningly,

> Remembrest thou what thou sayd yesternyght?
> Wylt thou abyde by the wordes agayne? (323–4)

Up comes a fifth courtier, Ryote, tawdry in dress and squalidly knowing in conversation, boasting of how he lives on his mistress's immoral earnings. Next the Dreamer witnesses a third secret conversation, between Disdayne and Dyssymulation, but this time he cannot hear what they are saying, though he 'dempte [judged] and drede theyr talkynge was not good' (426). He sees to his horror that Dyssymulation has two faces in his hood, a knife in one sleeve and a golden spoon of honey in the other. Dyssymulation commiserates with the Dreamer on the envy of which they are both victims, and utters many threats without ever making quite clear at whom they are directed or how they will be carried out. Lastly the Dreamer is greeted by Disceyte, who hints almost unintelligibly at a plot against him. Drede is by this time thoroughly terrified, imagines that he sees 'lewde felawes here and there' (528) coming to slay him, and desperately attempts to throw himself overboard; at which the dream comes to an end. He had thought at first, along with the other merchants, that

Favoure we have toughther than ony elme,
That wyll abyde and never frome us fall, (129–30)

but now he has learned just how deceptive the favour of the court is,
and he ends in terror, despair and attempted suicide.

The Dreamer is not a complete innocent; he can, for example, see
through the 'grete gentylnes' (176) of Favell to the 'doubtfull doublenes'
behind it. But he soon gets entirely out of his depth, and the sense of
the loss of any solid ground under his feet, the inability to find a reliable
truth in any direction, and the growing and all-too-justified paranoia,
are clearly developed out of the situation of the naive and bewildered
dreamer in earlier poems such as *The House of Fame*. There the naivety
was in relation to a heavenly other world; here, more frighteningly, it
relates to this world. The Dreamer is not being carried through the skies
by an eagle, or confronted by an angry Cupid; he is an inexperienced
and eager courtier, who finds reality itself dissolving into something
unpredictable and threatening. As C. S. Lewis has written, 'The subject
is a perennial one – the bewilderment, and finally the terror, of a man
at his first introduction to what theologians call "the World" and others
"the racket" or "real life"...almost any man in any profession can
recognize most of the encounters...'[24] It is worth noting, however, that
the Dreamer is considered specifically as a courtier; unlike Chaucer's
dreamers after *The Book of the Duchess*, he is not a court poet, at least
while he is dreaming. (Skelton does not take on that role as dreamer
until his later poem, *The Garland of Laurel*, by which time he had a
reputation as a poet and a career to look back on and quizzically justify.)
One scholar has asserted that 'Dread is, we know, a poet', and that 'the
purpose of the poem is to consider...the possibility, for the poet, of
moral action'.[25] But it is only in the waking sections that the narrator
is seriously treated as a poet. In the opening stanzas, as we have seen,
he is a poet longing to emulate the allegorical writers of the past, but
lacking the ability to do so; and his waking fears of making an unsuccessful attempt, as one

That clymmeth hyer than he may fotynge have;
What and he slyde downe, who shall hym save? (27–8)

offer an analogy to the experience of the dream, though his aspiration
and fall there belong to a different realm. And the moment he woke
from the dream, he 'Caughte penne and ynke, and wroth this lytyll boke'
(532); thus, like Chaucer in *The Parliament of Fowls*, he found that his
dream provided him with 'mater of to wryte', and solved his earlier
dilemma. But the identity he acquires in the dream, as Drede, belongs

to his experience as courtier, not as poet: there is no consideration in
The Bowge of Court of 'the possibility, *for the poet,* of moral action'. As
Renaissance courtier, Drede has naturally some acquaintance with *literae
humaniores,* and so Dyssymulation can flatter him by saying, 'I knowe
your vertu and your lytterkture' (449). But a joke made by Hervy Hafter
about his melancholy appearance –

> Tell me your mynde, me thynke ye make a verse,
> I coude it skan and ye wolde it reherse (244–5)

– surely depends for its full effect on our awareness of a separation
between Skelton as poet and Drede as courtier.

In becoming Drede, Skelton takes his place in an allegory of court
life. Usually, with a scrupulousness uncommon in those dream-poems
such as the *Roman de la Rose* and *The Book of the Duchess* where there
is no complete separation between poet and dreamer, he remains within
the limited point of view of Drede. Thus he takes care to explain how
he can overhear the sinister whispered conversations with which he is
surrounded: 'And I drewe nere to herke what they two sayde' (182, 296)
is a line repeated twice, and his inability to overhear what passes in the
third conversation, between Disdayne and Dyssymulation, marks a stage
in his collapse into helplessness and despair. Moreover, by a most
unusual development in personification-allegory, the Dreamer as Drede
is not merely an observer and victim, but has an occasional part to play
in the action as seen by the other personifications. For example, he tells
us that the seven 'subtyll persones' did not welcome his early attempts
to join in their amusements, because 'They sayde they hated for to dele
with Drede' (146). Part of the horror of his dream-experience is that
he is trapped in a state of fear so deep-rooted as to have become an
identity, which makes him from the beginning as unattractive to the
other figures in his dream as they are to him.

In this and other respects, Skelton seems to have tapped the experience of nightmare with a convincingness unknown in most earlier
dream-poetry. His poem feels like an account of an autumnal *insomnium*;
but at the same time it implicitly claims throughout to be more than a
sleeping fantasy, and to tell the truth about life at court. Its final stanza
makes explicit the ambiguous status of dreams which was hinted at in
the opening lines:

> I wolde therwith no man were myscontente;
> Besechynge you that shall it see or rede,
> In every poynte to be indyfferente,
> Syth all in substaunce of slumbrynge doth procede.
> I wyll not saye it is mater in dede,

But yet oftyme suche dremes be founde trewe:
Now constrewe ye what is the resydewe. (533–9)

The challenge offered by a dream-poem to its audience is familiar, but the nature of the dream itself has made the dilemma unusually sharp. We are left to decide for ourselves not just whether this dream is heavenly vision or subjective fantasy, but whether it depicts the everyday reality of our own world or is a mere paranoiac nightmare. The only acceptable answer to the poem's challenge is that it is both: it asserts that the real life of the court *is* a nightmare, from which there can be no escape by waking up. This is a new and frightening use for the dream-poem.

Douglas: 'The Palice of Honour'

The Palice of Honour, which was written in 1501, opens with a waking section in which the poet is in a paradisal garden, a Maytime landscape described largely in terms of art, and sharply distinguished, in the same manner as Dunbar, from the reality of Scottish weather:

God Eolus of wind list nocht appeir,
Nor auld Saturne, with his mortall speir
And bad aspect contrair till everie plant. (49–51)[26]

Here he hears a voice – 'I not was it a vision or fantone' (60) – singing in praise of May, and associating the month with the power of Nature. The poet dedicates himself to May, Nature and Venus, but at the same time feels terror at the mysterious voice, and, unable to 'sustene so amiabill a soun' (102), he attempts to leave the garden for his home. This inability to endure mysterious experiences is, as we have seen, common in medieval dreamers; here it is already apparent while the narrator is awake, and we are thus prepared for a special emphasis on his unfitness in the dream. There is something a little comic about an apparently grown man being frightened of an 'amiabill' voice in a garden, and the comedy is redoubled when he begins to dream. This happens almost immediately:

Out of the air come ane impressioun,
Throw quhais licht in extasie or swoun
Amyd the virgultis all in till a fary
As feminine so feblit fell I doun. (105–8)
virgultis bushes; *fary* daze

Extasie implies a religious experience, *swoun* something less grand, perhaps of merely medical interest; and this familiar uncertainty is continued later, as the Dreamer refers to his state now as an *extasie* (193) and now as a mere *fantasie* (358). So far, our best guess is likely to be that this is a love-vision, using the language of religious experience for secular purposes.

When the narrator comes to himself again, he finds himself 'in my sweven' (121) in a hideous and unnatural desert landscape, contrasting directly with the ideal landscape in which he was struck down. As that was 'depaint as paradice amiabill' (8), so this is a version of hell, with a river 'Like till Cochyte the river infernall' (138) running blood-red through waste rocks, and fish in it 'yelland as elvis' (146). Where the garden was full of flourishing flowers, this landscape has only rotting tree-stumps, and while Aeolus was silent in the garden, here 'The quhissilling wind blew mony bitter blast' (158).[27] We may be reminded of the desert in which Chaucer finds himself at the end of book I of *The House of Fame*, but here the landscape is elaborated into a full-scale nightmare, and we have no idea of its cause or meaning. Neither has the Dreamer; and Douglas's purpose appears to be to create an atmosphere of mystery, in which not only the Dreamer but the reader has to discover for himself the rationale underlying the sequence of events. The Dreamer for the present merely sees the unpleasant change as an example of the workings of Fortune, repeating three times 'Inconstant warld and quheill [wheel] contrarious!' (172, 182, 192). It is the first of a series of sharp contrasts, and it may be that Douglas himself was more interested in the effect of contrast than in a definite meaning underlying it. The Dreamer is further terrified at a sudden noise, 'As heird of beistis stamping with loud cry' (196), and hides himself in a stump. But he soon discovers that they are 'beistis rationall' (201) – a company of lords and ladies, damsels and prelates, surrounding a chariot-enthroned queen. When they have passed, he learns from two disreputable characters who are following them that the queen was Minerva, 'the Quene of Sapience' (241), accompanied by sybils, prophets, clerks and philosophers. So we have a further unexpected contrast: through the disordered wilderness moves the goddess of rational wisdom and her well-ordered train. The Dreamer's informants, who identify themselves as Sinon and Ahitophel, men who possessed wisdom but used it treacherously, tell him that the company are riding towards the palace of Honour. When asked how they come to be associated with it, they answer that 'Haill, eirdquaik and thunder / Ar oft in May, with mony schour of rane' (272–3), thereby suggesting a parallel with the earlier contrast between the May garden and the barren wilderness.

The Dreamer is a little comforted by this conversation, though he is still so nervous that

The stichling of a mous out of presence
Had bene to me mair ugsum than the hell. (308–9)

The stichling...presence The rustling of a mouse away from me; *ugsum* loath-some

We may be somewhat comforted ourselves by the Dreamer's self-depreciation, but we cannot be entirely at ease in a situation of such uncertainty. Things begin to clarify: the Dreamer tells us that he remained within his stump, hoping for 'sum signes or sum tokin / Of Lady Venus or hir companie' (314–15), and we seem to be confirmed in our guess that this is to be a love-vision, with the Dreamer in the usual role of timid but aspiring lover. Immediately a token appears; not of Venus but, with yet another contrast, of her opposite, Diana, the goddess of chastity. A hart runs past, torn by hounds, and the Dreamer recognizes it as a *signe* (320) of Actaeon, who was transformed into a hart and thus punished for seeing Diana bathing. Another company rides past to the palace of Honour, consisting of ladies dressed as huntswomen, surrounding Diana riding an elephant (a supposedly chaste beast); though this company contains 'bot few' (336). The Dreamer needs no informant this time: he is beginning to grasp the iconology of his dream.

He tells us more about the wilderness, with its serpents and stagnant water, and then there is once more a contrast: he sees a shining light and hears harmonious music. He digresses to explain why sound can be heard more clearly over water than over land, a passage that may remind us of the eagle's discourse on the theory of sound in *The House of Fame*. As there, the science is accurate by the standards of its time, but cannot be taken quite seriously: what conceivable relevance to the circumstances can be found in the information that fish cannot hear because 'as we se richt few of thame hes eiris' (377)? Douglas cuts himself short with 'Aneuch of this – I not quhat it may mene' (382), and then takes a whole stanza to return to the subject. Evidently he is making fun not only of himself as Dreamer but of the kind of poem which his dream constitutes: a vision which takes upon itself the role of an encyclopaedia, and supplies information relentlessly, whether or not it is desired. Such was the role played by the eagle as scientific informant in *The House of Fame*, but Douglas seems to be taking still further the element of burlesque, of self-mockery, that was found there.

The music is the herald of a third procession to Honour, and one which arouses the Dreamer's enthusiasm to the extent of a whole stanza of exclamations. This 'angellike and godlie companie', which 'me thocht a thing celestiall' (416–17), is the court of a third goddess, described at great and rapturous length. He wonders who she is, but once more his iconological learning comes to his rescue, when he sees that she is accompanied by a handsome blind man with a bow and arrows, whom he recognizes as 'Cupyd, the god maist dissavabill [deceiving]' (482). The goddess then must be Venus, and

> I knew that was the court sa variabill
> Of eirdly lufe, quhilk sendill standis stabill. (484–5)
>
> *sendill* seldom

There is clearly a conflict between knowledge and instinct in the Dreamer's response to this desired culmination of his vision. He proceeds with a further encyclopaedic passage, this time on the theory of music – a burlesque of the discussion of heavenly music in the *Somnium Scipionis*, which once more dissolves into self-mockery:

> Na mair I understude thir numbers fine,
> Be God, than dois a gekgo or a swine,
> Saif that me think sweit soundis gude to heir.[28] (517–19)
>
> *gekgo* cuckoo

Then he lists at considerable length the goddess's followers, beginning with her own lover, Mars, and proceeding through all the lovers – mostly unhappy – of history, legend, and fiction. Further evidence of inner conflict in the Dreamer follows: his description of this third court has been of far greater length than those of Minerva and Diana, it has been largely enthusiastic, he has seen *mirth* in the famous lovers, and yet their very *mirth* impels him to sing a 'lay' of misery. In it he bewails his own unhappy enslavement to love, along with 'this warldis frail unsteidfastnes' (610), and ends by cursing 'Cupyd and...fals Venus' (634) and all their court.

Although the Dreamer is still in hiding, the song is heard by the goddess. Venus bites her lip, the others rein in their horses, and they search from tree to tree for the singer. He crawls out in fear, and they taunt and torment this 'reclus imperfite' (645), and then lead him bound before Venus, who decides to try him for blasphemy against the religion of love. The trial follows the Scottish criminal procedure of the time, and this leads the Dreamer into an inconsistency which redoubles the absurd indignity of his situation. First he throws himself on the judge's mercy,

> Submittand me but ony langer pley
> Venus' mandate and plesure to obey, (676–7)
>
> *but* without

but when he finds that this is ineffective he objects that she is unfit to judge him, because she is a woman, and because he is a 'spirituall man'

(697), and should go before an ecclesiastical court. He can hardly expect this to cut much ice with Venus, since it would make him all the more her enemy, and indeed she contemptuously rejects his objection and makes it clear that he is to be tried not only as an individual but as a representative of all clerks, the treacherous opponents of her service. Gavin Douglas really was a cleric, and his admission of this role throws a new light on the mysteries of the dream so far. If the love-garden of the opening was transformed in his dream into a hideous wilderness, that is what it ought to have been all along to a celibate priest. The processions of Minerva and Diana, wisdom and chastity, indicated the ways to honour that were appropriate for him, yet he was less attracted by them than by the court of Venus. The conflict in his attitude towards Venus is just what might have been expected in a cleric who could not resist the pull of earthly love; and his rash condemnation of Venus and Cupid, along with the unsteadfastness of all earthly things, is the natural expression of one who is not only an unsuccessful lover but is barred from success in love by his commitment to religion.

Venus prepares to pronounce sentence, and the Dreamer is shown in an emotional crisis which is both comic and serious. He writhes in his skin, fearing not so much death as transformation into an animal, and recalling to himself the case of Actaeon and similar instances of the turning of men into beasts by pagan gods. Yet this would be a highly suitable punishment for a cleric who has followed Venus, and we may remember how much of the dream he has spent on all fours. He is so frightened that he can neither pray nor say his creed; and at this point of suspense the poem's first part ends. But at the beginning of the second part, as in the next instalment of a thriller, help comes from the very God to whom he could not pray,

> He that quhilk is eternall veritie,
> The glorious Lord, ringand in persounis thre. (775–6)
> *that quhilk* who; *ringand* reigning

He looks up and sees a 'hevinlie rout' (787) approaching, a court of 'eloquent fathers trew / And plesand ladyis' (793–4), playing on various instruments and singing 'Facund epistillis, quhilks quhylum Ovid wrait' (809) (eloquent epistles that Ovid once wrote). This is the 'court rethoricall' (835), at whose head is Calliope, and whose train includes a long list of poets, among them the famous Greeks and Romans, some Italians of the fourteenth and fifteenth centuries, and, from England, Chaucer, Gower and Lydgate. The Dreamer does not know why God should have sent this fourth court to save him, but the reason becomes clearer if we remember that in his encounter with Venus he has shown himself not only as a would-be lover and a priest, but in a third role, as a poet. His blasphemy against Venus has taken the form of a poem; and this is only one of several ways in which the encounter shows its derivation from Chaucer's *Prologue* to *The Legend of Good Women*. Chaucer represented himself as being arraigned before Cupid for writing *The Romaunt of the Rose* and *Troilus and Criseyde* – works of which his authorship must have been well known to the audience of the *Legend*. We do not know whether Douglas was well known as a poet to the audience of the *Palice*, still less whether his 'lay' against earthly love had originally been published as a separate poem. But Douglas at least asks us to imagine him in a similar dream-situation to Chaucer. Chaucer was saved from Cupid's anger by the intercession of Alcestis, and, as we saw, Alcestis in her earthly role as daisy was addressed as the mistress of the poet's wit – his muse. Since Douglas is a priest, his salvation must come from God; but since he is also a poet, it is highly appropriate that it should come in the form of a procession of poets, led by a muse. The rift between Philosophy and the Muses, with which Boethius begins his *De Consolatione*, has now been healed; by the early sixteenth century it was possible to have a greater confidence in poetry as a means to salvation. Calliope asks Venus what is going on, and when Venus explains that it is the trial of that 'subtell smy [rascal]' (944) Douglas for blasphemy, Calliope assures her that a mere fool cannot besmirch the honour of Venus, whose excellence is so widely known. With amusingly self-conscious magnanimity, Venus decides to be merciful, and she hands Douglas over to Calliope, on condition that he immediately composes a poem 'Tuitching my laude and his plesand releif' (996) (concerning my praise and his pleasing escape), and that he accepts the next command she makes him. Douglas is released, and at once writes and repeats the flattering poem demanded. Calliope says she is content with it, and Venus grudgingly 'said eik it was sum recompence' (1049). Venus and her court disappear, but the Muses remain.

The remainder of the poem is concerned above all with the poetic vocation, and with the path it opens to honour, an honour which proves to be higher than the wide-blown name and fame (961–3) with which Venus is so concerned. After the Dreamer has thanked Calliope, she sends him off to see 'wonderis moir' (1069), and assigns him as his personal guide 'ane sweit nimphe' (1071) from her court, whom we are presumably to understand as the symbol of Douglas's own modest share of the poetic gift. She takes him on a wide-ranging journey through the heavens, on apparently Pegasean horses, which 'flaw and raid nocht, as thocht me' (1085). In the course of it, he sees all the countries and rivers of the world, until at last he arrives at Hippocrene on Mount Helicon, the source of the highest poetic inspiration. This journey can be seen in a number of lights. Journeys to the heavens, from which the earth can be seen in true perspective, are a common theme of visionary writings from the *Somnium Scipionis* onwards. At the same time, this is a journey in thought or imagination, 'Als swift as thocht' (1077), like that described by Boethius's Philosophy, and burlesqued in *The House of Fame*. And thirdly, in its content, the journey is, as Mrs Bawcutt suggests, 'an allegory of a poet's education, a figurative account of studies which Boccaccio had considered essential for the aspiring poet'.[29] On Helicon the crowd is so thick that the Dreamer does not manage to drink from the sacred stream, but he does find the Muses again, refreshing themselves in a pavilion set in a paradisal landscape. Calliope calls on her 'clerk' Ovid to sing of the great men and deeds of the past, and he is followed by other poets, ancient and modern; thus the wide scope of poetry is illustrated.

The company ride on, and at last arrive at 'the finall end of our travaill' (1248), a mountain rising from a plain. Here Douglas protests his inability to write more, in words derived from those of St Paul in I Corinthians 2:9 ('That eye hath not seen, nor ear heard, neither hath it entered into the heart of man, what things God hath prepared for those that love him'):

> The hart may not think nor mannis toung say,
> The eir nocht heir nor yit the eye se may,
> It may not be imaginit with men
> The hevinlie blis, the perfite joy to ken
> Quhilk now I saw... (1255–9)

He goes on to echo another Pauline passage, that familiar one from II Corinthians about not knowing whether he was in the body or in the spirit:

> For quhidder I this in saull or bodie saw
> That wait I nocht, bot he that all dois knaw,
> The greit God wait, in everie thing perfite.
> Eik gif I wald this avisioun indite,
> Janglaris suld it bakbite and stand nane aw,
> Cry, 'Out on dremis, quhilks ar not worth ane mite!' (1264–9)
> *Janglaris* fault-finders

In *The House of Fame* Chaucer's echo of that passage was predominantly comic, and, in view of the much emphasized and displayed incapacity of Douglas's Dreamer, we may assume that there are comic overtones here too. But now the comedy is solely at the Dreamer's expense, and the vision of honour which is to follow offers an insight into heavenly values. The traditional ambiguous status of dreams is skilfully turned inside out: it is precisely because this is a vision of truth that *janglaris* will think it a worthless fantasy. Though Douglas's Dreamer has taken on the role of poet, he has not abandoned that of priest, and for him, incapable though he is of the highest vision, poetic and religious inspiration will be one and the same. Before proceeding, he invokes the Muses, who granted him to see 'this blis and perfite glorie' (1289).

Assisted by his nymph, the Dreamer climbs the single path up the slippery marble rock. But a burning gulf, 'Quhair mony wretchit creature lay deid' (1319), lies in the way, and, as he stands looking into it with teeth chattering, the nymph explains that they are those who laid claim to honour in early life but then succumbed to sloth. Seizing him by the hair, she pulls him farther up, and now, viewing the world from a greater height of inspiration than in his earlier heavenly journey, he sees it burning in 'ane fyrie rage' (1349), and a ship being wrecked, with only a few escaping from it. His guide explains that this is the ship of grace, and that only those who manage to cling to a plank of it will be saved. But again she urges him upwards, assuring him that what he sees will provide 'fouth of sentence' (1401) (abundance of meaning) (1401) for his poetry afterwards. He looks up and sees the palace of Honour itself, set in yet another paradisal plain, where the beasts do not prey on one another, and all fruits are always in season. In the 'first waird' (1442) they see knights in Venus's service performing 'deidis of armis for thair ladyis saikis' (1449), and then in an enclosed garden they come to Venus herself, enthroned with a mirror before her. Evidently she and her followers are capable of reaching the outskirts of Honour's palace, if not the 'principall place' (1450) itself. Once more the nymph warns the Dreamer, 'Quhat now thow seis, luik efterwart thow write' (1464): this dream is to follow the traditional function of providing material for subsequent poems. The warning provides a kind of excuse for the next section of the poem, which is most nearly encyclopaedic and least to the taste of our time. Looking in Venus's mirror, the Dreamer sees 'The deidis and fatis of everie eirdlie wicht' (1496), and the next 236 lines give a list of famous stories from Biblical and Classical sources, followed by games, folktales and sorcery. This further illustration of the scope of poetic *materia* lays special emphasis on the story of Aeneas, 'as Virgill weill discrives' (1631), and to that extent it is specially relevant to Douglas. Venus at last notices his presence, asks him how he crossed the gulf (to which he replies, 'Madame,... I not mair than ane scheip' (1737)), and reminds him of his agreement to fulfil her next command. She hands him a book, and tells him to translate it; and, although the book is not named, it must surely be Virgil's *Aeneid*, the translation of which was the chief work of Douglas's subsequent poetic life. In this sense, *The Palice of Honour*, like Chaucer's *Prologue* to the *Legend*, acts as a justification for the existence of a later poem. Since Aeneas was Venus's son, Douglas will be serving Venus as he had promised, though in a fashion more appropriate to a celibate.

The Dreamer is now taken back to the palace, where he sees Sinon and Ahitophel and others trying without success to climb the walls. The palace's golden gate has engraved on it 'All naturall thingis men may in eird consave' (1836), and, while he is standing wondering at this, his nymph, irritated at his 'doting' (1868), 'schot me in at the yet [gate]' (1865) – a clear reminiscence of the Dreamer's experience in *The Parliament of Fowls*. Inside, the palace is as brightly jewelled as the heavenly city of the Apocalypse, and is 'perfite paradise' (1899) to behold. They make for the great hall, and ascend ten steps of topaz, only to find the door shut. But the Dreamer peeps in through a chink, is dazzled by brilliant light, and sees how

> Enthronit sat ane God omnipotent,
> On quhais glorious visage as I blent,
> In extasie be his brichtnes atanis
> He smote me doun and brissit all my banis. (1921-4)
>
> *quhais* whose; *blent* gazed; *atanis* at once; *brissit* bruised

The suddenness of this moment of supreme vision is overwhelming. The imagery of paradise and heaven has been used so often before in the poem that we cannot have expected that this time it would lead to a genuine moment of religious vision. Poetic inspiration has brought the Dreamer to a glimpse of God, and his dream can now be finally defined as an *extasie*. But he is a poet, not a mystic, and the glimpse is too much for him. His nymph rudely reproves him for his weakness, and she is so familiar with divine mysteries that she laughs when he explains that

> the sicht
> Of yone Goddis grim fyrie visage bricht
> Ovirset my wit and all my spreitis swa,
> I micht not stand. (1948-51)
>
> *spreitis* powers

She proceeds to explain to him that in this realm the 'hevinlie King' (1972) sees honour not in earthly terms of 'estait of blude, micht or sic thing' (1975) but of virtue, which alone brings 'lestand honour cleir' (1997). Compared with this dream of truth, 'Prosperitie in eird is bot a dreme' (1983). This is the poem's climax on the level of doctrine, as the brief vision of God is its emotional climax. If we look back over the tradition of dreams and visions from this point, we can see *The Palice of Honour* as a poem which goes back to the *De Consolatione Philosophiae* and the *Somnium Scipionis* to provide an ending for Chaucer's unfinished *House of Fame*. Perhaps if Chaucer's 'man of gret auctorite' had been allowed to speak he would have made some such distinction between earthly fame and heavenly honour, and Chaucer's poem would have been completed, like the *Troilus* and *The Canterbury Tales*, with a section in which the unstable earthly concerns of the main body of the work would have been set against unchanging earthly values.

The Dreamer, like the narrator of *Pearl*, wishes he could have seen more of the heavenly mysteries; but he is still dreaming, and his nymph urges him to refresh himself first by visiting the garden where the Muses are gathering 'The sweit flureist colouris of rethoreis' (2066). To get there, he has to cross a tree laid over a moat; the nymph goes first, but he is frightened, falls off, and

> Quhat throw the birdis sang and this affray
> Out of my swoun I walknit quhair I lay
> In the garding, quhair I first doun fell.
> About I blent, for richt cleir was the day,
> Bot all this lustie plesance was away.
> Me thocht that fair herbrie maist like to hell
> In till compair of this ye hard me tell.
> Allace, allace, I thocht me than in pane,
> And langit sair for to have [swounyt] agane. (2089–97)
> *In till compair* in comparison with

The dream-world has more truth and beauty than the waking world, and Douglas bitterly wishes that he could have gathered some rhetorical colours himself, and have seen the punishment of those who offended against Honour. But he has to confine himself to writing a poem in praise of Honour, and an envoy dedicating his book to King James IV, 'quhais micht may humbill thing avance' (2160). Douglas was shortly advanced to the earthly honour of being Provost of St Giles's, Edinburgh. Cleric though he was, he had never pretended to be more than an earthly dreamer, frightened and ill at ease in the heavenly world of poetry and Honour.

Skelton: 'The Garland of Laurel'

The Garland of Laurel has much in common with *The Palice of Honour*. Both are poems by clerics, which use the dream-form as a way of thinking about the poetic vocation itself, and both set that vocation in the context of fame or honour, making particular use of Chaucer's *House of Fame* to do so – indeed, each of them might have as its sub-title, 'The House of Fame Refinished'. Each relates its concern with the poetic vocation in general to the specific literary career of its author, though Douglas is looking forward to his intended translation of the *Aeneid*, while Skelton is looking back over his work from near the end of his career.[30] Modern readers appear to have been baffled or repelled by both poems, and probably for the same reasons: that they depend for a full appreciation on our sharing in their authors' awareness of a long tradition of dream-poetry, which they do not merely copy but modify; and both derive from that tradition a mockery of the poet-Dreamer which does not cancel out high claims for the profession to which he aspires. *The Garland of Laurel* in particular has been seriously under-rated; even C. S. Lewis has described it as merely 'decorative allegory' and has asserted that 'All that is of value in this production is contained in the seven lyric addresses to ladies which are inserted at the end'.[31] As the *Garland* begins, with a cumbrously magnificent astronomical *circum-locutio*, one may suspect that the faithful old medieval dream-allegory is being trundled out for one more, positively last appearance. But as one reads on, one realizes that for Skelton the dream-poem was still a vigorous literary form, traditional of course, but capable of setting the tradition itself in quite a new light. Skelton's relationship to literary tradition is somewhat similar to T. S. Eliot's. Both are poets who value tradition very highly precisely because their sensibilities and their works are (in relation to their respective pasts) modern. The truly traditional poet is one who has not fully objectified the concept of tradition: he simply follows tradition because the possibility of doing otherwise never occurs to him. Lydgate, in *The Temple of Glass* and elsewhere, is a poet of this kind. But Skelton, like Eliot, invokes the idea of tradition very consciously, and makes it serve the purposes of his individual talent. In *The Garland of Laurel* he invokes the same triad of England poets – Gower, Chaucer, Lydgate – who are mentioned by Dunbar in *The Goldyn Targe* and by Douglas in *The Palice of Honour*, in order that they may support Skelton's own claim to literary fame. The use of the literary tradition they represent is that it should reach its laureate culmination in John Skelton. Skelton, being a writer of lively intelligence, saw the humour of this situation, and in the *Garland* treats his own ambitions with amusing irony, though he bates nothing of his claims for poetry itself.

The subject of *The Garland of Laurel*, then, is the relation between poetry and fame; and to say that is already to imply that it is likely to be deeply indebted to Chaucer's *House of Fame*, and to take over from

Chaucer the use of the dream-poem as a means of discussing the poet's own role and standing. Since Skelton, unlike Douglas, does not make any distinction between heavenly honour and earthly fame, but simply assumes that the inspired poet deserves fame on earth, it is closer to Chaucer than *The Palice of Honour* is. The *Garland* begins with the narrator meditating on mutability, while leaning against the remains of an oak-tree destroyed in a gale – a powerful emblem of the instability of things, even those of seemingly invincible strength. As he is doing so, he falls half-asleep and dreams, he knows not whether through 'ymagynacyon', through 'humors superflue', or by 'fatall persuacyon' (31–4).[32] This amounts to saying that he does not know whether his dream is a *somnium animale, naturale* or *coeleste*, but the Chaucerian uncertainty is taken still further, because he defines the 'humors super-flue' as those that come from 'drykyng over-depe', and later in the poem poetic inspiration itself is associated with Bacchus, the god of wine. Whatever the cause, 'As one in a trans or in an extasy' (37), he dreams that he sees a richly decorated pavilion, within which the Queen of Fame is addressing Dame Pallas. Pallas is the Greek name for Minerva, with whom we have become familiar in *The Kingis Quair* and *The Palice of Honour* as the goddess of wisdom. The Queen asserts that Pallas has ordered her to give Skelton a place within her court, and yet, she says, he is 'wonder slake' (69),

> And wyll not endevour hymselfe to purchase
> The favour of ladys with wordis electe. (75–6)

Skelton is thus introduced from the beginning as a poet. The Queen admits that he (unlike Douglas in the *Palice*) has tasted Helicon, but it is not enough, evidently, for him to be thus inspired and to be favoured by wisdom: he ought to be seeking fame and at the same time conferring it on ladies. The assumption, as with Chaucer, is that the poet is the servant of his noble audience, and that his purpose should be to please the ladies who are prominent in it. Pallas defends Skelton by saying that if he should 'gloryously pullishe his matter' (83) he would be accused of flattery, while if he should write 'true and plaine' (85) he would share the dangers of Ovid and Juvenal. Pallas thus seems to imply that Skelton is not only a love-poet, but a commentator on politics and society, as indeed he was, and as Chaucer in general was not. The dream is evidently to be a wish-fulfilling self-justification; all the better for Skelton if we can also accept it as a vision of truth. Pallas goes on to point out that Fame favours men quite arbitrarily – 'As wele foly as wysdome oft ye do avaunce' (180) – and indeed that she seems to prefer the

foolish and the wicked: a conception very close to that of Chaucer's
Fame. The Queen does not deny this, but she still wishes to know 'With
laureat tryumphe why Skelton sholde be crownde?' (217). And so Pallas
sends Aeolus to summon all the poets, to see if Skelton comes among
them.

The jostling crowd of poets is described with a liveliness that may
remind us of *The Bowge of Court*, though this is a more cheerful mob,
which implies no threat to the Dreamer:

> There was suyng to the Quene of Fame;
> He plucked hym backe, and he went afore;
> 'Nay, holde thy tunge,' quod another, 'let me have the name!'
> 'Make rowme,' sayd another, 'ye prese all to sore!'
> Sume sayd, 'Holde thy peas, thou getest here no more!' (253–7)

Skelton inevitably *is* among them, because it is his dream, and he has
to be present in order to dream of them: the dream, which is also a poem,
itself exemplifies his claim to a place among the poets. With them come
minstrels, who have an Orphic power over nature, and make the very
oak-trees dance; indeed, the oak-stump against which Skelton is still
leaning inside his dream suddenly leaps a hundred feet back, thus
making him the victim of his own imagination. The poets are led by
Apollo, who is lamenting the transformation of his beloved Daphne into
a laurel-tree; in her memory, he establishes the laurel as the emblem
of poets. There follows a long list of poets, in which Skelton emphasizes
the part played by Bacchus in poetic inspiration, repeating as refrain
the lines,

> But blessed Bacchus, the pleasant god of wyne,
> Of closters engrosyd with his ruddy flotis
> These orators and poetes refresshed there throtis. (334–6, etc.)
>
> *engrosyd* enriched

There is a considerable overlap between Skelton's lists and that of
Douglas in the *Palice*. Skelton's 'orators and poetes' are mostly classical,
including prose-writers such as Quintilian, Cicero and Plutarch, and also
Boethius and Macrobius 'that did trete / Of Scipion's dreme' (368–9);
then come a few modern writers of Latin; and lastly the usual English
triad of Gower, Chaucer and Lydgate. Of these Skelton remarks patron-
izingly that 'Thei wantid nothynge but the laurell' (397), for they, unlike
Skelton himself in real life, had not received this academic distinction.
Each of these English poets in turn assures Skelton that he deserves a
place in Fame's court, and he answers each with becoming modesty –
a modesty which, of course, the nature of the poem contradicts. But
at last, as he puts on a show of reluctance, a poetic equivalent to *nolo*

episcopari, they force him into the pavilion where Pallas is sitting. I do not doubt that Skelton intended his audience to find his humility out of character. Pallas orders that Skelton should be conveyed to the bejewelled palace of the Queen of Fame, which he then describes. To it messengers come rushing in from all over the world, in a splendid Skeltonic re-creation of the equivalent Chaucerian scene, now made full of half-understood snatches of conversation and vague suspicions of double-dealing. The three English poets drily comment, 'Lo, syr, now ye may se / Of this high courte the dayly besines' (518–19). And they leave Skelton in the charge of Dame Occupation, Fame's registrar, who greets him with elaborately aureate courtesy, and promises to broadcast his name.

Occupation takes the Dreamer into a field where he sees gates which are 'issuis and portis from all maner of nacyons' (580), and on the other side of which are crowds of seekers after fame unsuccessfully trying to get in. Then he hears sudden gunfire, which does great damage among them, leaving them ragged, dazed and limping. (One may suspect that the passage contains allusions to some of Skelton's own enemies or rivals.) At this moment a mist descends, like a cloud passing over the moon on a winter night. When it clears again, a most dreamlike transformation-scene has occurred, and the Dreamer finds himself in a traditionally paradisal garden. At its centre is a laurel tree, with a phoenix nesting in its branches. The evergreen laurel has already been established as the emblem of poetic fame, and to this the phoenix adds immortality. The garden is that of the Muses, who are dancing round the tree to music made by the bard Iopas. Once more we may recall *The Palice of Honour*; but Skelton sees a higher destiny for poetry than Douglas, for Iopas (borrowed from book 1 of the *Aeneid*) is singing of the origin of all things and the nature of the cosmic order. For Skelton, the poet in his ideal role and dignity is quite literally one of those seers and visionaries with whom this study of dream-poetry began. He is taking the dream-poem back to its primitive roots. But, characteristically, from this high level Skelton sinks once again to satire against a certain 'blunderar...that playth didil diddil' (740), an adversary whom he names only allegorically, as Envious Rancour. Then once more the course of the poem changes, suddenly and casually:

> Thus talkyng we went forth in at a postern gate;
> Turnyng on the ryght hande, by a windyng stayre,
> She brought me to a goodly chaumber of astate,
> Where the noble Cowntes of Surrey in a chayre
> Sat honorably, to whome did repaire
> Of ladys a beve with all dew reverence:
> Syt downe, fayre ladys, and do your diligence! (766–72)

It is an enchanting moment, somewhat similar in effect to the interactions of real life and fiction that are found later in masques. Inside his dream, Skelton is led by a personification into a real room occupied not by other personifications but by real people. The Countess of Surrey was Skelton's actual patroness, and in all probability we should imagine this poem being read aloud for the first time to her and her ladies; and, to their surprise, they find themselves enclosed within the poet's fiction, and directly addressed by him: 'Syt downe, fayre ladys, and do your diligence!' (implying perhaps, 'Get on with your needlework').

The Countess is instructing the ladies to set about making a laurel for Skelton, because he always reports well of them in the court of Fame, and never says shame of them – except of those who are no ladies. This way of putting it implies the two aspects of poetic fame treated by Chaucer in *The House of Fame*: the poet gains fame, symbolized by the laurel, by writing, but also confers fame, good or bad, on those he writes about. The ladies set to work with great bustle and activity,

> With, 'Reche me that skane of tewly sylk!'
> And, 'Wynde me that botowme of such an hew!' (799–800)

And so Occupation tells Skelton in return to devise some 'goodly conseyt' (814) for the ladies,

> Commensyng your proces after there degre,
> To iche of them rendryng thankis commendable,
> With sentence fructuous and termes covenable. (819–21)
> *after* according to; *covenable* appropriate

At the beginning of the poem, the Queen of Fame had complained that Skelton would not endeavour to 'purchase / The favour of ladys with wordis electe'; now he is going to make good this omission, and thereby both gain the right to fame for himself (according to traditional courtly conceptions of the function of poetry), and grant fame to the ladies whom he celebrates. There follow his complimentary poems, beginning with one addressed to the countess herself. The poems to the ladies of highest rank are in rime royal, and are somewhat formal, though that to Lady Muriel Howard is pleasantly teasing in tone. After these come lyrical poems in short lines addressed to the lesser ladies, and the best of these are indeed ravishingly beautiful, and fully deserve Lewis's praise. They have truly conferred fame on their subjects: the names of these ladies would be entirely forgotten were it not for these poems addressed to them: Margery Wentworth –

> With margerain jentyll,
> The flowre of goodlyhede,

Embrowdred the mantill
Is of your maydenhede. (906-9)

margerain majoram

– Margaret Tylney, Jane Blennerhasset, Margaret Hussey, Gertrude Statham, Isabel Knight, and Isabel Pennell:

Enuwyd your colowre
Is lyke the dasy flowre
After the Aprill showre;
Sterre of the morow gray,
The blossom on the spray,
The fresshest flowre of May. (985-90)

Enuwyd tinted

The lyrics achieve an exquisitely delicate poise in the relationship they establish between the poet and his circle of patrons. The triumph of tone is all the more remarkable in a poet as jagged as Skelton often is; here at least he manages to allude publicly to private matters, without any sense of intrusion or discomfort.

When the lyrics are over, Occupation tells the Dreamer to put on the laurel the ladies have made for him, because he is summoned by Aeolus to appear before the Queen of Fame. As he goes, we get another charmingly private moment of reality, as another aspect of life at Sheriff Hutton castle is drawn into the sphere of dream, or poetic fiction:

Castyng my syght the chambre aboute,
To se how duly ich thyng in ordre was,
Towarde the dore, as we were comyng oute,
I sawe Maister Newton sit with his compas,
His plummet, his pensell, his spectacles of glas,
Dyvysynge in pycture by his industrious wit
Of my laurell the proces every whitte. (1093-9)

Doubtless the picture Master Newton was creating really existed. Now the Dreamer is greeted once more by Chaucer, Gower and Lydgate, who praise the laurel as being 'the goodlyest / That ever they saw, and wrought it was the best' (1112-13). Thus the compliment is diverted from Skelton himself to his patroness and the other ladies who made the garland. But by this stage of the poem one begins to suspect that 'the laurel' has come to refer not just to the garland Skelton as dreamer is wearing but also to the poem called after it which Skelton as poet is writing. That too is well-wrought, and, if not made by the Countess and her circle, is at least inspired by them. He appears before the Queen of Fame, who wishes to know what claim he has to the 'laureat triumphe' (1126) which is prepared for him. The answer lies in a book compiled by Occupation, which records all of Skelton's works, a self-advertisement

217

reminiscent of the Chaucer bibliography in the *Prologue* to *The Legend of Good Women*. The catalogue in question is a delightful late-medieval volume, whose margins are full of characteristically florid and realistic illuminations – grasshoppers, wasps, butterflies, peacock tails, flowers, and 'slymy snaylis' (1160). The list is enormously long, and includes a number of works which are no longer extant. Perhaps the Countess had asked for it; perhaps Skelton was determined to give it. At the end, Occupation 'of the laurell... made rehersall' (1503) – and that statement could mean either that she referred to the laurel garland on Skelton's brow, or that she mentioned the very poem in which she appears, the latest and greatest of Skelton's works, which is itself the justification for his triumph in the palace of Fame. At the very mention of the laurel, all those present shout out in applause:

> All orators and poetis, with other grete and smale,
>
> A thowsande thowsande, I trowe, to my dome,
> *Triumpha, triumpha!* they cryid all aboute!
> Of triumpettis and clariouns the noyse went to Rome;
> The starry hevyn, methought, shoke with the showte;
> The grownde gronid and tremblid, the noyse was so stowte.
> The Quene of Fame commaundid shett fast the boke,
> And therwith sodenly out of my dreme I woke. (1505–11)
> *dome* judgment

The poet's wish-fulfilment has at last over-reached itself, and, with an ingenious twist of the device by which some physical sensation within the dream awakes the dreamer, the thunderous applause brings his dream-triumph to an end, and it is the book of the dream as well as the book within the dream that is to be shut fast. Needless to say, Skelton is here once more making fun of himself: his vanity is as much a literary device as Chaucer's modesty, though no doubt both grew out of the actual life-styles of the poets as men. Here the exaggerated triumph is rightly broken by the realization that it could only happen in a dream. The poem itself is not quite over yet; it fades out gradually with Skelton's habitual group of envoys in English, French and Latin. I would emphasize in conclusion that *The Garland of Laurel*, for all its 'modern' self-advertisement and self-mockery, remains in touch with the earliest origins of dream-poetry in the claim of poets to be seers and prophets. In the reign of Henry VIII such claims could be made only when elaborately guarded, but Skelton was not merely joking when he asserted a visionary power.

NOTES

1. Dreams and visions

1 George Kane, *The Autobiographical Fallacy in Chaucer and Langland Studies* (Chambers Memorial Lecture, London, 1965), p. 11.

2 James Wimsatt, *Chaucer and the French Love Poets* (Chapel Hill, 1968), pp. 125 –6.

3 E.g. J. H. Fisher, *John Gower: Moral Philosopher and Friend of Chaucer* (London, 1965), p. 191, and R. W. Frank, *Chaucer and the Legend of Good Women* (Cambridge, Mass., 1972), pp. 4–5.

4 From the Chaucerian translation. All Chaucer quotations are taken from *The Works of Geoffrey Chaucer*, ed. F. N. Robinson (Cambridge, Mass., 1957).

5 *The Floure and the Leafe and The Assembly of Ladies*, ed. D. A. Pearsall (London, 1962), p. 57.

6 *Writing Degree Zero*, trans. A. Lavers and C. Smith (London, 1967), p. 68.

7 P. M. Kean, *Chaucer and the Making of English Poetry* (London, 1972), vol. I, p. 23. See also Gervase Mathew, *The Court of Richard II* (London, 1968), pp. 3ff.

8 *Feeling and Form* (London, 1953), p. 413.

9 *Poetics*, 1450a.

10 N. K. Chadwick, *Poetry and Prophecy* (Cambridge, 1942), pp. 91–2.

11 *Aeneid* VI. 640–1, trans. W. F. J. Knight (Harmondsworth, 1956).

12 From Macrobius, *Commentary on the Dream of Scipio*, trans. W. H. Stahl (New York, 1952). The dream-classification is in chapter III, pp. 87ff.

13 There is no evidence to support James Winny's recent speculation that this type of dream 'seems to offer a close parallel to the state of imaginative excitement in which the poet apprehends, or is given, the matter of his poem' (*Chaucer's Dream-Poems* (London, 1973), p. 31).

14 See C. R. Evans and E. A. Newman, 'Dreaming: an Analogy from Computers', *New Scientist*, no. 419 (1964), pp. 577–9.

15 J. S. Lincoln, *The Dream in Primitive Cultures* (London, 1935), passim, and E. R. Dodds, *The Greeks and the Irrational* (Berkeley, 1951), pp. 102–34.

16 All Biblical quotations are taken from the Douay translation of the Vulgate.

17 English translation from M. R. James, *The Apocryphal New Testament* (Oxford, 1924), pp. 525–55.

18 Latin text in *Patrologia Latina*, vol. CXXV, cols. 1115–20.

19 Bede, *A History of the English Church and People*, trans. Leo Sherley-Price, rev. edn (Harmondsworth, 1968), pp. 291–2.

20 On the treatment of hell in medieval French literature, see D. D. R. Owen, *The Vision of Hell* (Edinburgh, 1970).

21 M. W. Bloomsfield, *Piers Plowman as a Fourteenth-Century Apocalypse* (New Brunswick, 1961), p. 48.

219

22 Ed. Robert Spindler (Leipzig, 1927), 11. 128, 163.
23 Ed. P. J. Bawcutt, *The Shorter Poems of Gavin Douglas* (Edinburgh, 1967).
24 *European Literature and the Latin Middle Ages*, trans. W. R. Trask (New York, 1953), chapter. x.
25 Quoted from Chaucer's translation. The flight is described in book IV, pr. 1 and m.1. On the sensation of flight in dreams, see Sigmund Freud, *The Interpretation of Dreams*, trans. James Strachey (London, 1954), pp. 272–3.
26 English translation from D. M. Moffat, *The Complaint of Nature* (New York, 1908). The Latin text can be found in *The Anglo-Latin Satirical Poets and Epigrammatists of the Twelfth Century*, ed. Thomas Wright (London, 1872), vol. II.
27 See Winthrop Wetherbee, *Platonism and Poetry in the Twelfth Century* (Princeton, 1972), pp. 188–210.
28 Noted by C. S. Lewis, *Studies in Medieval and Renaissance Literature* (Cambridge, 1966), p. 169.
29 Cited by J. B. Friedman, *Orpheus in the Middle Ages* (Cambridge, Mass., 1970), p. 10.
30 Wetherbee, *Platonism and Poetry*, p. 209.
31 *The Allegory of Love* (Oxford, 1936), p. 88.
32 See R. W. Southern, *Medieval Humanism and Other Studies* (Oxford, 1970), pp. 61–85.
33 E.g. G. Paré, *Les idées et les lettres au XIIIe siècle* (Montreal, 1947); A. M. F. Gunn, *The Mirror of Love* (Lubbock, 1952); J. V. Fleming, *The Roman de la Rose* (Princeton, 1969). I have made use of these without detailed acknowledgment, as also of the sections on the *Roman de la Rose* in D. W. Robertson, *A Preface to Chaucer* (Oxford, 1963), pp. 91–104 and 196–207, and Rosemond Tuve, *Allegorical Imagery* (Princeton, 1966), pp. 233–84.
34 French text ed. F. Lecoy, 3 vols (Paris, 1965–70); English translation by Charles Dahlberg, *The Romance of the Rose* (Princeton, 1971).
35 C. S. Lewis, *The Allegory of Love*, p. 125. Jean de Meun seems to have seen the fountain of Narcissus as implying self-love, because, near the end of his continuation, he implicitly compares the Dreamer with Pygmalion, who fell in love with an image he had himself created, and makes Pygmalion compare himself with Narcissus (20846ff.). But Guillaume did not necessarily have all this in mind.
36 'The letter' is the literal sense of Scripture, here Genesis 1:26–7.
37 *A Defence of the People of England*, in *Complete Prose Works of John Milton*, vol. IV, part 1 (New Haven, 1966), p. 439.
38 John Bayley, *The Characters of Love* (London, 1960), pp. 72–3.
39 *The Rise of Romance* (Oxford, 1971), pp. 77, 80–1.
40 Ed. Lecoy, vol. I, p. xxi.
41 This point has been made by L. J. Friedman, '"Jean de Meung," Antifeminism, and "Bourgeois Realism",' *Modern Philology*, vol. LVII (1959–60), pp. 13–23.
42 Quoted by J. F. Benton, in *The Meaning of Courtly Love*, ed. F. X. Newman (Albany, New York, 1968), pp. 28–9 and 37.
43 Gunn, *Mirror of Love*, p. 462.
44 Cf. Chaucer's *Pardoner's Tale* and the Towneley *Secunda Pastorum*.

45 Quotations from Machaut from *Oeuvres de Guillaume Machaut,* ed. E. Hoepffner (Paris, 1908–21).
46 Quotations from Watriquet de Couvin from *Dits de Watriquet de Couvin,* ed. A. Scheler (Brussels, 1868).
47 This is the term used by Wimsatt, *Chaucer and the French Love Poets.*
48 Quotations from Froissart from *Oeuvres de Froissart,* ed. A. Scheler (Brussels, 1870–2).
49 There is an apparent exception in the *De Consolatione Philosophiae,* where Boethius introduces himself in the opening metrical section as a poet. But Philosophy's first act is to drive the Muses from his bedside: he can become a visionary only by ceasing to be a poet.

2. Chaucer

1 C. G. Jung, *Modern Man in Search of a Soul* (London, 1933), p. 16.
2 The statement is provoked by Troilus's nightmares, which are realistically described at v. 246–59 in a passage added by Chaucer to his sources. I have discussed another dream in *Troilus and Criseyde,* that of Criseyde in book II, in *Criticism and Medieval Poetry,* 2nd edn (London, 1972), pp. 139–47.
3 D. W. Robertson, 'The Historical Setting of Chaucer's *Book of the Duchess*', in *Medieval Studies in Honor of U. T. Holmes* (Chapel Hill, 1965), pp. 169–95.
4 Though most editors, believing a line to have been omitted after 479, give a total of 1334.
5 E.g. J. B. Severs, 'Chaucer's Self-Portrait in the *Book of the Duchess*', *Philological Quarterly,* vol. XLIII (1964), pp. 27–39.
6 *Chaucer's Early Poetry* (London, 1963), p. 30. Clemen had offered a similar view of Chaucer in the earlier version of this book, *Der junge Chaucer* (Köln, 1938).
7 *Gothic* (Harmondsworth, 1968), p. 115.
8 Cf. Jung's definition of 'genuine symbols' (in the arts as much as in dreams) as 'the best possible expressions of something as yet unknown – bridges thrown out towards an invisible shore' (*Contributions to Analytical Psychology* (London, 1928), p. 239).
9 *Chaucer and the Mediaeval Sciences,* 2nd edn (London, 1960), chapter 8.
10 Latin original in *Patrologia Latina,* vol. CLXXXIV, col. 1300.
11 *English Writings of Richard Rolle,* ed. H. E. Allen (Oxford, 1931), p. 93.
12 *The Interpretation of Dreams,* pp. 165 and 218.
13 For discussion, see W. O. Sypherd, *Studies in Chaucer's Hous of Fame* (London, 1907), p. 10; M. W. Stearns, 'Chaucer Mentions a Book', *Modern Language Notes,* vol. LVII (1942), 28–31; Wimsatt, *Chaucer and the French Love Poets,* pp. 84–5.
14 Suggested by B. H. Bronson, '*The Book of the Duchess* Re-opened', *Publications of the Modern Language Association of America,* vol. LXVII (1952), pp. 863–81.
15 *The Interpretation of Dreams,* pp. 179, 293.
16 Winny, *Chaucer's Dream Poems,* p. 35; Kane, *The Autobiographical Fallacy,* p. 19.
17 *The Interpretation of Dreams,* p. 266.
18 Ella Freeman Sharpe, *Dream Analysis* (London, 1937), p. 59.
19 E.g. in his essay 'On the Relation of Analytical Psychology to Poetic Art', in *Contributions to Analytical Psychology.*
20 D. W. Robertson writes that 'the dream vision as a poetic form...is... certainly not conducive to dream "realism"' (in *Companion to Chaucer Studies,*

ed. Beryl Rowland (Toronto, 1968), p. 338). But the presence of elements of 'dream realism' in medieval dream-poems has been studied, though without much penetration, by Constance B. Hieatt, *The Realism of Dream Visions* (The Hague, 1967).

21 Numerous attempts have been made to solve this riddle, ranging from Skeat's suggestion that it is a compliment to Edward III to the assertion that 'Octovyen' is a numerological pun, meaning 'Christ coming' (B. F. Huppé and D. W. Robertson, *Fruyt and Chaf* (Princeton, 1963), p. 49, developed further by R. A. Peck, 'Theme and Number in Chaucer's *Book of the Duchess*', in *Silent Poetry*, ed. Alastair Fowler (London, 1970), p. 100).

22 Chaucer's description of the puppy is derived from two of Machaut's poems, the *Jugement dou Roy de Navarre* and the *Dit dou Lyon*. The puppy itself has been variously interpreted as symbolic of marital infidelity, the priesthood, flattery, and dialectic. J. B. Friedman sensibly remarks that 'Like many familiar objects recurrent in the literature of the Middle Ages, the dog appears in so many different ways that there cannot accurately be said to be a "tradition of the dog" to cast symbolic light upon his every appearance in medieval literature' ('The Dreamer, the Whelp and Consolation in the *Book of the Duchess*', *Chaucer Review*, vol. III (1968–9), pp. 145–62; at p. 149). My remarks relate simply to the part the puppy plays in the action of this poem.

23 Several scholars, and notably J. E. Grennen, '*Hert-huntyng* in the *Book of the Duchess*,' *Modern Language Quarterly*, vol. XXV (1964), pp. 131–9, have suggested that the hunt has a symbolic significance, and have noticed the pun on *hert*, though they have arrived at very diverse conclusions as to the meaning of these elements in the poem as a whole.

24 *Introductory Lectures on Psycho-Analysis*, trans. Joan Riviere, 2nd edn (London, 1929), pp. 148–9.

25 Ibid. p. 145.

26 Sharpe, *Dream Analysis*, p. 157.

27 'The Story of Asdiwal', in *The Structural Study of Myth and Totemism*, ed. Edmund Leach (London, 1967), p. 21.

28 *Chaucer and His Poetry* (Cambridge, Mass., 1915), pp. 48, 50.

29 *Art and Tradition in Sir Gawain and the Green Knight* (New Brunswick, 1965), pp. 180–1.

30 For example, in the *Jugement dou Roy de Navarre* Machaut as participant is so absorbed in hunting that he fails to notice the lady who wishes to complain about the judgement given in his earlier poem, and yet as narrator he is able to tell us what the lady and her squire were saying to each other. Later in the same poem, however, with a certain self-consciousness, he explains that he is able to report what the king and his advisers said when they left him to consider their verdict, because a friend informed him.

31 E.g., J. R. Kreuzer, 'The Dreamer in *The Book of the Duchess*', *Publications of the Modern Language Association of America*, vol. LXVI (1951), pp. 543–7, and Bronson, in *Publications of the Modern Language Association of America*, vol. LXVII.

32 Cf. John Lawlor, 'The Pattern of Consolation in *The Book of the Duchess*', *Speculum*, vol. XXXI (1956), 626–48, and *Chaucer* (London, 1968), pp. 21–6.

33 Marshall McLuhan, *The Gutenberg Galaxy* (London, 1962), p. 136.

34 *The Allegory of Love*, p. 170; *Chaucer and the Making of English Poetry*, vol. I, p. 45.

35 Cf. Sheila M. Delany, *Chaucer's House of Fame* (Chicago, 1972), p. 44: 'That the Narrator's position as dreamer and as poet is the same suggests that the dream is not only analogous to the composition but may be a metaphor for it – or, more accurately, for the poetic conception embodied in the work. The process of dreaming becomes nearly synonymous with the creative act.' Also Winny, *Chaucer's Dream-Poems*, p. 35: 'The...contemporary interest in dreams encouraged the poet to relate his imaginative experiences as if he had dreamt them, and to use conventional figures of the dream-poem to embody his imaginative awareness.'

36 M. W. Bloomfield, *Essays and Explorations* (Cambridge, Mass., 1970), p. 184.

37 See J. M. Steadman, 'Chaucer's Eagle: a Contemplative Symbol', *Publications of the Modern Language Association of America*, vol. LXXV (1960), pp. 153–9. The eagle has been the subject of much scholarly comment, not all of it relevant to the poem; but for some ingenious suggestions, see J. Leyerle, 'Chaucer's Windy Eagle', *University of Toronto Quarterly*, vol. XL (1971), pp. 247–65.

38 Lying behind this may perhaps be discerned the explanation of the music of the spheres in the *Somnium Scipionis*.

39 C. A. Muscatine, *Chaucer and the French Tradition* (Berkeley, 1957), p. 246.

40 Robert Henryson, *The Testament of Cresseid*, ed. Denton Fox (London, 1968), line 463.

41 This point is made by J. A. W. Bennett, *Chaucer's Book of Fame* (Oxford, 1968), p. 150.

42 Ibid. p. 153.

43 See Clemen, *Chaucer's Early Poetry*, pp. 114–16.

44 Winny, *Chaucer's Dream-Poems*, p. 149.

45 The chief source is Dante, *Inferno* II. 7–9, which confirms that by 'Thought' Chaucer means memory. Winny, *Chaucer's Dream-Poems*, pp. 33–4, is entirely mistaken in asserting that 'Thought' here means imagination and that 'Chaucer seems to reject firmly the idea that the dream has been impressed on his mind from outside by some kind of supernatural agency, and asserts that it has been produced by the purposeful workings of his own mental forces.'

46 Closely based on Dante, *Paradiso* I. 13–27.

47 T. S. Eliot, *The Love Song of J. Alfred Prufrock*.

48 As suggested by D. M. Bevington, 'The Obtuse Narrator in Chaucer's *House of Fame*', *Speculum*, vol. XXXVI (1961), pp. 288–98.

49 Suggested by Bennett, *Chaucer's Book of Fame*, p. 187.

50 *The Social History of Art* (London, 1951), vol. I, p. 220.

51 J. L. Lowes, *Geoffrey Chaucer* (Oxford, 1934), p. 117.

52 In this Chaucer is continuing a tradition that goes far back in medieval courtly poetry, though it rarely achieved conscious realization. Cf. E. I. Condren, 'The Troubadour and his Labor of Love', *Mediaeval Studies*, vol. XXXIV (1972), pp. 174–95: 'Many troubadour lyrics seem indeed to speak about a new and rarefied concept of love – about *fin' amors*. But several of them also use the language of love to describe the poet's search for poetry. Similarly, the poet's anguish and frustration in love are frequently co-subjects with his inability to create songs' (p. 175).

53 *Contributions to Analytical Psychology*, p. 232.

54 Noted by D. S. Brewer, ed., *The Parlement of Foulys* (London, 1960), p. 103.

55 *The Parlement of Foules: An Interpretation* (Oxford, 1957), p. 54.

56 G. D. Economou, *The Goddess Natura in Medieval Literature* (Cambridge, Mass., 1972), p. 136.
57 *The Savage Mind* (London, 1966), p. 204.
58 Ibid. p. 107.
59 R. O. Payne, *The Key of Remembrance* (New Haven, 1963), p. 145.
60 F. R. Leavis, 'T. S. Eliot's Later Poetry', in *Education and the University*, 2nd edn (London, 1948), p. 88.
61 It is interestingly similar to totemism as seen by Lévi-Strauss, though in play, not in earnest; cf. *The Savage Mind*, pp. 75–6.
62 See James Wimsatt, *The Marguerite Poetry of Guillaume de Machaut* (Chapel Hill, 1970).
63 Or perhaps we ought to imagine the scene of the dream as being the earthly meadow in which the Dreamer falls asleep, and to which the God and his company have come on a visit from paradise. The earthly setting is so paradisal that it scarcely matters.
64 See note 11, above.
65 Frank, *Chaucer and the Legend of Good Women*, p. 22.

3. The alliterative tradition

1 It probably includes the two homiletic poems *Patience* and *Purity*, as well as *Pearl* and *Sir Gawain*. I have discussed it as a body in my *The Gawain-Poet* (Cambridge, 1970), which includes a more detailed interpretation of *Pearl* than would be appropriate in the present book.
2 See P. M. Kean, *The Pearl: An Interpretation* (London, 1967), pp. 120–32.
3 This taste in art is discussed by Millard Meiss, *French Painting in the Time of Jean de Berry: The Late Fourteenth Century and the Patronage of the Duke* (London, 1967), chapter VII, section 2; quotations from p. 146.
4 Quotations from *Pearl* are from the edition of E. V. Gordon (Oxford, 1953).
5 C. G. Jung and C. Kerényi, *Introduction to a Science of Mythology* (London, 1951), pp. 109, 115. The relevance of this passage to *Pearl* is noted by Paul Piehler, *The Visionary Landscape* (London, 1971), pp. 157–8. The similarity with *Pearl* is remarkable, though the indefiniteness of Jung's account, and the absence of documentation from reports of specific dreams, make one reluctant to insist very strongly on the 'realism' of this aspect of *Pearl*.
6 Augustine, *Confessions* IX. 25; Bernard, *Sermones in Cantica Canticorum* XXXI. 6, trans. S. J. Eales, *Life and Works of Saint Bernard* (London, 1896), vol. IV (Latin original in *Patrologia Latina*, vol. CLXXXIII, col. 943).
7 *De Eruditione Hominis Interioris* II. 2 (Latin original in *Patrologia Latina*, vol. CXCVI, cols. 1299–300).
8 Punctuation of this line suggested by Kean, *The Pearl: An Interpretation*, p. 29.
9 *The Works of Sir Thomas Malory*, ed. E. Vinaver, 2nd edn (Oxford, 1967), pp. 1034–5.
10 *De Genesi ad Litteram*, *Patrologia Latina*, vol. XXXIV, cols. 458ff. See Edward Wilson, 'The "Gostly Drem" in *Pearl*', *Neuphilologische Mitteilungen*, vol. LXIX (1968), pp. 90–101, which also points out that St John's vision was put in this category by the fourteenth-century English *Chastising of God's Children*.
11 *Sermones in Cantica Canticorum* XLI. 3 (*Patrologia Latina*, vol. CLXXXIII, col. 986).
12 Ibid. LII. 3 (col. 1031).

13 *The Scale of Perfection*, ed. Evelyn Underhill (London, 1923), pp. 424–5.
14 Ibid. p. 305.
15 Quotation from G. G. Coulton, *Pearl Rendered into Modern English* (London, 1906), p. vii. For the second view see, e.g., D. W. Robertson, 'The Pearl as a Symbol', *Modern Language Notes*, vol. LXV (1950), pp. 155–61, and many other recent studies.
16 See Elizabeth Salter, 'Medieval Poetry and the Figural View of Reality', *Proceedings of the British Academy*, vol. LIV (1968), pp. 73–92.
17 See Norman Davis, 'A Note on *Pearl*', in *The Middle English Pearl: Critical Essays*, ed. John Conley (Notre Dame, 1970), pp. 325–34.
18 This is denied by Sister M. V. Hillman, ed. *The Pearl* (Notre Dame, 1961), passim, but her own interpretation of the poem creates more problems than it solves.
19 *The Scale of Perfection*, p. 23.
20 On date and priority, see *The Parlement of the Thre Ages*, ed. M. Y. Offord (London, 1959), pp. xxxiii–xxxviii, and S. S. Hussey, 'Langland's Reading of Alliterative Poetry', *Modern Language Review*, vol. LX (1965), pp. 163–70.
21 Quotations from *Wynnere and Wastoure*, ed. Sir Israel Gollancz (London, 1920); but I have sometimes disregarded Gollancz's numerous emendations and gone back to the manuscript readings as he records them.
22 Suggested by Gollancz, ed. *Wynnere and Wastoure*, Preface, and Nevill Coghill, 'The Pardon of Piers Plowman', *Proceedings of the British Academy*, vol. XXX (1944), pp. 303–57, at p. 305.
23 Quotations from *The Parlement of the Thre Ages*, ed. Offord (Thornton manuscript).
24 In the following paragraph I am indebted to suggestions made in two recent articles: R. A. Peck, 'The Careful Hunter in *The Parlement of the Thre Ages*', *ELH*, vol. XXXIX (1972), pp. 333–41, and R. A. Waldron, 'The Prologue to *The Parlement of the Thre Ages*', *Neuphilologische Mitteilungen*, vol. LXXIII (1972), pp. 786–94.
25 Waldron, in *Neuphilologische Mitteilungen*, vol. LXXIII, p. 794.
26 Chambers published a series of articles, but his position is most fully stated in his book, *Man's Unconquerable Mind* (London, 1939), chapters IV and V. Of more recent work on *Piers Plowman*, I have been most influenced by John Lawlor, *Piers Plowman: An Essay in Criticism* (London, 1962), Charles Muscatine, *Poetry and Crisis in the Age of Chaucer* (Notre Dame, 1972), chapter III, and Elizabeth D. Kirk, *The Dream Thought of Piers Plowman* (New Haven, 1972).
27 See George Kane, *Piers Plowman: the Evidence for Authorship* (London, 1965).
28 A-text quoted from *Piers Plowman: The A Version*, ed. George Kane (London, 1960), B- and C-texts from *The Vision of William Concerning Piers the Plowman in Three Parallel Texts* (Oxford, 1886).
29 E. T. Donaldson, *Piers Plowman: The C-Text and Its Poet* (New Haven, 1949), chapter VII
30 In the manuscript printed by Skeat, the following line reads, 'For bi kuynde knowynge in herte comseth ther a fitte' (For a fitt [i.e. division of the poem] will arise from natural knowledge in the heart). Kane's reading is no doubt more authentic, but Skeat's at least testifies that one scribe recognized that the passage was about the author as poet.

31 Langland came to see that an uneasy conscience on this matter could be made a central theme in his poem, and in the C-text he inserts at an earlier stage an autobiographical passage in which this point is put to the Dreamer in a forcefully expanded form by as important a personification as Reason. The Dreamer wakes 'whan ich wonede on Cornehull' (C VI. 1), and, while he is 'romynge in remembraunce' (C VI. 11), Reason interrogates him about the usefulness of his life. The Dreamer is forced to make the dubious excuse that he is too weak and too tall for manual work, and to admit that he has no estates or rich relations to support him. His only tools are the prayers he says for his patrons, and his only defence is his inner certainty that Christ wishes him to live such a life and Christ's saying that 'Not in bread alone doth man live' (Matthew 4:4). He refrains, however, from completing the verse with 'but in every word that proceedeth from the mouth of God' and thereby claiming the defence of divine inspiration for his poem.

32 As Mrs Kirk points out (*The Dream Thought of Piers Plowman*, pp. 47–8), if the audience was to understand this passage, it must have known that the poet's name was Will.

33 Cf. 1 Thessalonians 5:21.

34 *Confessio Amantis* VI. 1246–7, ed. G. C. Macaulay (London, 1899–1902).

35 See Bloomfield, *Piers Plowman as a Fourteenth-Century Apocalypse*, pp. 171–2.

36 Noted by Elizabeth Salter and Derek Pearsall, eds., *Piers Plowman* (London, 1967), p. 173.

37 There are valuable studies of such parallels by Elizabeth Salter in her '*Piers Plowman* and the Pilgrimage to Truth', *Essays and Studies*, NS vol. XI (1958), pp. 1–16, and, with special reference to sleeping and dreaming, in her *Piers Plowman: An Introduction* (Oxford, 1962), pp. 58–62. From a different point of view, parallels have been suggested with Julian of Norwich and with Rolle by Geoffrey Shepherd, 'The Nature of Alliterative Poetry in Late Medieval England', *Proceedings of the British Academy*, vol. LVI (1970), pp. 1–22, at pp. 15–18. Shepherd writes of the presence in *Piers Plowman* of 'a series of illuminations, arbitrary in their initial occurrence, inexplicable in their succession, but accepted by the poet as compelling and authoritative' (p. 19). He sees these as belonging to *Piers Plowman* as an alliterative poem; I would argue that they belong to it as a dream-poem.

38 Ed. Grace Warrack (London, 1901), p. 118.

39 *Incendium Amoris*, ed. Margaret Deanesly (Manchester, 1915), p. 190; trans. Allen, *English Writings of Richard Rolle*, pp. xxvi–xxvii.

40 The C-text adds a second vision of this kind, when Will is at his prayers in church (C VI. 105ff.), replacing one which in B begins when he is saying prayers by the wayside (B v. 5ff.).

41 *Sermones in Cantica Canticorum* XVIII. 6 (*Patrologia Latina*, vol. CLXXXIII, col. 862).

42 *The Scale of Perfection*, pp. 429, 434.

43 Ed. M. Day and R. Steele (London, 1936). Cf. passages in *Piers Plowman* such as C XXI. 360–1, where the Dreamer apologises for a digression on lying, 'That ich ne segge as ich seih, suynge my teme'.

44 Possibly the poet attributes the assurance to Reason because in the C-text of *Piers Plowman* it had been this personification who questioned the Dreamer's way of life (C VI. 11ff.).

45 Ed. Sir I. Gollancz (London, 1930). I have sometimes abandoned Gollancz's emendations and returned to the manuscript readings.

46 See *Death and Liffe*, ed. J. H. Hanford and J. M. Steadman, *Studies in Philology*, vol. xv (1918), pp. 221–94, at pp. 249–51.

4. The Chaucerian tradition

1 Ed. John Norton-Smith, *John Lydgate: Poems* (Oxford, 1966). I am much indebted to Mr Norton-Smith's notes on the poem.

2 *John Lydgate: Poems*, pp. 177–8.

3 Otherwise known as *The Boke of Cupide*, and probably written 1386–91. See V. J. Scattergood, 'The Authorship of *The Boke of Cupide*', *Anglia*, vol. LXXXII (1964), pp. 137–49.

4 *The Boke of Cupide*, ed. V. J. Scattergood, *The Works of Sir John Clanvowe* (Cambridge, 1975).

5 H. S. Bennett, *Chaucer and the Fifteenth Century* (Oxford, 1945), p. 131. For an interesting attempt at more detailed interpretation, see David E. Lampe, 'Tradition and Meaning in *The Cuckoo and the Nightingale*' in *The Art and Age of Geoffrey Chaucer*, ed. J. Gardner and N. Joost (Illinois, 1967), pp. 49–62.

6 The one scholar who has recognized this is Aage Brusendorff, *The Chaucer Tradition* (Copenhagen, 1925), p. 444: 'It is very likely that the poet was a personal pupil of Chaucer; at any rate his *Bok of Cupid* shows him as one of the understanding few who already in Chaucer's own lifetime perceived the possibilities of the new style the master had introduced, and tried to develop it through independent work'.

7 I.e. 'foolish curious cry'; but there may be a pun on the indecent sense of *queynte*.

8 Scattergood points out that this incident may derive from Jean de Condé's *Messe des Oiseaus*, where the hawk drives the cuckoo away. If so, it would indicate that Clanvowe was a follower not only of Chaucer but of the French tradition which Chaucer himself followed. The saying which Scattergood quotes from *Fulgens and Lucres*, that he who 'throwyth stone or stycke' at the cuckoo is likely to 'synge that byrdes songe', indicates not just that it was thought 'unlucky to throw things at the cuckoo' (*Works of Sir John Clanvowe*, p. 85), but that the narrator is himself likely to be cuckolded. In the very act of defending the God of Love's spokesman, he unknowingly shows himself up as the God's victim.

9 Douglas Gray, in *The Middle Ages*, ed. W. F. Bolton (London, 1970), pp. 325–6.

10 See V. J. Scattergood, '*The Two Ways*: An Unpublished Religious Treatise by Sir John Clanvowe', *English Philological Studies*, vol. x (1967), pp. 33–56.

11 Ed. John Norton-Smith (Oxford, 1971) and Matthew P. McDiarmid (London, 1973). Quotations are taken from the former.

12 Ed. M. M. Gray (Edinburgh, 1912).

13 John MacQueen argues that the existence of the prologue shows that this fable must originally have been published separately (*Robert Henryson: A Study of the Major Narrative Poems* (Oxford, 1967), p. 168); but it seems natural that Henryson's ambiguous justification of his enterprise should appear at its centre.

14 Ed. H. Harvey Wood, *The Poems and Fables of Robert Henryson*, 2nd edn (Edinburgh, 1958).

15 *Virgil's Aeneid...by Gavin Douglas*, ed. David F. C. Coldwell, vol. IV (Edinburgh, 1960).

16 Poem-numbers and quotations from *The Poems of William Dunbar*, ed. W. Mackay Mackenzie (London, 1932).

17 For the *Liber*, see p. 57 above.

18 Tom Scott, *Dunbar: A Critical Exposition of the Poems* (Edinburgh, 1966), pp. 271–3.

19 John Speirs, *The Scots Literary Tradition*, 2nd edn (London, 1962), p. 56; Scott, *Dunbar: A Critical Exposition of the Poems*, p. 48. There is a more favourable account in C. S. Lewis, *English Literature in the Sixteenth Century* (Oxford, 1954), pp. 91–2.

20 A later example of a Scottish dream-poem which shows an awareness of the contrast between the real weather and the climate of literary convention is David Lyndsay's *Dreme*, in which the poet walks on the seashore in January, meets Flora in disguise, and hears the lark reproaching Aurora and Phoebus for their absence; then he sleeps and dreams.

21 By a further paradox, when the ship originally arrived it was described in images belonging not to art but to nature – its sail was 'quhite as blossum upon spray', its mast-top 'brycht as the stern [star] of day', and its movement 'As falcoune swift desyrouse of hir pray' (51–4).

22 Ed. Robert S. Kinsman, *John Skelton: Poems* (Oxford, 1969). Kinsman, evidently following A. R. Heiserman, *Skelton and Satire* (Chicago, 1961), p. 17, finds an earlier analogy in Hoccleve's *Regement of Princes*; but that is not a dream-poem.

23 *Policraticus*, p. 90. Cf. Heiserman, *Skelton and Satire* p. 32.

24 *English Literature in the Sixteenth Century*, p. 135.

25 S. E. Fish, *John Skelton's Poetry* (New Haven, 1965), pp. 68 and 79, n. 9. Cf. Heiserman, *Skelton and Satire*, p. 63: 'the narrators of such satires are by convention anxious writers'.

26 Ed. Bawcutt, *The Shorter Poems of Gavin Douglas*. I quote from the Edinburgh text, and am much indebted to Mrs Bawcutt's admirably sensible introduction.

27 Mrs Bawcutt notes numerous other parallels between the landscapes (*The Shorter Poems of Gavin Douglas*, p. xl).

28 Douglas may be recalling here Henryson's joke about his inability to understand heavenly music (*Orpheus and Eurydice*, 240–2).

29 *The Shorter Poems of Gavin Douglas*, pp. xlii–xliii, citing *De Genealogia Deorum* XIV. vii.

30 This implies acceptance of the date 1523 for Skelton's poem, although it has been argued (see Kinsman, *John Skelton: Poems*, p. 195) that the astronomical opening best fits 1495, which also has the advantage of falling in the one period when the Howards (to one of whom the poem is dedicated) are known to have resided at Sheriff Hutton Castle (where part of it is set) (see M. J. Tucker, *English Language Notes*, vol. IV (1967), pp. 254–9). But since a major purpose of the poem as we have it is to supply a Skelton bibliography, including works as late as 1522, it seems safer to assume that, if the astronomical opening is accurate, it derives from an earlier and different version of the poem, about which we otherwise know nothing. The extant *Garland of Laurel* is by its very nature a work from near the end of its author's career.

31 *The Allegory of Love*, p. 252; *English Literature in the Sixteenth Century*, p. 141.

32 *The Poetical Works of John Skelton*, ed. A. Dyce (London, 1848).

BOOKLIST

In each section, a list of texts is followed by a list of scholarly and critical works. In the lists of texts, the following abbreviations are used:

CMTS   Clarendon Medieval and Tudor Series
EETS OS   Early English Text Society Original Series
STS   Scottish Text Society

1. Dreams and visions

Alanus de Insulis, *De Planctu Naturae*, in *The Anglo-Latin Satirical Poets and Epigrammatists of the Twelfth Century*, ed. Thomas Wright (London, 1872), vol. II; English translation by D. M. Moffat, *The Complaint of Nature* (New York, 1908)

Boethius, *De Consolatione Philosophiae*, ed. and trans. H. F. Stewart and E. K. Rand (London, 1918)

Jean Froissart, *Oeuvres*, ed. A. Scheler (Brussels, 1870–2)

Guillaume de Lorris and Jean de Meun, *Roman de la Rose*, ed. F. Lecoy (Classiques Français du Moyen Age) (Paris, 1965–70); English translation by Charles Dahlberg, *The Romance of the Rose* (Princeton, 1971)

Guillaume Machaut, *Oeuvres*, ed. E. Hoepffner (Société des Anciens Textes Français) (Paris, 1908–21)

Macrobius, *Commentary on the Dream of Scipio*, trans. William H. Stahl (New York, 1952)

Watriquet de Couvin, *Dits*, ed. A. Scheler (Brussels, 1868)

N. K. Chadwick, *Poetry and Prophecy* (Cambridge, 1942)

J. V. Fleming, *The Roman de la Rose* (Princeton, 1969)

Sigmund Freud, *The Interpretation of Dreams*, trans. James Strachey (London, 1954)
    Introductory Lectures on Psycho-Analysis, trans. Joan Riviere, 2nd edn (London, 1929)

M. R. Green, Montague Ullman and E. S. Tauber, 'Dreaming and Modern Dream Theory', in *Modern Psychoanalysis*, ed. Judd Marmor (New York, 1968)

A. M. F. Gunn, *The Mirror of Love* (Lubbock, 1952)

Constance B. Hieatt, *The Realism of Dream Visions* (The Hague, 1967)

C. G. Jung, *Contributions to Analytical Psychology* (London, 1928)
    Modern Man in Search of a Soul (London, 1933)

George Kane, *The Autobiographical Fallacy in Chaucer and Langland Studies* (London, 1965)

Ernest Langlois, *Origines et sources du Roman de la Rose* (Paris, 1891)
C. S. Lewis, *The Allegory of Love* (Oxford, 1936)
J. S. Lincoln, *The Dream in Primitive Cultures* (London, 1935)
D. D. R. Owen, *The Vision of Hell* (Edinburgh, 1970)
H. R. Patch, *The Other World* (Cambridge, Mass., 1950)
Paul Piehler, *The Visionary Landscape* (London, 1971)
Ella Freeman Sharpe, *Dream Analysis* (London, 1937)
Rosemond Tuve, *Allegorical Imagery* (Princeton, 1966)
Winthrop Wetherbee, *Platonism and Poetry in the Twelfth Century* (Princeton, 1972)

2. Chaucer

Geoffrey Chaucer, *Works*, ed. F. N. Robinson, 2nd edn (Cambridge, Mass., 1957)
    The Parlement of Foulys, ed. D. S. Brewer (London, 1960)

J. A. W. Bennett, *Chaucer's Book of Fame* (Oxford, 1968)
    The Parlement of Foules: An Interpretation (Oxford, 1957)
Wolfgang Clemen, *Chaucer's Early Poetry* (London, 1963)
W. C. Curry, *Chaucer and the Mediaeval Sciences*, 2nd edn (London, 1960)
Sheila M. Delany, *Chaucer's House of Fame* (Chicago, 1972)
Dorothy Everett, 'Chaucer's Love Visions', in her *Essays on Middle English Literature* (Oxford, 1955)
R. W. Frank, *Chaucer and the Legend of Good Women* (Cambridge, Mass., 1972)
B. F. Huppé and D. W. Robertson, *Fruyt and Chaf* (Princeton, 1963)
P. M. Kean, *Chaucer and the Making of English Poetry* (London, 1972)
G. L. Kittredge, *Chaucer and His Poetry* (Cambridge, Mass., 1915)
B. G. Koonce, *Chaucer and the Tradition of Fame* (Princeton, 1966)
John Lawlor, *Chaucer* (London, 1968)
J. L. Lowes, *Geoffrey Chaucer* (Oxford, 1934)
Charles Muscatine, *Chaucer and the French Tradition* (Berkeley, 1957)
Robert O. Payne, *The Key of Remembrance* (New Haven, 1963)
W. O. Sypherd, *Studies in Chaucer's Hous of Fame* (London, 1907)
J. I. Wimsatt, *Chaucer and the French Love Poets* (Chapel Hill, 1968)
James Winny, *Chaucer's Dream-Poems* (London, 1973)

3. The alliterative tradition

Death and Liffe, ed. Sir Israel Gollancz (London, 1930)
William Langland, *Piers Plowman: The A Version*, ed. George Kane (London, 1960)
    The Vision of William Concerning Piers the Plowman in Three Parallel Texts (Oxford, 1886)
Mum and the Sothsegger, ed. Mabel Day and Richard Steele, EETS OS 199 (London, 1936)
The Parlement of the Thre Ages, ed. M. Y. Offord, EETS OS 246 (London, 1959)
Pearl, ed. E. V. Gordon (Oxford, 1953)
Wynnere and Wastoure, ed. Sir Israel Gollancz (London, 1920)

Ian Bishop, *Pearl in Its Setting* (Oxford, 1968)
Morton W. Bloomfield, *Piers Plowman as a Fourteenth-Century Apocalypse* (New Brunswick, 1961)

R. W. Chambers, *Man's Unconquerable Mind* (London, 1939)
E. T. Donaldson, *Piers Plowman: The C-Text and Its Poet* (New Haven, 1949)
Dorothy Everett, 'The Alliterative Revival', in her *Essays on Middle English Literature* (Oxford, 1955)
P. M. Kean, *The Pearl: An Interpretation* (London, 1967)
Elizabeth D. Kirk, *The Dream Thought of Piers Plowman* (New Haven, 1972)
John Lawlor, *Piers Plowman: An Essay in Criticism* (London, 1962)
C. A. Muscatine, *Poetry and Crisis in the Age of Chaucer* (Notre Dame, 1972)
J. P. Oakden, *Alliterative Poetry in Middle English* (Manchester, 1930–35)
Elizabeth Salter, *Piers Plowman: An Introduction* (Oxford, 1962)
A. C. Spearing, *The Gawain-Poet: A Critical Study* (Cambridge, 1970)

4. The Chaucerian tradition

John Clanvowe, *The Cuckoo and the Nightingale*, ed. V. J. Scattergood, *The Works of Sir John Clanvowe* (Cambridge, 1975)
Gavin Douglas, *The Palice of Honour*, ed. P. J. Bawcutt, *The Shorter Poems of Gavin Douglas*, STS (Edinburgh, 1967)
    Virgil's Aeneid, ed. David F. C. Coldwell, STS (Edinburgh, 1960)
William Dunbar, *Poems*, ed. W. Mackay Mackenzie (London, 1932)
Robert Henryson, *Poems and Fables*, ed. H. Harvey Wood, 2nd edn (Edinburgh, 1958)
James I of Scotland, *The Kingis Quair*, ed. John Norton-Smith, CMTS (Oxford, 1971)
Lancelot of the Laik, ed. M. M. Gray, STS (Edinburgh, 1912)
John Lydgate, *The Temple of Glass*, ed. John Norton-Smith, *John Lydgate: Poems*, CMTS (Oxford, 1966)
John Skelton, *The Bowge of Court*, ed. Robert S. Kinsman, *John Skelton: Poems* CMTS (Oxford, 1969)
    The Garland of Laurel, ed. Alexander Dyce, *The Poetical Works of John Skelton* (London, 1848)

H. S. Bennett, *Chaucer and the Fifteenth Century* (Oxford, 1945)
Aage Brusendorff, *The Chaucer Tradition* (Copenhagen, 1925)
S. E. Fish, *John Skelton's Poetry* (New Haven, 1965)
Denton Fox, 'The Scottish Chaucerians', in *Chaucer and Chaucerians*, ed. D. S. Brewer (London, 1966)
A. R. Heiserman, *Skelton and Satire* (Chicago, 1961)
C. S. Lewis, *English Literature in the Sixteenth Century* (Oxford, 1954)
Derek Pearsall, 'The English Chaucerians', in *Chaucer and Chaucerians*, ed. D. S. Brewer (London, 1966)
    John Lydgate (London, 1970)
Tom Scott, *Dunbar: A Critical Exposition of the Poems* (Edinburgh, 1966)

INDEX